6/6/08

Edward Bond and the Dramatic Child

Edward Bond's plays for young people

Edward Bond and the Dramatic Child

Edward Bond's plays for young people

Edited by David Davis

Trentham Books

Stoke on Trent, UK and Sterling, USA

Trentham Books Limited
Westview House   22883 Quicksilver Drive
734 London Road   Sterling
Oakhill   VA 20166-2012
Stoke on Trent   USA
Staffordshire
England ST4 5NP

First published 2005

British Library Cataloguing-in-Publication Data
A catalogue record for this book is available from the
British Library

ISBN-13: 978-1-85856-312-1
ISBN-10: 1-85856-312-7

Cover photo by John Doona of Edward Bond with students and
staff involved in the TAMESIDE ARTS EDUCATION INITIATIVE
at Egerton Park Arts College Theatre, Manchester.

Designed and typeset by Trentham Print Design Ltd., Chester and
printed in Great Britain by Cromwell Press Ltd., Wiltshire.

Contents

To the dramatic children –
agents of the future

Contributors

David Allen is Artistic Director of the Midland Actors Theatre. Productions for MAT include *Waiting for Godot*, 2000, *Lady Chatterley's Lover*, 2001, *The Children*, 2003 and *Macbeth*, 2004. He is the author of numerous books and articles on acting, including *Stanislavski for Beginners*, (1999) and *Performing Chekhov*, (2000).

Edward Bond is recognised by many as the most important living playwright in the UK. 'Edward Bond is a great playwright – many, particularly in continental Europe, would say the greatest living English playwright' (*Independent*). His plays have been performed in Algeria, Argentina, Australia, Austria, Belgium, Benin, Brazil, Bulgaria, Burkina Fasso, Canada, China, Croatia, Czech Republic, Denmark, Egypt, England, Estonia, Finland, France, Georgia, Germany, Greece, Holland, Hong Kong, Hungary, Iceland, India, Ireland, Israel, Italy, Ivory Coast, Japan, Latvia, Lithuania, Macedonia, Malta, Morocco, New Zealand, Nigeria, Norway, Panama, Palestine, Poland, Portugal, Romania, Russia, Slovakia, South Africa, Spain, Sweden, Switzerland, Tunisia, USA, Wales and Yugoslavia. His most productive working relationship in theatre in the UK over recent years has been with Big Brum Theatre in Education Company, Birmingham.

Chris Cooper has worked in Theatre in Education since 1988 when he became an actor/teacher with the Dukes TIE, Lancaster. He has been Artistic Director at Big Brum Theatre-in-Education Company since 1999. Chris is also the author of six plays.

Tony Coult has worked as actor and writer in Community Theatre, Theatre in Education and Young People's Theatre since 1973. He has taught Theatre Studies, Theatre-in-Education and Playwriting at colleges and universities, most recently at Loughborough University. He has written a series of historical dramas for BBC Radio 4. He wrote the first study published in the UK about Edward Bond's work, and has written an introduction to Brian Friel's plays, published by Faber. He co-edited *The Welfare State Handbook* with Baz Kershaw and he contributes regular articles on drama and theatre studies to *e-Magazine*, published by the English and Media Centre, London. Together with Darren

Rapier, he runs weekly drama workshops at the Snowsfield Adolescent Unit and Evelina School, at Guy's Hospital, London.

David Davis is Professor of Drama in Education at the University of Central England where he was the founder and until recently, director of the International Centre for Studies in Drama in Education and course leader for MA, MPhil and PhD studies in Drama in Education. Now he works only with his MPhil and PhD students and researches into Drama and Theatre in Education at UCE. He taught for fifteen years as a drama teacher in secondary schools.

John Doona is a teacher of Drama and a professional theatre writer. He is currently Director of Theatre and Community Arts at a specialist performing arts college, Egerton Park, in Manchester. His writing has been seen at the Royal Court Young People's Theatre, the Riverside Studios and more recently on BBC Radio 4. He works with secondary and primary school staff to promote the development of meaningful drama. In 2000 he directed Bond's *The Crime of the Twenty-First century* for Manchester's Bare Witness Community Theatre Company.

Kate Katafiasz is Senior Lecturer in Drama at Newman College of Higher Education in Birmingham. She was for many years a teacher of Drama at secondary school level. She became interested in Bond's work as a result of his collaboration with Big Brum, NATD and at the University of Central England in the 1990s, where he was Patron of the International Centre for Studies in Drama in Education.

Bill Roper teaches Social Psychology in the Faculty of Law, Humanities and Social Sciences at the University of Central England in Birmingham. He has published in the area of the social and psychological dimensions of drama, the arts and education for several years. Recent papers, several with David Davis, have focused on learning, the self, intelligence, discourses, and imagination and the human mind. His commitment is to an approach to human psychology that makes transformations possible.

Introduction

David Davis

'Hier ist kein warum' (Primo Levi)

If This is a Man
You who live safe
In your warm houses,
You who find, returning in the evening,
Hot food and friendly faces:
    Consider if this is a man
    Who works in the mud
    Who does not know peace
    Who fights for a scrap of bread
    Who dies because of a yes or a no.
    Consider if this is a woman,
    Without hair and without name
    With no more strength to remember,
    Her eyes empty and her womb cold
    Like a frog in winter.
Meditate that this came about:
I commend these words to you.
Carve them in your hearts
At home, in the street,
Going to bed, rising;
Repeat them to your children,
    Or may your house fall apart,
    May illness impede you,
    May your children turn their faces from you.

(Primo Levi, 1958)

Spoon
(for Noëlle Cazenave)

All the people of this world would know it when they saw it
It is a spoon
A being from another world would not know

You could stir all the waters of the world's dark ocean with this white
spoon

The handle fits the human hand
The bowl could carry food to the human mouth

This white spoon would stir all the black waters of the world
It is not white – a sickly zinc-tin mottled grey
It would seem white in the black water

It has been strengthened with a moulded rib running along the handle
The handle is stamped 1942 the year of manufacture
SS insignia – eagled spread over a swastika
Number 22376
The arm that lifted it was tattooed with the same number

This white spoon would stir all the waters of the world's dark seas

The number is scratched on the other side of the handle
Security in terror
To lose it is starvation
To steal it death - property of the Reich

This white spoon would stir all the black waters of the world

Two rough arrows scratched near the end of the handle point nowhere
Or perhaps they are another sign
Before the woman died she gave it to her granddaughter
An Auschwitz spoon
The young girl handed it to me wrapped in a cloth

There is always a spoon

Fierce cruel rampaging ravaging vaunting
Destroying annihilating ravening
History a vice crushing bones to the marrow

Yet there is a spoon

Sartorial uniforms tapping feet on the platform before the overdue train
Death fidgeting in office
Ordered detailed listed book-kept scheduled
Tearing the world from its socket

There is a spoon

Maniacal ruthless violent vicious
Fierce barbaric obliterating
Ripping the ligaments

There is a spoon
This spoon stirs all the waters of the world's black ocean
To the last tear black with soot – to the last salt drop
Breaks the black salt encrusted on wooden piles
This spoon stirs the waters

(Edward Bond, 2004)

n 1944, two years after the spoon was manufactured, Primo Levi was deported to Auschwitz. He may have seen or even touched this spoon. It forms only one of the many threads that connect Edward Bond to Auschwitz and the atrocities of German fascism. It is possible that at the very time that Levi was being transported to Auschwitz, German bombers were trying to kill Edward Bond in the East End of London (see his chapter 'Something of Myself'). For Bond, Auschwitz became a defining act in the barbarity of the twentieth century; not that there were not other barbarous acts; Hiroshima, Nagasaki, wars, torture, pillaging and rape – the twentieth century is littered with them; and the killing continues not only in wars but in artificial famines as a consequence of western prosperity and the needs of globalisation. But the sheer size and rational planning of the genocide of more than 6,000,000 Jews, socialists, communists, trade unionists, gypsies and homosexuals still commands horrifying central attention.

Levi appears to be uttering a curse at the end of his poem but this is not how he was. He would not let himself be poisoned by hatred or the desire for revenge, but he never forgave what was done to him (Levi, 1989:xiv). Similarly, Bond has taken up artistic cudgels against barbarians, both open and disguised, yet is the most gentle of people who hates violence. But because the world is dominated by violence and injustice he insists it must be dealt with in his plays. His drive to tell the truth and call a spade a spade has led him to be seen as a person who seeks to be merely confrontational, but this is the opposite of the truth. He confronts us with reality and we often do not like it. We fight back and then he *will* confront us, to challenge us to open our eyes. He will defend himself if attacked: he is not a pacifist. But like Levi, Bond's heroes would be people like the Italian civilian worker in Auschwitz, Lorenzo, who

...brought me a piece of bread and the remainder of his ration every day for six months; he gave me a vest of his, full of patches; he wrote a postcard on my behalf to Italy and brought me the reply. For all this he neither asked nor accepted any reward, because he was good and simple and did not think that one did good for a reward... I believe that it was really due to Lorenzo that I am alive today; and not so much for his material aid, as for his having constantly reminded me by his presence, by his natural and plain manner of being good, that there still existed a just world outside our own, something and someone still pure and whole, not corrupt, not savage, extraneous to hatred and terror; something difficult to define, a remote possibility of good, but for which it was worth surviving. (Levi, 1996:125-127)

This sounds like one of Bond's characters: in every one of his plays there is a person who is working for humanity.

Levi also recounts an incident when, driven by thirst, he broke off an icicle outside the window of the hut but 'a large, heavy guard' snatched it away from him.

'Warum?' I asked him in my poor German. 'Hier ist kein warum' he replied, pushing me inside with a shove.' ('Why?' 'There is no why here.') (Levi, 1996:35)

That there was no why in Auschwitz has become Bond's *leitmotif*: Auschwitz was a wholly rational operation. Reason without humanising imagination cannot lead to a future filled with humanising value.

This is a theme taken up recently by Ariel Dorfman, the Chilean writer. Writing in the *Guardian* after the first revelations of the torture and humiliation of imprisoned Iraqis (May 8, 2004), he asks 'Is torture ever justified?' As he recounts, it is the question asked of the saintly Alyosha by his brother Ivan in Dostoevsky's *The Brothers Karamazov*. If you could bring humanity eternal happiness, would you consent to the torture to death of only one small creature, only one small child? Alyosha softly replies, 'No, I would not consent'. Dorfman continues:

He is telling us that torture is not a crime committed only against a body, but also a crime committed against the imagination. It presupposes, it re- quires, it craves the abrogation of our capacity to imagine someone else's suffering, to dehumanise him or her so much that their pain is not our pain. It demands this of the torturer, placing the victim outside and beyond any form of compassion or empathy, but also demands of everyone else the same distancing, the same numbness, those who know and close their eyes, those who do not want to know and close their eyes, those who close their eyes and ears and hearts.

Not to close our eyes, ears and hearts has again been a central theme of Bond's life work. He has not chosen the call to arms of the political parties, who would be addressing a class or social group, and instead has chosen to turn his attention to our individual responsibilities for each other. In an important sense he would say that we are all responsible for each other, for the world as a whole. In a recent unpublished personal letter he wrote:

> I am not in a political party (inevitably I must add, nor was Brecht) – because I think that rightly carries a specific obligation, that you should as a writer express the particular party line – which I wouldn't mind doing, but as a writer I want to always spend my limited time, energy and resources on asking the most fundamental questions: *Why* politics? *Why* is Auschwitz 'wrong'? (or *Why* not Auschwitz) *Why* does humanness matter? *Why* not robotise ourselves? (which in fact we can't do, but *why* can't we do it?).

He finds in each individual the search for justice from our birth onwards: each human has a 'right to be' almost inbuilt in the genetic make-up and each human infant starts life afresh with 'radical innocence'. This makes Bond basically an optimist in outlook. Even in his grimmest plays, such as his latest and perhaps his greatest play to date, *Born*, soon to be published in volume eight of the *Collected Plays*, there is the positive and the solid grounds for hope. Standing out against the domination of human thinking by forms of ideology, forms of transcendental authority, whether they be religious, national or political in form, can be a lonely and frightening experience. After Van Gogh, Bond calls it facing the terror of the 'blank canvas', facing the 'gap' where the human individual has to make his own mark. And it is here, in the gap, that the imagination has to seek reason to find human value and justice. Once we are able to sense that we stand with all those who have fought for a human future, the fear goes.

The fear of living in the gap is the theme taken up by Erich Fromm in his book *Fear of Freedom*, dealing with the question of how the people of his country could have followed Hitler. Here Fromm writes:

> It is the thesis of this book that modern man, freed from the bonds of pre-individualistic society, which simultaneously gave him security and limited him, has not gained freedom in the positive sense of the realisation of his individual self; that is, the expression of his intellectual, emotional and sensuous potentialities. Freedom, though it has brought him independence and rationality, has made him isolated and, thereby, anxious and powerless. This isolation is unbearable and the alternatives he is confronted with are either to escape from the burden of this freedom into new dependencies and submission, or to advance to the full realisation of positive freedom which is based upon the uniqueness and individuality of man. (Fromm, 1991:x)

This reference to individuality should not be mistaken for individualism. Fromm is a social psychologist and Bond sees the individual as intrinsically social and needing to act for the social. The quote at the start of his play *The Crime of the Twenty-First Century* is Thatcher's 'There is no such thing as society' and the play explores the implications of the forces behind such a statement and the struggle against them. In fact Bond's roots are in his working-class childhood and he identifies strongly with his class. His thinking is grounded in Marxism but he has been concerned to find or re-find a living form of dialectical thinking and practice. He must have been horrified by the dead hand of the Stalinist corruption of Marxism which he came across in the fifties and sixties. What he has sought to find, not through an academic treatise on the philosophy of Marxism but by his living fresh thinking, is a form of dialectical materialist thought which cannot just be dry reasoning but must embody the living force of imagination and must be freshly worked for by the individual. As Marx writes:

> The chief defect of all hitherto existing materialism – that of Feurbach included – is that the thing, reality, sensuousness, is conceived only in the form of the *object* or of *contemplation*, but not as *human sensuous activity, practice, not subjectively*. (Marx, 1950:95) [Emphasis in original]

Bond's genius has been to find a form of theatre that can face the individual with his or her social responsibilities.

I have tried so far in this introduction to place Bond in his site in the twentieth and twenty first centuries. He has faced the responsibilities which flow from his understanding of the world around him; responsibilities which each of us needs to face. His art is concerned with how this can be done without preaching at the audience, without using propaganda, without taking a 'holier than thou' stance. This has involved him in creating a new form of theatre and has led him to stringent criticism of Stanislavski and Brecht, whose approaches to theatre cannot do the job required of them today (or even yesterday). He recognises that he and Brecht would have been in the same concentration camp together, given different historical circumstances, but this does not stop him from being harshly critical. In fact he has had to be more harsh to urge people to take note of what he is saying.

Bond's plays have been produced in at least fifty-five countries. He told me recently these are only the countries he is sure of. He hears regularly of other performances, sometimes in remote parts of the world. There have been no major productions of his plays by a national company in Britain for many years. This is because he has lost all confidence in institutions like the National Theatre and the Royal Shakespeare Company. He has refused them permission to stage his plays even though The Court, the Royal National Theatre and the Royal Shakespeare Company have regularly asked him. He finds these theatres stuck in antiquated forms of dead theatre. Without an understanding of how his new form of theatre works and without the will to learn from him, his plays just won't work; they don't lend themselves to Stanislavskian or Brechtian approaches. Instead Big Brum have premiered his new plays, which were specifically written for them.

His main home has recently been in France. ('Like Brecht I have spent my middle years in exile' (Bond, 2000:171). The *Théâtre National de la Colline* in Paris and others have championed his work[1] and in Europe he is regarded as a leading playwright. His longer plays are now written for France and other mainland European countries. His disappointment with mainstream theatre in Britain has been replaced by great joy and admiration of the drama he has seen by young people. He regularly writes for groups of school children and students and lends his support to their work. His main home in this country has been with Big Brum Theatre in Education Company in Birmingham. He has written four plays for them and worked with them on how to perform them and the sort of acting they demand. The company has given him some sort of base to try out ideas and he greatly values his relationship with them.

Even though this book is concerned with Bond's plays for young people, we have worked to understand his theory and practice as fully as we can. This is required for all his plays. The plays for young people are not watered down versions of adult plays. They make the same demands on the director, actors and designers and young audiences as do his other plays.

On reading this book

This book deals only with the published plays that Bond has written for young people. Centrally this has involved a mutually creative relationship with Big Brum Theatre in Education Company and the four plays he has written for them: *At the Inland Sea, Eleven Vests, Have I None, and The Balancing Act*. Other subjects include *The Children*, written for youth theatre and for any number of young people who are encouraged to improvise around a certain number of given lines; *Tuesday* written for BBC Education TV; and his working relationship with Egerton Park Arts College in Manchester.

The chapters of the book can be read in any order. I have interwoven the two theory chapters (those by Kate Katafiasz and Bill Roper) with the other chapters in the book, rather than separate them out. There could have been a theory section, a section on Bond's work with Big Brum Theatre in Education Company and a section with case studies. In the end this seemed to be counter-productive. I would encourage readers to start where their interest takes them first. The chapters should work together and re-inforce each other as they are read. I have deliberately allowed repetition of explanations of terms. For example, there is overlap between entries in the Glossary and in Bond's own section on 'Drama Devices'. There are also places in the text where some contributors make their own explanation of terms even though other contributors have done so and they are also in the Glossary. Because these are terms for a new form of theatre, they are not immediately accessible and need explanation and working at by the reader, just as do coming to grips with Stanislavski's units and objectives or Brecht's *Verfremdungseffekt* and epic theatre.

Some people find Bond's theoretical writings difficult to start with and we hope this book will open some doors to students and drama teachers who are new to his work.

The book starts with Bond's *Something of Myself*, which is a brilliant exposition of the notion of site, human responsibility and how his theatre works, largely in the form of a memoir of his childhood. Tony Coult, in *Building the Common Future*, then provides a general introduction to the plays for young people by looking at the role of infants and young people in his plays and provides a general introduction to Bond's work. Kate Katafiasz's chapter, *Alienation is the 'Theatre of Auschwitz'*, on how Bond's new art form works, is fundamental to an understanding of this. She sets out an exposition of what is new in Bond against the emergence of main art forms in the twentieth century. Edward called it 'groundbreaking' when he read it. Chris Cooper, the artistic director of Big Brum, writes in *Edward Bond and the Big Brum Plays* of the many years of productive working relationship they have had with Bond. He writes in some detail of the four productions and the challenges to the company they posed. John Doona in the *Sheet of Glass* writes of the experiences made by the students at his school and the other schools who worked on the Edward Bond Project. In a second chapter by Tony Coult, *Arguments With Authority*, he analyses the themes of the play, *Tuesday*, against an account of the production of the play for the BBC. This is a useful account of Bond's work in TV as there are not many accounts of his work for this medium. *Imagination and Self in*

Edward Bond's Work by Bill Roper is certainly the most detailed examination available of the theory of self and imagination which underlies Bond's plays. Anyone really wanting to get to grips with these aspects of Bond's theorising, particularly as illustrated in *The Hidden Plot* (Bond, 2000), will be advised to set aside some time to read this chapter. David Allen writes a case study of the work he did with his theatre company, Midland Actors Theatre, and some teenagers in a school over the period of a week. They worked on and then performed *The Children*. Finally I contribute a chapter on *Edward Bond and Drama in Education*, which proposes the argument that we need to return to early Heathcote to find forms of drama in education which come closest to the sort of theatre that Bond is advocating. Edward Bond has also contributed a list of his *Drama Devices* which is supplemented by a glossary of terms used in his drama. A number of recent unpublished letters by Edward Bond are to be found at the end of the book. They provide useful accounts of some of the terms he has invented for his theatre.

References

Bond, E. (2000) *The Hidden Plot*, Methuen, London

Fromm, E. (1991/1942) *The Fear of Freedom*, Routledge, London

Levi, P. (1989) *The Drowned and the Saved*, Abacus

Levi, P. (1996/1963) *If This is a Man*, Vintage

Marx, K. (1950/1888) 'Theses on Feurbach' in *Ludwig Feurbach and the End of Classical German Philosophy*, Foreign Language Publishing House, Moscow

Notes

1 'In France, where nowadays he is the British author most performed....' (my translation from *Le Monde* date unknown but after 21.4.02, as this date is mentioned in another review of his play *Eleven Vests* on the same page).

1

Something of Myself

Edward Bond

I think I can remember a lamp lighter lighting gas lamps in a London street. Certainly our flat was lit by gas mantles. When the second World War began my two sisters and I were evacuated to Cornwall. In those days England was still in its ancient verdure. We went by train. It seemed as long as a journey to Siberia. We had parcel labels tied to our lapels. We were each issued with a packet of sandwiches and barley sugar. I sat on my packet. The sandwiches were squashed and the barley sugar sticky. We dared each other to stick our heads out of the windows. A passing train might knock them off. Very late we came to Penzance. The crowd of evacuees was put into the large classical town hall. People came and picked those they would take in. It was something like a slave market. My elder sister was seven. In London an instruction had been given that I should be billeted with her. We did not know this. She was chosen early. Later the Women's Voluntary Service volunteers could not find her. I waited. The WVS vanished. Perhaps each thought someone else was taking care of me. Such hitches happen when so much has to be organised. I was alone in the great hall. As they say, the silence echoed. I stood there. Then I set off. I walked outside down the vast stone steps. My only luggage was my gas mask in its case. The street seemed empty. There was no light because of the war black-out. I think I heard the sea. A policeman stopped me. In a strange accent he said 'Where yoo off to boy?' I said 'London.' Which was true – it seemed the nearest place though it was a world distant. He took me back to the town hall. I was accused of trying to run away. Strange that they thought such a tiny child could have had such an heroic will. I was restored to my sister. We were billeted in the same house. The people were 'posh' and to us the place palatial. I must have sensed the woman's barrenness. I made a point of saying 'Good night mum!' It was a sensation. I may even have been very smart and said 'mummy'. It was not a conscious 'sin'. In my innocence I thought I was the apple of temptation itself. I developed the habit of nocturnal micturition – I pissed the bed. We were banished to the council houses. My sister never complained.

In this safe haven diphtheria broke out. It still killed. I know what it was like to be trapped in a medieval plague. We picked wayside flowers for children's funerals. My sister was a 'carrier'. She had the bacillus but did not develop the disease. We were split up and forbidden to touch. Once we met in the lane. She had hard-boiled sweets. A wartime luxury. We debated whether she might safely give me one or would it kill me? We decided for – a sweet was a sweet. But she did not hand it to me. She threw it. I picked it up from the ground.

There were no cars. The smithy was beside the stream that ran under the road at the bottom of the village. A medieval saint had built his hermitage there. The huge farm horses stood to wait in the clear water. The old men round the fire, the anvil, bellows, the hoofs pared down with a heavy knife, the hiss and reek of hot iron on hoofs, the hammering of nails, the thick manes over the eyes, the everlasting patience – the harshly factual combined with the mysterious. I have an intimate acquaintance with Homer.

The land lay in prehistoric silence. Trees and hedges were vast. I saw fighter-planes like smudges of silver duelling so high they were in a world even more silent than mine. I caught scabies. There was no puss, no effusion. The sores itched. My hands were bound in bandage. If you scratched the sores they put out tiny tendrils trying to join up. Something burrowing under the skin. In London it was quiet. The raids had not come. We were sent home in time for them – the blitz. I was bombed night after night after night. I dreaded the coming darkness. The siren. A long silence. Then the background hum and rumble. The pock-pock-pock and crash of guns. The searchlights raised like fingers beseeching the sky. Then the bombs fell. A thin even whine from far away. Then a juddering rush – a roaring crammed into a small space – an explosion of pure noiseless sound – passed through you and into the earth. Already the next thin whistle had started. This one must hit you. It cannot be so close and not hit you. Each time. It lifted up the top of your head as if it was a lid and jumped inside. In the morning we collected shrapnel in the streets. There was a lot. Heavy and jagged. For safety I was sent away to my grandparents in the fens. London fell quiet. I came back in time for the V1s – pilotless flying bombs. You heard the ramshackled rumbustuous engine. Then you saw it. The engine cut out. A silence as the bomb fell. It disappeared behind the roofs. You counted the seconds. Bang. We discussed what to do if you saw one coming straight at you – run towards it or away. The V2s were next. They gave no warning. If it was day you might be in the street. The explosion summed up all explosions. The smithy's hammering of nails magnified to the limit. In a way the more distant explosions were sadder. Less shock, you contemplated the meaning. In the newspapers about then the first pictures of concentration camps. Then two atom bombs.

On the last day of war we ran to the sweet shop. We thought rationing was over. The sweetshop owner shouted. He accused us of not using our ration coupons at his shop in the war and now we expected to wallow in luxury. Anyway rationing wasn't over. I went home. On the radio Churchill announced peace. A voice in my head told me 'So you will live.' We thought violence was at an end. Not even adults would be so foolish again. Later when bombs were dropped in the first Gulf War I spoke at a peace rally. I used an obscenity. I hadn't intended to. I'd never spoken obscenely before in public. The word spoke itself. It was an after-shock from forty years before. I do not remember the sound of bombs. If I close my eyes and listen I hear it. In all its baroque horror. If I did not hear it I would have lost my self. It was my soul that swore.

There was no time for real education. We needed and were given distraction and reassurance. Years later – I was ten – a teacher who had been evacuated with us visited our school to say goodbye. She was going to live abroad. I'd left for the day to go home. She ran after me in the street for two miles. She stopped me and said 'You remember me!' I looked blank. 'Yes ! – you called me the lady with the golden smile.' I didn't remember her at all. A look of despair – of sudden age – of war – passed over her face. It went immediately. She smiled. It didn't matter. We had helped each other then.

Later sometimes my lack of formal education troubled me. I made a circumlocution when I didn't know how to pronounce a word I knew by sight. I did not want to appear ignorant. I did it even after I'd met highly educated people – often with influence and power – who managed to be shallow and thick in equal proportions at the same time. A lot of learning may be a dangerous thing. As the war was ending I was sent to a 'proper' junior school. To understand what happened on my first day you must remember that I had no education and was very innocent. The schoolmistress made me stand up. She stared at me. She said 'What are seven nines?' I had never been asked anything so extraordinary in my life. War cannot prepare you for everything. I said 'Why do you want to know?' The class burst out laughing. Unintentionally I had made her ridiculous in the eyes of her victims. In the hubbub I tried to put it right. I fumbled trying to count on my fingers. She screamed 'Look at him!' and imitated me grotesquely. Her tongue flickered. She was the snake that is afraid of other snakes. Later the time came to sit the 'eleven plus'. I saw children being led into a room. Their shoes were better than mine. I wouldn't have passed anyway. It would have been a waste of paper in a time of scarcity. Last year at an acting workshop in Paris I referred to Lazarus. A young actress said 'For those of us who have no culture could you say who Lazarus was?' Immediately I said 'If there were a God he could be no more intelligent than you. For him two and two would still be four. If he saw a tree he could only see what you see. Given that, the rest is nothing!' She was a good actress. I was shocked that she could 'put herself down'. No doubt God might have had more experience than she, but who is to say if he'd learnt anything from it? What I told her was true.

At fourteen I went in a school party to the Cambridge theatre in Camden Town. It was part of a scheme of visits started by the Labour Government. I saw Wolfit as Macbeth. Fifty years later I remember the play and Wolfit in detail. He was a revelation. He put together what the bombs had broken apart. Now it would be difficult for an actor to be so good on stage. There is no repertory apprenticeship. TV and film have made most stage acting insipid, and reductive intellectual theories have made it irrelevant. I had been ill treated – mostly unintentionally – by people who would have denied the ill treatment. Witches foretell Macbeth his future. They do not appear after the first two-thirds of the play. That is astonishing. A lesser writer would have brought them back at the end to gloat over their victim – and the audience – and fly off to snare the next one. They do not appear because Macbeth has taken responsibility for his own actions. Even if it had been the devil who had tempted him, I do not think he would have appeared again. The devil would have been afraid of him – not of his crimes (trivial compared to those even I had seen) but of his honesty. Macbeth was a villain. He did not pretend otherwise to himself. I found in that honesty a great goodness. I had learnt by then – and have since confirmed – that most people deceive themselves. It is far better to lie to others than to yourself. The first is dishonesty, the second is corruption. The corrupt – unlike Macbeth – can never regret their stupidities and come to hate their cruelties. He educated me. If only more teachers were like Macbeth. Afterwards it was just a matter of acquiring some facts.

I read. There were no books at home of course. My father couldn't read. School books were mysterious. They talked of 'quad' and 'prep'. Later I found out this was public school jargon. I used the local library. This frightened my mother ('bringing nasty things into the house. . .'). I would catch an infection from other people's germs. Unknowingly she was afraid I would be infected by ideas. It was still essential to know your place. Only trouble-makers tried 'to get above themselves'. They were unhappy and a danger to those who depended on them. It was all right to 'better yourself' if it meant winning your superiors' approval so that they gave you a slightly more responsible job. But you had to know the limits. You didn't get their job. The working-class survived through self-repression. They enforced it on each other by scorn and guilt. Both were used very subtly because they had to do a lot of work. Any wider interest was a threat. I know the look of scorn well. The eyes seem to stare at you but really they are sightless and the face is blank. The scorner is avoiding looking at himself. Scorn gave great satisfaction but at the same time it made for anger. I saw that often the fists were clenched. You learnt to turn your need for freedom into defence of your prison. It is the half story of history. All 'culture' was pretentious fake, yet at the same time arcane knowledge the 'nobs' understood but you never would. Now the situation has changed. Mass 'culture' is everyone's entitlement. Your prison is your fun palace. Enjoy it! The process is reversed to achieve the same effect. When one foot is tired from kicking use the other. The young are disaffected, but increasingly the economy provides ersatz satisfactions. They are trapped in cash linearity. We take less care over meaning than any society in the past. We are the first society not to have created a culture, we are parasitic on other cultures. Post-modernism is a mirage. And the undeclared discontent is even greater because now it is less necessary.

I kept it quiet when I started to write. It would make those around me anxious. I felt guilty. I still do. I ought to write nice slick plays that make money. Have a holiday home in the sun and a knighthood. Others have wanted me to write plays to a rigid formula that ask no questions because they have all the answers. Do I really still feel guilty? Yes, faintly – or to be more exact, vaguely. But now it's a provocation I enjoy defying. I regret only when I cause actors or directors trouble. They try to make the text work but it won't collude with the tricks and evasions they have come to use to survive. I am never angry but sometimes they grow incandescent with rage. Once – at the beginning – I thought there was a real 'culture'. It would be based on Macbeth's honesty. See it and say it. That's all I did in my first play. I was genuinely surprised at the uproar. On the first night there were fist fights. The critics scorned – I think they clenched their fists so hard they were in danger of breaking their own knuckles. It was the last play prosecuted by the censor. My next play was the last to be completely banned. I find it deeply satisfying that the censorship should fall to a working-class writer. Just retribution for centuries of arrogance. I have the strengths of my class and am not dismayed by its weaknesses. I am true to it when I write.

My first plays were staged by the Royal Court. Then it was a place of cultural upheaval. Some of its writers became reactionary. At the beginning all of them were fighting a poisoning parasite. I called it the o-beast-ity. Now like most of our theatres the Court is assiduously petit-bourgeois. For a long time it has sought the remunerative blessing of the capitalist market. You express your need for freedom by building your prison. The censor is Hollywood and shock is a fashion accessory. This is not the fault of the new writers. Their abilities are wasted. They have nowhere to learn the tool kit of drama. Directors' 'workshops' are useless. You might as well train for the Grand National on the wooden horses of a merry-go-round.

In *The Sea*, a young girl's fiancé is drowned. She talks of her sense of loss. Thirty years ago an American director came to tell me how he would direct the play. He liked it. 'But of course we gotta get shot of all that stuff the girl says. No one talks like that'. I demurred. I had written the speech after listening to someone in mourning. A little later the play was staged at a school. I can't remember which school or the young actress's name. She was not a trained actress. She sat on the stage and said the lines. She would have been at home on the stage with Wolfit. I see and hear her now. I think the part could not be acted better. She might never have been in another play, but the speech would always have been of use to her even after she'd forgotten the words. She had created it. When they are allowed, young people are always good in my plays. It is to try to explain why that is so that I have written about my early life at the beginning of this essay. I was a happy child. It was not a calm contented happiness. It was fierce and electric and relentless and unwaveringly optimistic. It stays with me and is why I write. I may understand nothing, but I have learnt what it is necessary to try to understand. Otherwise there is scorn, anger and self-deception. You may think you need those things to survive. No, even the taint of them corrupts.

* * *

The Children is a play for two adults and a group of young people aged eleven to fifteen. It starts with a long monologue by a boy or girl. In this production it was a boy. He has a large doll. The sort of grotesque toy you may win at Bingo (for some reason it's often a panda). We called it the puppet. The boy takes it to a waste lot to throw into a stream. His mother insists he get rid of it. He's too old for it. He tries to persuade the puppet that it's for the best. He gives it sweets. He takes his comb from its pocket – he's used its pocket to hold his own things. As he talks he explains a lot about himself. He can throw the puppet in the stream only after he has struck it with bricks. The incident relates to an actual murder. In some productions the puppet is a 'central object' cathexed with the play's meaning. In less-careful productions it's just a nice piece of 'art'.

This production was in a Bucharest prison. The prisoners were males between twelve and twenty. The offences of many of them were serious. Some were murderers. Their society was impoverished. A few nouveaux riche drove Mercedes. The prisoners were keen to act. It was an 'internal escape'. They had discussed and cast the play and learnt their few set speeches. The first acting rehearsal began. The young prisoner came on with the puppet. He could not speak. Stage fright? The others encouraged him. Prompted him with the text. Made suggestions. Hold the puppet like this. Take it over there. No, his voice had gone. Prisoners shout whisper or sing. They don't lose their voice. He had learnt his text but when he picked up the puppet he could not speak. He was dumb.

Imagination creates reality. The *extreme situation* recathexed the puppet. The prisoner had turned the puppet into the body of the person he had murdered. The murderer is holding his victim's body. The body is not there but the *reality* of the body is there. If he attacks it with a knife there will be straw or plastic stuffing and it will have the entrails' *reality*. He will re-commit the murder but its meaning will be unchanged. The murderer faces what Van Gogh knew as the panic, the terror, of the white canvas. The white canvas is the barrier to be crossed. There is no ideological or conventional description on it. The gap is empty. On this side of the barrier is an accident, the puppet and the dumbness. On the other side is 'accident time'– in which the actor finds the invisible object he may act. But the prisoner cannot – he is dumb. His paralysis spreads to the others. The director, the adult actors – even the prison officers and a visiting psychiatrist – are lost. A sense of catastrophe. The good intentions falling apart. Perhaps prison doors must remain shut, you cannot open them and nothing can be done. Silence.

Another prisoner took the puppet from him. He is the audience. He is also an offender who shares the young murderer's *extreme*. He knows what to do. He says 'I'll be the puppet. Talk to me.' He takes the puppet's place.

Death is recathexed. The dead body is alive – the prisoner is not really the body but he is its *life*. The murderer talks. He tells the prisoner how he will kill him. He tries to tell him why. He argues with himself and reaches a conclusion. He might have made excuses, gone deeper into corruption, but I think he didn't. He had dramatised the situation so that he could find his innocence. He said 'Now I must kill you – because that is what I did.' Then he jumped to the end of the play, where he's forgiven by a ghost – dressed in the puppet's clothes – of the boy he murders in the play. He said 'And before I kill you, you must forgive me.' The other prisoner said 'I forgive you' and the rehearsal went on. For a year the psychiatrist had tried to get the prisoner to speak about the murder. Nothing. Today he said everything. The professionals had been at a loss. It was another prisoner – who perhaps had been written off as a 'no-hoper' – who understood what needed to be done.

The murderer had never been at a play. He was not guided by existing dramatic forms. Yet in prison he made drama a human resource. What he dramatised was the honesty of Macbeth. For just long enough he wore his victim's shroud – and then he murdered for the first time. Every child – every audience – is on the prisoner's site. They are not murderers but they have to create a life in an unjust world and their extremity may be even greater than the murderer's. If we can't understand this our barbarism has begun and we might as well go back to our jee-jaws and weapons and wait for the end.

The murderer in the prison in Bucharest had invented modern drama.

2

Building the common future:
Edward Bond and the rhythms of learning

Tony Coult

One of the more significant, and until this book largely unnoticed, journeys in the world of modern drama has been the gradual but inexorable forging together, often through thickets of mis-representation, of the dramatist Edward Bond, and the world of Theatre for Young People. It's a curious fact that most commentators on theatre and drama write about Bond either as the victim of shameful neglect by the panjandrums of the arts in this country, or as a spent force artistically, over-whelmed by his political commitment. The latter idea is probably im-permeable to reason but it is certainly true that the contrary winds of theatrical fashion seem to keep his recent, most highly developed work ever off the shoreline of the British Isles.

There is an element of truth in the neglect idea, of course. It is partly Bond's own doing. If France and other European countries, rather than Britain, have regularly championed his work in recent years, it is partly because of the writer's constructive quarrel with the major producing houses. In no uncertain terms, the National, the RSC and even the Royal Court theatres have, at various times, been told that they are not welcome to produce his work. Yet the truth is that year after year Bond plays are still premiered in this country and, far from being sniffily noticed as used to be the way, are simply ignored. The reason is that these plays – a whole body of work – are written for community groups, youth theatres and theatre-in-education companies, the kinds of groups that metropolitan-aspirant critics charac-terise as worthy at best, amateurish at worst. Certainly a Bond premiere at the National Theatre appears to carry more cultural weight than one in a Nechells comprehensive. This may seem obvious but it is nevertheless strange – or ought to be seen as such.

There are precedents amongst Bond's generation of writers for this kind of community involvement, most notably in Arnold Wesker's creation of the Centre 42 project in the 1960s and John Arden/Margeretta D'Arcy's projects of community festivals in Yorkshire, and their continual involvement during the 1970s with radical political companies, particularly over the Irish war. One writer of these times, and a graduate with Bond and Arden of the Royal Court Theatre's Writers Group from the late 50s, Ann Jellicoe, went on to devote herself more or less completely to the idea of community drama. These writers' characteristic works find a reflection in these side-projects – Wesker's commitment to the humanising effects of art, expressed in plays like *Roots* and *Their Very Own* and *Golden City*, is given public form in the trade union-backed (and trade union-abandoned) Centre 42 project. Arden/D'Arcy's challenge to notions of communal order and disorder, and class power, in plays like *Serjeant Musgrave's Dance* and *The Ballygombeen Bequest* leads them into the oppositional theatre work of the theatre company 7:84 and CAST (Cartoon Archetypal Slogan Theatre).

Bond's case is subtly different because his journey from a relatively conventional model of artistic independence towards the body of work represented by the Young People's Theatre/Theatre in Education movement is almost unprecedented amongst significant artists today. And it results in an unambiguous and ongoing project that has none of the scent of disillusion or lapsed interest that others of his cohort seem to have experienced. The journey of this dramatist towards that body of work is also a two-way one, as the TiE/DiE (Theatre in Education/Drama in Education) fields themselves transformed and evolved towards shared territory, artistically and politically. That this convergence of concerns takes place over a period of significant social and political upheaval – approximately the last thirty years of the twentieth century – is also significant, and in outlining some of that convergence, we inevitably have to consider some of the living history that was driving Bond and TiE/YPT (Young People's Theatre) into collaborative cohabitation.

If Wesker's and Arden/D'Arcy's characteristic playwriting is reflected in their community activities, so too, and powerfully, is Bond's. From very early on, his plays are concerned with the rhythms of learning, and the effect on young people of the inhibiting and corrupting culture that Bond identifies as lurking at the heart of modern capitalist-individualist society.

It is no particular surprise that people in the Arts and in Education should want to chew at similar problems in the objective world. What is unusual is the direct and ongoing collaboration that has resulted.

Bond is an auto-didact. His early immersion in the London theatre scene of the late 1950s/early 1960s was a conscious process of self-education. Similarly, his decision to give creative time to work with young people in the 1980s was more than just an act of civic responsibility. It was a decision based in part on what he felt he could learn from young people and their kaleidoscope of concerns, hopes and anxieties. Lastly, at least up to the present, the phase of work in which his energies in this country are channelled largely into work for young people is a confirmation that his most urgent value as an artist is to the community of educators. That community may be understood in very different ways, and is certainly not limited to 'teachers'. However, it is clear that Bond has constructed a bridge between art and education and in a way that, initiated by a major artist, is rare and valuable.

The fate of children – infants, children, adolescents – has been at the heart of Bond's 'project' well before his move towards the world of education. There are playwrights-a-plenty who can create powerful images of a corrupt and dangerous modernity, inimical to humanity and justice. What Bond offers in addition is a built-in set of tools with which to do more than be shocked or confirmed in our anger and distress. These are the tools of education and they are present in the plays because the writer has always been fired by the processes by which we learn and fail to learn. These processes of course happen to all people all the time but they are most visible and urgent for young people.

> 1. A child's mind should not be described as a circle of light that increases as the child learns. Its mind is a totality and it brings the world into it bit by bit as if increasing the brightness... (Bond, 1995)

This sensuous imagining of a fundamental learning process illustrates Bond's ability to address important ideas, not just for drama, but for all human progress. In his world-view the two are fatefully interwoven. Much of his most recent theoretical and contemplative writing about drama starts with the child. 'I must become a child, hungry and stripped and shivering in blood, I must open my eyes and see.' (Bond, 1971)

Children haunt Edward Bond's plays, and the rhythms of birth and growth to adulthood are the bedrock of his work. There are good reasons for this. Children and childhood haunt our society and its culture in a way that we seem increasingly ambiguous about, and Bond's career-long exploration of that dynamic triangle bounded by imagination, justice and change has frequently invoked the child as a stimulus to explore that disturbing ambiguity.

The child is a literary and cultural archetype that is perhaps open to abuse as a short-cut to significance. In the Christian art of the Renaissance and after, the identification of all children with the Christ-child establishes a tradition of childhood as a time of innocence, of 'sinless ness'. (It also legitimises the possibility of violence against children who vary from the sinless path...) The dawning realisation, after Freud, that this innocence was largely about adult wish-fulfilment has resulted today in something of a mirror-image, equally overwrought, of childhood as a haunted land of abuse and threat. Never mind the Land of Lost Content, as Housman saw it, now we live with the horror of contentment that never existed. It takes a Marxist perspective to remind us that the models of Heavenly or Hellish childhood apply differently to the typical childhood of a handloom weaver and that of the squire's child, and it would certainly be helpful if current educational debates could even consider the role of the commodification of childhood by market force [*sic*] as a factor.

Bond isn't the only dramatist to invoke The Child. Beckett's *Waiting for Godot*, on every syllabus in sight, is regarded as the quintessential twentieth century play, powerfully evoking a feeling of pessimistic stasis and existential angst. This condition, it is said, is brought about by a Western, technocratic culture that has shed faith like a discarded chrysalis but has replaced it with nothing. The thing that is supposed to become a butterfly is cruelly exposed, unprotected, fatally vulnerable. Beckett's tramps first mused (in 1952, year of the first H-Bomb) upon the futility of a world where two atomic bombs had just offered the possibility of a real apocalypse, as well as the first reality of a genetic poisoning that corrupted the very idea of human continuity. No wonder they embrace the notion that 'We give birth astride of a grave' and that stoic humour is all that is available to the bravest, and degrees of self-delusion to the rest of us! If this is the play that characterises the modern world, or at least its culture's view of the world, its use of the child may well have something to teach us. So what do we find? That the Boy is a marginal character, a semi-slave errand boy for a tyrant. Cowed and damaged, this Boy is indeed a symbol of a pervasive tyranny's effects and we can, for the fleeting moments he is with us, feel 'sorry' for him. The problem, for Bond, is that the Boy has no potential for change and is therefore sentimentally unreal, fit only to be pitied:

> The theatre we have (not the one we ought to have) puts on stage, as great opponent, foe and friend, of the protagonists, not devils or gods – but babies, the sugar of sentimentality: its icon is the little messenger boy in Godot' (Bond, 1996)

The impotence and passivity of the Boy derives not from his own situation as Dickensian potboy, a Smike after the Second World War, but from the playwright's own use of the symbol of Child. The Boy may have come from somewhere vague, Pozzo's realm, but more importantly he has nowhere to go. That is perhaps why Bond's famous argument with Beckettism, begun in the 1950s, is so fundamental to him. *Waiting for Godot* could be – *should* be – the Boy's play. Not in order to rescue or redeem the Boy (in the arms of an authorial Nicholas Nickleby) but to use the one obvious source of dynamism in the play at least to challenge, if not to determine, the play's meanings.

Beckett was an inevitable influence on any young writer in the 1950s. For Bond, he soon became a flag under which he could refuse to serve. The cause was not a worthy one, philosophically. Far more worthy, and initially useful to Bond, was Brecht. The 1956 visit of the Berliner Ensemble to England, and the final materialisation of the semi-mythical *Augsberger* from behind the Iron Curtain, was a powerful stimulus to a swathe of young artists of a notion of drama as socially engaged and politically active: the very same notion and example that was beginning to engage the pioneers of the Educational Drama movement in the UK. Bond's later challenge to Brecht's influence is, arguably, even more potent for him than the German's early influence.

Edward Bond's dramatic poetry about childhood differs from Beckett's as dynamism differs from stasis. For a start, Bond's vision assumes a seamless connection between childhood and adult experience. Childhood, it suggests, is not another country but the state in which we all live. In this he is implicitly rejecting more Wordsworthian ideas of childhood, a time that has 'the glory and the freshness of a dream'. The essential characteristic of being a child is the potential to take on board experience, process it, and act upon it – to change. Taken as a whole, Bond's work is concerned with the human capacity to learn from often overwhelming experience, and the capacity of institutions to frustrate or assimilate that learning to its own purposes. The capacity to learn, to self-educate and to judge what is false learning and what true, is the thrust of all his work. In this regard the idea of a body of work divided neatly into 'adult' and 'child/youth' departments is too neat. Only in the institutions that produce the work does it really hold up.

Taking the sweep of that work from the 1960s to the present, it is possible to see broad patterns in his use of the child/young person. Like others of his playwriting generation, including Potter, Pinter, Wesker, and Nicholls, childhood was marked by direct experience of war. Bond, Pinter and Wesker, all Londoners, were evacuated from the capital as it came under attack from the Luftwaffe, a process of uprooting from family and normality that would need to be absorbed and processed by any sensitive child. We need to remember that by the late stages of the war, the V1 and V2 attacks were quite likely to succeed in destroying London and their child-hood environments and their families' lives. The fragility of childhood experience and the possibility of atrocity round the corner was no abstract concern for this generation. Bond, in particular, speaks powerfully of his experience of being bombed. In an early and revealing interview, he describes the experience of a bomb or missile exploding near him in Finsbury Park:

> ...there was suddenly this enormous sort of bang which one can't describe, you know, because it's so... a noise almost inside you. I went along to the park and saw all the trees stripped bare, and picked up this little bird with its head blown off. I would think, very much, that was one of the reasons why I wrote that scene in *Saved*. (Bond, 1972)

That short description seems to prefigure, in its intensity and web of meanings, a characteristic working method that he later coins a Theatre Event, in a conscious departure from Brecht's Alienation Effect. The ruined body of the bird, the stripped trees, both creatures of air, have a material connection with the thing that has come from out of the air to devastate them in the 1940s. The image of the dead bird in the park resurfaces in the 1960s, transformed into the Saved baby in the park: the balloon attached to the pram, a flag signalling its vulnerability, and possibly distantly evoking memories of barrage balloons over London. The same insistent questions are demanded of reality – 'what killed the baby/the bird and why?'

Both of Bond's early published plays, *The Pope's Wedding* and *Saved*, revolve around an intense desire to know and to learn about events that are deeply troubling. Scopey, in *The Pope's Wedding*, whose name nudges us into this 'looking' territory becomes obsessed with a reclusive figure whom he falsely believes has answers to his anxieties about the narrow, class-bounded rural backwater in which he lives. Alen is the innocent object of this misdirected interrogative energy, and ends up murdered because of it. From the outset Bond creates a situation where his character observes but can only stare obsessively, almost fetishistically, at what he sees. He fails to learn from what he sees, as a child should learn – dynamically. In this, he is the Beckettian figure, not the faux-mysterious tramp Alen! Scopey cannot transfer what he sees into new understanding.

Bond is laying out in this play – his first to be performed – early and profound concern with the processes of learning, both as human instinct and in the more formalised arena we might call education. Scopey remains locked in his mistake, but Len, in *Saved*, (again the name nudges us towards the word), learns, or at least moves towards learning. It is the possibility of change and progression, on the basis of seeing, experiencing, and understanding the worst, that drives these plays. There's no conventional resolution to these problems built into the play: the task of resolution is handed over to the audience. In a sense what Bond does is to turn his audience into watching children. As Len is, we are made into voyeurs. We are made complicit in child murder. Like Len, we have been voyeurs at an atrocity. In instinctively measuring ourselves against Len, as we must surely do, we have a choice to stare in shocked fascination, or to understand and perhaps absorb that understanding into action. Bond's plays almost always have an open-ended energy, replacing the adult pleasures of resolution and certainty with the child's tendency, indeed necessity, to push out, explore, test boundaries, question realities.

In *Narrow Road to the Deep North* (1968) Bond makes an early main focus of the play an image that recurs frequently from now on. It is a bundle, a peasant means of carrying, protecting and controlling an infant. (Peasants need to take the baby with them: work cannot be interrupted by a crawling, danger-prone infant.) This image is common in Bond, Sometimes it is transformed into a more disturbing version, like the 'white worm' that is the entrepreneur's chauffeur, kidnapped in *The Worlds*, bound and wrapped like a helpless infant, and fed with a tube. It is the combination of protection and restraint that makes for a fruitful stage image. Its ambiguity is challenging, and intensely provoking.

In that first group of plays from *Saved* to *The Sea* – the 'Question Plays' as Bond defines them, this basic rhythm of learning and demanding answers to existential and political questions is pursued to the point where the open-endedness is given almost literal force in the interrupted last sentence of the learner, Willy, ('Will he?') in *The Sea* who, like Len, Arthur in *Early Morning*, or Lear in *Lear*, have to find the child's absence of illusions in order to restart their quest for maturity, whether fruitful or futile. Though even when it is futile, as it is perhaps for Lear, it need not be futile for the witnessing audience. Where there are children, infants or adolescents and in-betweens, in this group of plays, they are mainly victims, not yet active agents. It is in placing the audience in role as a child-learner that the theme of childhood is most present.

By the 1970s Bond's work was becoming familiar, and useful, to a student generation growing up with the political consequences of the Vietnam and Cambodian wars, the economic fall-out from the oil price rise caused by the Arab-Israeli Yom Kippur war, and, domestically, the ongoing war in Ireland, whose consequences were being felt in mainland Britain. There was a sense now that Bond was addressing issues directly touching on the concerns of young people. One significant production in 1972 was the Leeds-based student group Last Knockings' production of *Lear*, the first ever after the Royal Court premiere. In the atmosphere of 'comedown' from 60s euphoria, with the harsh pressing reality of political crises at home and abroad, questions of political power and revolutionary challenge to the state and status quo were intensely relevant, and a student and youth generation were keenly aware of their importance. Members of the Last Knockings group were also active in the Interplay community and youth arts group. Bond visited the group, met local people and maintained a relationship with the company as an advisor. The above named exceptions apart, such a contact between grass roots organisations and a major British artist were rare, to say the least.

Responding to the same sets of social and political events throughout the 1970s, the Theatre in Education movement was developing a set of techniques based on the active participation of young people, usually in role, within a dramatic action. The work's main imperative at this time tended to be to educate about the workings of a society that fostered inequality and injustice, usually by dealing with issues like racism, or environment. Theatre in Education had sprung from the relationship between local theatres and local schools in the 1960s, and many of the actor-teachers who made up the new Theatre in Education teams had teacher training. They also carried with them much of the idealism and optimism of that decade and sought to apply these to the developing political crises of the 1970s.

These were problems to which Bond responded more obliquely, at least at first sight, in his next group of plays – the plays of explorations of culture, *Bingo, The Fool* and *The Woman*. Children are important but peripheral, except in the sense that these too are plays of learning and delusion. The old man in *Bingo* is infantilised by wartime wounds, Patty in *The Fool* contrasts her own pain in child-rearing with her poet husband's artistic pain, and Astyanax, the child of Trojan Cassandra, is killed by the victorious

Greeks in *The Woman*. It is with another play, *The Bundle*, first performed in 1978, the same year as *The Woman*, that the imagery of the infant comes literally centre-stage and into the title. Reworking the narrative material of *Narrow Road to the Deep North*, the play is set in a conflation of the literary and art-historical landscape of medieval Japan and the Cambridgeshire/ Suffolk fenlands, familiar to Bond from his family history and his own home. It is worth noting that another East Anglia-based artist, Benjamin Britten, used a similar conflation in his 1964 Parable for Church, *Curlew River*, and a similar narrative device of a Fenland ferryman. Britten is also an artist concerned with the corruption of childhood by social injustice but, like Bond's contemporary Dennis Potter, his moral vision is based on a simple, powerful regret for a lost innocence stolen by an act of violence. Bond's vision is both more contradictory and confrontational, involving the audience far more directly in the moral judgements made by his *Bundle* characters.

In a climactic scene, the audience is directly implicated in problems of personal responsibility. In a medieval Japan, a young man deliberately hurls an abandoned baby into the river so that he should not be distracted by human sympathy from pursuing his destiny as a revolutionary leader. Bond opens up the way to a new kind of play that anticipates parallel developments in the practice of Theatre in Education. This child-murder is not a recipe for action but the imagining of a terrible dilemma that the young man, and the audience, have to deal with. In a preface to the play, Bond writes of a new approach to the problems of playwriting:

> The 'dramatisation of the analysis instead of the story', in both the choice and the ordering of the scenes and in the incidents dramatically emphasised in the scenes, is a way of reinstating meaning in literature...But these dramatisations must not exist in their own right as dramatic effects. They demonstrate those crises in a story when the audience are asked to be not passive victims or witnesses, but interpreters of experience, agents of the future, restoring meaning to action by recreating self-consciousness. At these moments the audience are superior to the actors: they are on the real stage. (Bond, 1978)

To those familiar with the Theatre in Education model, it will be clear, I suspect, how close this approach is to that of a well-achieved Theatre in Education programme, if not yet in specifics but in the sense of empowering the audience and expecting them to work with the material, not simply to observe it, Scopey-like.

The Bundle is a pivotal play and it coincided with a period when Bond was deliberately involving himself in teaching situations. In 1978 he was supported by Northern Arts to be a Visiting Fellow, based at Newcastle University. His work there with students and Workers' Educational Association members resulted in his play *The Worlds*. Interviewed in 1980, Bond spoke of the personal imperatives that took him to these new situations:

> I certainly felt that I wanted to get off the rails that it seemed to me a lot of contemporary theatre is on. I felt that I wanted to broaden my experience ...to put myself in very problematic situations and find out how to deal with them. (Bond, 1980)

In the same interview it is clear that Bond is happy to embrace the responsibilities of a teacher, a role that is clearly defining itself and moving him towards the world of Drama and Theatre in Education:

> I try to make my sessions really rather difficult and to leave people unsatisfied – which I can do quite well!... You are the teacher – whether you like it or not. And they are the kids – whether they like it or not. And you can't actually say 'I'm one of you' or 'Let's be social together' or whatever. The relationship is different from that. It's a very dramatic relationship, and you have to polarise, I think. And press the relationship. (*ibid*)

The Worlds was re-staged by the Activists youth theatre, based at the Royal Court but serving a sizable area of south-western London. The production, directed by Bond, was another measure of his emerging commitment to young people's drama. He was also running workshops for Activists members and in the set of papers written at the time, he begins to outline ideas for a new way of performing his plays. In a poem, part of the Activists Papers collection, he writes these lines:

> The life of one man is explained by the lives of all men
> You don't need to understand his character
> You need to understand his life
> [...]
> You must act all men
> That is the theatre of reason
> Act this understanding
> Act learning
> [...]
> Let your playing show that you understand history
> The changes that men make and that make men
>
> (Bond, 1980)

In these ideas and sentiments there is an echo, or reflection, of what is going on amongst the new breed of actor-teachers, themselves aspiring to be stimuli of active learning. Here an accomplished TiE actor-teacher reflecting on her craft, looks for a similar holistic approach that takes into account the whole function and context of her acting:

> ... I find I can't get a proper relationship to the part unless I'm constantly reminding myself of the relationship of my character to the piece of theatre or to the programme as a whole because that can affect the way that you play the part. You can interpret a character usually in quite a variety of different ways and the interpretation that you eventually select, I think, depends on quite a lot of different factors. Obviously first of all your relationship to it and understanding of it, then the interaction that you have with the other actors i.e. other characters, and then what it is that the company as a whole is trying to say with the piece; what responses they want the audience to have, should, I think, dictate the ways in which you play it. (Jarvis 1983)

By 1982, Edward Bond had written *Derek* for the Royal Shakespeare Theatre's Youth Festival and was beginning work on the fiercely ambitious trilogy for the Royal Shakespeare Company, to be grouped together as *The War Plays*. Britain was by now deep into the period of social and economic disturbance under the right-wing leadership of Prime Minister Margaret Thatcher. By that Orwell-mythologised year, 1984, the Miners' Strike and its crushing by a triumphalist state exposed the true intention of a government that, thanks to its clear inability to deal with the Irish war, was itself nearly wiped out by the Brighton IRA bomb. What is clear is that neither TiE nor Bond as respectively, collective and individual dramatists, could be disengaged personally and artistically from the onslaught on liberal and progressive ideas during this time. For both Bond and the TiE movement, the churning social tensions of that period seemed to edge each towards respective crises from which they were to emerge, in some ways, revivified, although this was not at all obvious at the time. Many in the TiE movement could foresee only the eradication of their work and Bond even suggested that such was his disillusion with the state of theatre, he might go and raise sheep in Australia instead! In 1984 he abandoned his work on the RSC productions of *The War Plays*, unable to reconcile his artistic objectives with the institutional demands of the company. These seemed like dark days.

In the following year, 1985, conflicts over methodology and political ideology caused a wounding split in the TiE movement. The destructive pressures on funding by the Thatcher government took their toll on commitment and morale, as in all probability they were designed to do. The

Education Reform Act, and the rate-capping of local councils, brought to an end the support of many companies by local authorities. A re-alignment and closing of ranks of TiE companies began to take place as numbers dwindled. A significant bloc of TiE workers emerged who had a grounding in the Drama in Education theories and practice of Dorothy Heathcote and Gavin Bolton and it was these that made strong connections with the path that Bond was now on. Bond's commentary on *The War Plays* included a discussion of his ideas about the 'Theatre Event', his way of relating the meanings implicit in individual moments of the play to the play as a whole. This reflected a concurrent concern within TiE companies to take control of imagery and symbolism, as in key programmes like Leeds TiE's *Raj* and Cockpit TiE's *Ways of Change*. This was itself a concern absorbed from the work of Heathcote and Bolton. Bond's one produced work from 1985 was a short unpublished scenario, called *Burns*, for performance in schools, commissioned by New Midlands Dance Company.

Following the collapse of his working relationship with the RSC, what is effectively a whole new phase of work began. Professionally, it was characterised by a tendency to distance himself from the major UK producing companies. From the late 1980s to the present, Edward Bond's work is premiered by semi-professional or amateur companies (e.g. *Human Cannon*, 1986, by Quantum Theatre in Manchester, *Coffee*, 1996, by Rational Theatre, Glamorgan) or by Youth Theatre or TiE companies (e.g. *Jackets*, 1989, Leicester Haymarket Outreach company, *At The Inland Sea*, 1995, Big Brum TiE, Birmingham). In a 1996 interview Geoff Gillham, director of *At The Inland Sea* and one of TiE's earliest enthusiasts for Bond's work, outlined in a 1996 interview some of the ways in which the movement and the dramatist had converged, in accordance with the new historical realities of the 1990s:

> ... in a sense TiE has moved away from a very specific focus. This is what we want you to go away with, more a 'web of connections' for the teachers to draw out afterwards. There has been a striking convergence with TiE, a move away from a tight focus. At The Inland Sea deals with imagination, ideology, Auschwitz, by implication the development of fascism in Europe and the world now, looking at what it is to be human... They're very big concepts. All that area of content is meshed... now there's a move away from a tight focus. Now we're in a period after the political revolution in the Soviet Union, fluidity and instability in the world, things in a lot of change. Very fundamental things are being raised but not necessarily in a direct political sense. (Gillham,1996)

The startling, enlightening and provocative set of one hundred and thirteen *Notes on Imagination* is a key text – his plays apart – for understanding Bond. In these he elaborates, often playfully, on what has become a central concern in recent years, the practical utility of the Human Imagination. The work he has created for Big Brum for young people is the embodiment of this concern. The first of these, *At The Inland Sea*, represents the end of the twin journeys that Bond and the TiE movement have taken together, but of course it is also a new beginning, a new crossroads. 1997 saw *Eleven Vests* written for Big Brum. It is a play that confronts head-on, but un-mechanically, the ethos of school and its connection to wider violence in society. At the time of writing, 2004, the Bond-Big Brum collaboration has given birth to *The Balancing Act*, a play for young people that perfectly sums up the fruitful situation the writer now finds himself in.

The Balancing Act embodies a delightful paradox: a deeply serious play about the end of the world that is larkily inventive and vigorously comic, the world of *Saved* reconstituted in the style of *The League of Gentlemen*. It is a play that opens with a girl using her imagination, and her capacity to symbolise, to contain and protect herself from the pain of a mad world. The whole play spins off wildly from this act of creative imagination, as it becomes clear that the imaginative world created is both Bond's and the character's. He is not illustrating for us something he has witnessed or experienced about the way we live our lives, as would be the case in more conventional concerned playwriting, but sharing a rich and ever-changing theatrical metaphor that plays with ideas. The play is play-ful, but it is not frivolous. There's too much at stake – literally one false step and the world ends! Sometimes the play feels like one of those powerfully eerie Chris Morris surrealistic satires on a world tipping out of kilter.

But what gives Bond's vision real humanistic muscle is the politicised understanding of injustice that has always fuelled his writing, and an un-shakeable confidence in the potential, particularly amongst the young, for a re-visioning of the world, and a re-making of it, thanks to the human capacity to imagine. This is a writer who shuns cynicism in his maturity, as right at the beginning of his career he shunned Beckett's nihilistic pity. There is a sweet irony in the realisation that a 70 year-old, as he will be in the year these words are written, is potentially the most exciting and challenging writer of drama for young people in the new century.

Edward Bond has continued to support organisations such as the National Association for the Teaching of Drama, and broken new ground with the play written for a mixed cast of children and adult professionals, *The Chil-*

dren, performed by schools in Cambridgeshire. The threads of Bond's commitment to art, young people, education and a defiantly oppositional socialistic politics are powerfully and succinctly expressed in this letter of support to protesting drama students. It enfolds a critique of society's mistrust of education, a statement of drama's urgency, and a practical gesture of support to young people. It is characteristically, in all these ways, 'Bondian':

> To the students from Rose Bruford college acting in defence of their education on Sunday June 21st:
>
> We are facing a crisis involving the whole of society – the way we live together, the way adults care for the young and the young care for the old, what happens when we are sick or workless, the way we understand ourselves. Naturally the crisis is severest at the points where society forms itself and is held together. One of these points is education.
>
> Many rationalisations are given for the changes in education. The truth is that young people are increasingly being educated to fit into an economic structure and not to question it, though it destroys communities and devastates the earth. Young people are being educated to be powerless.
>
> Drama is the ancient art by which human beings recreate themselves. It is the source of the self-knowledge that saves us from ignorance of others and so it is the basis of community. No one chooses a life in theatre unless at a deep level they wish to increase their own humanity and make society more just. It is a tragedy that so often our trivialised theatre betrays them.
>
> In this 'age of the image', theatre becomes more important. Audiences – especially of TV, because it is convenient – are obsessive. Yet they betray their secret contempt for the triviality of what obsesses them by calling actors and directors 'luvvies'.
>
> So you are struggling not only for your own education but for the future of your profession. More than that, you are fighting for the common future. The state of a democracy is shown by the state of its theatres. As our drama becomes shallower, our society becomes crueller, more ignorant and unjust. Anyone in or outside theatre who understands what is happening and fears what may happen, should stand at your side. (Bond, 1998)

References

Bond, E (1971) *Lear* London, Methuen

Bond, E (1972) 'Drama and The Dialectics of Violence', *Theatre Quarterly* Vol II No.5 Jan – Mar.1972 pps 4-14

Bond, E (1978) 'A Note on Dramatic Method' in Bond, E *The Bundle*, London, Methuen

Bond, E(1980) 'Advice to Actors' The Activists Papers, in *The Worlds*, with The Activists Papers, London, Eyre Methuen

Bond, E (1995) 'Notes on Imagination' in Bond, E *Coffee*, London, Methuen

Bond, E (1996) Letter to David Thacker, *Edward Bond Letters III*, ed. Ian Stuart, Amsterdam Harwood

Bond , E (1998) unpublished document

Jarvis (1983) Janice Jarvis (in discussion with Roger Chamberlain) 'Acting in Theatre-in-Education', *SCYPT Journal*, Number 11 September 1983 pps 14-25

Gillham G. (1996) Interview, unpublished, with Tony Coult

3

Alienation is the 'Theatre of Auschwitz':
an exploration of form in Edward Bond's theatre

Kate Katafiasz

With this shocking remark, Bond brings together two of the most apparently contradictory forces of the twentieth century: fascism and the communist dramaturgy of Bertolt Brecht. It is a profoundly disturbing, not to say incendiary collision of opposites, undermining conventional thought on both drama and politics in an instant.

The statement seems to suggest some sort of *functional* association between alienation and Auschwitz: as though both serve the same end. Given that alienation derives from a form of theatre passionately opposed to fascism, this seems grossly unfair. As Bond himself has it:

> I called the theatre of the A-effect the theatre of Auschwitz. Obviously I do not mean this in a simple sense. In a simple sense it is the opposite of true. The Nazis at Auschwitz would have exterminated Brecht not staged him. Brecht spent his energies and his life trying to make hell-holes such as Auschwitz – or the Gulag – impossible. (Bond, 2000:171)

So how does this functional association operate? What are the complexities hinted at by Bond's phrase 'not ... in a simple sense?'

It is the project of this chapter to try to unpack the historical and functional complexities: in doing so I hope to illuminate how and why the *intentions* of key innovatory practitioners like Brecht, came to be so seriously counterproductive in *effect* and consequently why drama has to develop radically differently. In his book on theatre theory, *The Hidden Plot* (Bond, 2000:10-19), Bond discusses different dramatic structures from the twentieth century: by elaborating on some of his thinking here, I hope to enable the reader to grasp why drama had to develop as it did, yet why past practitioners are subject to Bond's sometimes devastating critique. This will give the rationale for Bond's own dramaturgical innovations, which I will analyse in the latter part of the chapter. It is only by getting to grips with the discoveries, illusions and misconceptions of twentieth century drama that radical drama can progress usefully in the twenty-first century. It is clearly in the interests of such progression that Bond has thrown this challenging and intriguing remark into the dramaturgical arena.

Why does Bond attack dramatic alienation so unequivocally? It has excellent credentials: it arose partly out of a desperate need for clarity in the face of the ideological obfuscations of the trenches of the First World War. Why on earth did millions of young men from both sides willingly sign up to be slaughtered? Writing in Germany relatively soon after the event in 1928, Ernst Toller states that they were somehow hoodwinked by their elders' murderous ideology: 'the same elders who did nothing to prevent the war but, tricking it out in romanticism, pitilessly and unfeelingly sent battalion after battalion of young German manhood out to die' (Toller, 1995: 95). It is now widely recognised that the First World War was a war of attrition over capitalist markets fought in the name of God, King and Country. Why were prevailing artistic structures unable to expose the old ideologies?

Realism

To make an audience face its own ideological beliefs, the dramatic form must challenge, not confirm or confuse, the relationship between reason and imagination. The realist plays of Strindberg, Ibsen and Chekhov often depict characters who have difficulty distinguishing between the rational and the imaginative; Miss Julie, Hedda Gabler and Liuba Ranyevskaya all imagine that their aristocratic status makes them invulnerable. But they are either ahead of social change, in the case of Miss Julie, who imagines she can be sexually liberated *and* aristocratic, or lagging imaginatively behind it like Ranyevskaya, who cannot modify her aristocratic largesse even in the face of destitution. Putting emotion at the heart of the performance (in the manner of a Stanislavski trained actor) blurs the distinction between the real social issues at stake in the drama, as society shifts from feudal to capitalist values, and the imagined world of the characters. When emotion justifies action, the action becomes more reasonable and so the status quo goes unchallenged. When emotional justification precedes action, stasis is confirmed: this happens because of that: we understand and it seems reasonable to us. Whereas when a character acts unreasonably (as Julie, Hedda and Liuba unquestionably do!) a need for creative thinking (change) is implied: we don't understand – we must think! The consistency of actions endowed by objectives and through lines can work in direct opposition to the writers' efforts at creating a productive *dis*juncture for the audience. I would argue that the *characters* in realist drama are confused and cannot distinguish between the rational and the imaginative precisely in order to enable *their audiences* to consider the distinction. Stanislavski's system puts the audience in the same confused state as the characters, denying them the vital opportunity to reassess the relationship between reason and imagination. As Bond puts it:

> The audiences' imaginations do not create, the stage imagines for them. It is as if the stage took a photograph of its dead audience, and then they saw themselves reflected in their glassy eye. (Bond, 2000: 41)

Expressionism and Formalism

Playwrights clearly needed to modify dramatic structure to put their audiences in a more analytical place. The post-First World War European avant-garde realised that an emphasis on plausibility in drama imposes imaginative stasis on its audiences: the stage can only imagine things as they appear to be: it can neither anticipate or illustrate change. Two distinct trends emerged: one, in Germany, to illustrate the rational and urgent need for social change as fascism gained ground; the other, in the Soviet Union, where society *had* changed, fore-grounded the role of the imagination.

German Expressionism focused intently on the social and the rational in which the 'accidental private person' is revealed to be an explicitly social 'type'.

> In style, expressionism was pregnant, almost telegraphic, always shunning the peripheral and always probing to the centre of things. In expressionistic drama man is no accidental private person. He is a type posited for many, and ignoring the limits of superficial characterisation. Man was skinned in the expectation that somewhere under his skin was his soul. (Toller, 1995: 96)

The drive here was to illuminate the essence, to expose what was hidden beneath ideological surfaces, so that the tragedy of the war could never be repeated. In Soviet Russia, the social changes had been breathtaking: a slave-owning feudal state as late as 1861, Russia had attempted capitalist transformation and in 1917 became the first Communist state. As Lenin puts it in 1911, in the thick of the process before the revolution: 'Here in Russia everything has been turned upside down and is only just taking shape. What was turned upside down was serfdom and the whole of the old order that went with it.' (Lenin, 1996: 43). This extraordinarily radical social change needed correspondingly radical changes in dramatic form to give people insight into the changed realities: imagination had to catch up!

Early Soviet writers, theatre practitioners and film-makers (their movement became known as 'Formalism' because of their preoccupation with artistic form) discovered that disturbing realist graphic representation by splitting images, cutting and splicing film sequences, they could create disturbing juxtapositions. When time and space are dislodged in this way, the audience is challenged to reconnect them and so the mind of the onlooker comes to the fore in the process. The process is rational because the audience attempts to link cause with effect, but it is also imaginative. Realism shows all: here, what is *not* shown is what is significant. Realism had been unable to involve the audience in this dynamically rational and imaginative – conceptual – manner. You can see how artistic structure became a fascination for the Formalists: when you tamper with graphic representation and get an audience to think, the rather crude 'echo effect' of emotion in realist drama (when the audience feels what the characters feel) metamorphoses into the creation of *value*. Concepts of the world are held in the mind. Yet, because they involve human values, concepts are connected with society. They cannot be graphically represented but they can be invoked using these disrupted structures. Eisenstein's analysis of a child's drawing of 'lighting a stove' illustrates this most effectively:

> Everything is depicted in tolerable proportions and with great care: firewood, stove, chimney. But in the middle of the room there is an enormous rectangle crossed with zig-zags. What are they? They turn out to be 'matches'. Bearing in mind the crucial importance of these matches for the process depicted, the child gives them the appropriate scale. (Eisenstein, 1999: 19)

Semantics, or the reordering of the way the image signals itself, is shown to affect its meaning. Attention is drawn to something not technically present: the mind of the onlooker. The changed structure of the representational scale in the drawing dramatically changes the thought processes of the onlooker: Formalist artists like Eisenstein consciously manipulated the structure of their work to achieve this effect.

The Formalists were denounced, and ultimately they and their movement were destroyed by Stalin, for their focus on *literary* structures rather than *social* or class structures: the implicit connection between the two had not been understood. Brecht's dramaturgy emerges perhaps out of a well-intentioned attempt to reconcile the formalist structures, invented by his dead Soviet colleagues, with the demands of their political masters. '*Ostranenie*' is the creative oddness generated for the onlooker by the gap in between the Formalists' disconnected images. In Brecht's hands it becomes the '*Verfremdungseffekt*', the juxtaposition of literary imagination with social reality. Just as Stanislavski employs emotion to blur the distinction between fact and fiction making everything plausible, Brecht *separates* the real from the imagined by alienating emotion: in this mirror, you look so strange you don't know yourself!

Epic Theatre: Formalism *with* Expressionism

The problem lies essentially in the difficulties of expressing and signifying reality simultaneously: it is like asking us what we see and telling us what it is at the same time.

Brecht's project is to demonstrate that capitalist – and feudal – social structures, such as social class and inequality are neither natural nor God-given, but are constructed by humans and so can be altered by humans. This is often delivered via the central metaphor, prevalent in many of his plays, of a mother whose maternal instincts are tantamount to suicide in an inhuman society; or as Roland Barthes puts it: 'How to be good in a bad society?' (Barthes 1996: 139). Unless the audience are alienated from the action, they are blind to the social dimension, as were the early audiences of *Mother Courage*, in Zurich; they sympathised with Courage and saw her as standing 'with her great mother's heart outside the confines of history, indeed in eternity' (Brecht 1983: xxii): nothing could have been more off the mark, as far as Brecht was concerned! It is as if an idealist form preoccupied with the manipulation of time and space, and a materialist content bent on social analysis, wrestle with each other for communicative supremacy. This makes our responses to Courage and her plight surprisingly ambiguous.

Brecht's problem here is how to prize apart our sympathetic understanding of Courage from her virulently destructive ideology; we have watched her faith in commerce destroy her children one by one and now we see it destroying her. He does this by giving us the 'Gestic split' (Counsell, 1996:104). Because Brecht cannot allow his audiences to emote in ways he would see as inappropriate, he invents the Gestus, a device to generate a clear distinction between social reality and the fictional perspective of the play.

At the end of Brecht's Berliner Ensemble production of *Mother Courage*, Helene Weigel begins the final scene hunched over her daughter Kattrin's corpse, which she cradles and sings to as if it were a living baby. She has treated the living girl so badly that the way she caresses the corpse appals us: we feel she may have gone mad because she doesn't seem able to accept that Kattrin is dead. We abhor her sentiment because it is so misplaced. Then she goes into business mode, taking charge, covering the corpse and paying for the funeral with exaggerated dignity: her superior airs are totally misplaced because her situation – pulling the cart alone – is extreme. She bows low to the peasant and his son but refuses to bow to the peasant's wife. Then she bows very low to Kattrin's corpse as they carry it out. Her final 'bow', though, is to the cart: she bends double with the effort of getting the cart moving alone. This repeated bow shows her perceived social status is in stark contrast to her actual status: she is not superior as she imagines herself to be, but destitute. Her delusion – the gap between her perceptions and what we can see to be reality – is ultimately what alienates us: we cannot sympathise with her in her delusion, we can only rationalise about it.

Alienation: The Gestic Split

In the gestus, the repeated bowing, we see two discourses operating: the story discourse, or view from the play world (Courage's sense of superiority as a businesswoman amongst peasants), and the social discourse, which is intended to show that the text (story) is not truth but opinion. It is actually very hard for her to pull her cart alone. According to Counsell, this 'is the basis of Brecht's democratisation of the auditorium.' (Counsell, 1996:105). This view echoes the critic Roland Barthes' who has it that Brechtian dramaturgy 'postulates that... the responsibility of a dramatic art is not so much to express reality as signify it.' (Barthes 1996: 139). This is a stance with which I would take issue because I contend that Brecht does presume to insist on a particular response. This is not a split image as Eisenstein would have known it, with a gap to dwell upon, but the actor (reality) commenting on the character (story). Here reason and imagination are separated into two discourses. This is alienating emotionally: you cannot sympathise with Courage unless you deny that rationally she is the cause of her own situation. The problem, as I hope to demonstrate, is one of structure: whatever the good intentions of the writer, when you pit reason (actor) against imagination (character), you put your audience in a double bind: although you appear to offer your audience a 'democratic' choice of discourses, one set of signs invalidates the other.

This is how it works: as Fortier usefully puts it, 'the actor has a double role on stage as both character and actor/demonstrator' (Fortier, 1997: 25). Thus the actor might communicate one discourse, Courage's own perspective on things, as she bows to one person and not another; and another discourse, this time the actor's perspective, showing Courage's real plight as she is forced to bow lowest to the actual weight of her cart, revealing the character's weakness to the audience. Her attitude is hopeful, but her actions reveal how close she is to death. The actor shows the audience what Courage, in her ideologically-bound state cannot see: that the very thing she depends on for her life, getting her cart to its regimental market, is killing her. As she moves slowly forward, dragging her cart, Courage sees her action as giving her life: the audience sees it is killing her. Brecht intended for the audience, 'some exercise in complex seeing – though it is perhaps more important to be able to think above the stream than to think in the stream.' (Brecht, 1964: 44).

The rational discourse *is intended* to predominate over the imaginative one. This is the only way Brecht can prise ideology away from story. Alienation exposes the ideology by interrupting the story and letting the world (actor) show the audience how it really is. Ideology is exposed but at the cost of devaluing the human. Though the two discourses have been shown together, and to some degree inform each other, logically the imaginative has been shown to be fallacious: Mother Courage may *think* she can get back into business but we know better: we can see she will soon die. The story discourse cannot be trusted: Brecht draws on the authority of signs from outside the story, authored by the actor not the character, to ultimately communicate meaning to his audience. The imagination cannot influence reason as it does in Eisenstein's observation of the child's drawing, in which it is *reasonable* for the child's values to count. For Brecht reason has to influence imagination. We are consigned to a world of instrumental, not human value: the values of Auschwitz.

Alienation: The Gestic Split and Double Bind Theory

When reason is disassociated from imagination a strange process is set in train. Each member of the audience is split. To which set of signs should we respond? The story discourse engages us emotionally, we see as Courage sees, her situation is our situation: we are emotionally connected but socially myopic. Everything is tragic. The early Zurich audiences must have gone wholeheartedly for this response; they were in denial about their social reality, like Courage.

Or we can respond to the social discourse: in this event we understand Courage's situation, not Courage. *She* is responsible for her own predicament – her stupid inhuman values have put her where she is. But our need to pity Courage is very powerful! Her situation in capitalist society is our situation. The gestic split alienates us from ourselves: we can neither pity nor understand either Courage or ourselves. This is confusing: the emotion conjured by our engagement with Courage cannot coexist with the social discourse, so the choice of discourses is only illusory. It is not *reasonable* to pity her. When emotion is made entirely reasonable, as with the Stanislavski system, as we have seen, we cannot question the status quo: we just live it as the unchanging human condition. But when emotion cannot be rationalised we cannot engage our*selves* with our situation: to use Bond's term (Bond, 2000:47-50) it is as if we leave the 'site' of the drama, of the self, feeling as though we can stand outside our emotional framework, put it to one side and just be rational and unbiased. Instead of sympathising with Courage we disapprove of her – and also disapprove of that part of ourselves that identified with her. We are repulsed by Courage and her values and so cannot possibly come to terms with the fact that they are our values: if we accepted that they were our own values, we could change them. As it is we cannot *use* our knowledge: it is very frustrating! Alienation makes us helpless because it divorces us from ourselves and takes us outside of our social situation. We become invisible to ourselves: when we lose our insight our sanity is in question.

Imagining we can 'think above the stream', where reason predominates over imagination, puts us in a very psychologically and socially dangerous place. It is a classic double bind scenario in which the mind is schizophrenically confused and cannot make sense of the world: it either inhabits a trance-like state governed by metaphor – the story discourse, or it rationalises coldly and psychopathically. A double bind occurs whenever reason negates emotion (Bateson *et al.* 1956: 251-264). As Bond puts it, 'If situations could speak for themselves, drama would not be possible.' (Bond, 2000: 40). Far from generating 'complex seeing', as he intended, Brecht generates *either* myopia or grandiosity. His dramaturgy – particularly the gestus – functions in a way directly comparable with the following paradoxical command: do not read this! The onlooker responds (words are to be read) but the response is immediately invalidated. What is asked is at odds with what is implied. This separates reason from emotion. We have emotions but we cannot know them and so use them creatively. What happens to our emotional response? Where does the feeling go? It cannot be connected to anything, made sense of or conceptualised, so the *self* is invalidated: the mind cannot engage humanly with the world if the *self* is not incorporated. It is a surprisingly brutal scenario: when pity is made irrational we are in Auschwitz where human values do not exist. Far from empowering us, as some would claim Brecht intended, the process of alienation puts us in an ambivalent inertia: we either emote sentimentally, irrationally, or reason unfeelingly, genocidally. Either way, we are helpless in the face of fact. What is striking about this is how familiar the schizoid double bind is to us culturally in the post-modern era: it is as if Brecht pre-figures Derrida.

Alienation and Deconstruction

Brecht and Derrida may seem, superficially, to be in opposition to each other. Derrida's statement '*il n'ya pas dehors le texte*' (Derrida, 1967), there is nothing outside the text, seems to contradict Brecht's project whereby alienation strives to allow its audience to stand inside the 'text' and outside of it at the same time. Brecht seems to think that the mind can be made objective, as in his well-known example of the 'Street Scene' (Brecht 1964: 121), in which an uninvolved witness narrates the story of an accident to deliver a clear point of view to his audience. For Derrida, in contrast, the arts can only 'play' with the imagination, which can never be brought to bear on reality (Derrida, 2000:102). Yet I would argue that alienation and deconstruction *function* in the same way because they both disconnect reason from imagination. They are different sides of the same disabling methodology. It is highly ironic that just as Brecht the modernist separated reason from imagination to highlight the rational, much contemporary post-modern art separates them to capture the imaginative.

Deconstruction can deliver the rational *or* the imaginative. It cannot seem to do both. It is in some ways thanks to deconstruction that we are culturally equipped to shake off the ideologies of (God), king and country: it shows us logically that wars are fought for commodities. But in the past societies derived their sense of human value from a belief in God: as Bond puts it, the truth derived from a lie (Bond, 2003). Deconstruction reveals the lie, and erases the value that went with it: we have no value because we have no God. Exposing the lie erased the truth along with it. As feudal values finally give way to capitalist structures, as God steps out of the picture and is replaced by the ruthless nihilism of the markets, what becomes of human values? Deconstruction usefully brings us face to face with the difficult notion that there is nothing 'out there' to tell us how to be human: it forces us to face unpalatable facts about our social history as we grasp how feudal and capitalist societies cloak injustice with ideology. It is just that the process of deconstruction destroys value. Under capitalism we sense that blood ought *not* to be cheaper than oil, but reason alone, without God, cannot tell us *why* not exactly. Imagination dramatises by putting us into a situation. It lets us ponder, 'what if it were *my* blood?' To be human in this way we need to connect ourselves with the world, to reason imaginatively. It is why we have drama. Deconstruction, in separating reason from imagination, disconnects us from ourselves and thus destroys our capacity to value humanity: it is in this sense anti-drama.

Yet deconstruction has its uses. Deconstructing manufactured objects shows us our society, our situation and values: it is as if these are semantically encoded in the object by the social production process and in the mind by the process of language acquisition. Taking the object apart seems to reveal the social code. Deconstruction demonstrates how ideology interacts with history and to what ends: it delivers Brecht's agenda in that we see that there is nothing accidental or inevitable about the process that constructs our social situation. Bond says that the whole of society is in a cup: we can see Auschwitz in a bottle of pop (Bond, 2003). If we deconstruct a bottle of pop we become aware of the social processes involved in its manufacture: labour is undervalued, the shareholders reap the profits, marketing sells an empty dream, the contents are bad for us but we have to buy it because our economy depends on our continued consumption. Drinking pop destroys our teeth, makes us fat and ultimately can kill us, but it benefits the economy. Our society is organised to facilitate this: it makes us *want* to behave, like Courage, in self-destructive market-serving ways. There is no need for the SS in our death camp.

So we 'dramatise the map' when we deconstruct objects (Bond, 2003) and the mind sees its situation, though not its self, without ideology clouding the issue. But when we deconstruct an object produced by society it is as if we deconstruct ourselves along with it because the thought process, by disconnecting reason from imagination, disconnects us culturally from ourselves, and each other. When we separate reason from imagination we separate the self from society. In response to a rational analysis from our doctor or dentist about the health hazards of drinking pop, we might individually try to give it up and not allow our children to drink it. We watch the rest of society consuming it and feel as helpless as we did watching Mother Courage killing herself over her cart. It does nothing to change society. Deconstruction takes apart our human potency, our connectedness with and so our ability to influence society. We are either inside society and unable to see it or outside it and unable to change it: the point is, of course, to change it.

Bond: Dramatist in the Post-Modern Context

We have seen how Bond's theoretical writing in *The Hidden Plot* signals his extreme dissatisfaction with the practitioners and dramatic structures of the twentieth century: old structures such as alienation techniques are not only inadequate, but *virulent* when used in the post-modern context. It is also tempting to dismiss the insights of post-modernism because deconstruction appears to leave us so helpless in the face of market-driven brutalism. But if we can grasp the *mechanisms* at work when we use alienation and deconstruction, the way in which the double bind divorces reason from imagination, then we can appreciate how in Bond's hands the process is subtly yet radically reversed.

Bond, in contrast to Brecht, acknowledges that people, because of their different experiences, need to 'see things differently'. For instance, while Brecht considers it possible for a witness to a street incident to demonstrate what happened with the express purpose of assigning responsibility (Brecht, 1964: 121), Bond says your perception of the street accident may be different 'if you have a car yourself or if you have a close friend who had an accident: people bring their life to their decisions' (Bond, 2003). To deconstructionists and post modernists, this indicates that our perception is hopelessly skewed and the mind can never engage properly with the world because pure objectivity is unattainable. But Bond's dramaturgy, essentially experiential in nature, respects the mind as a rational and imaginative holism. His dramatic devices allow for individual differences in perception and response, but also allow virulent cultural and ideological associations to be challenged.

Alienation takes away significance. Everything we see on stage at the end of *Mother Courage* is valueless, reduced to its instrumental value. In the penultimate scene we have seen Kattrin save the city of Halle from attack, a scene of heroism and enormous human tragic value. Brechtian alienation takes a humanly significant subject and creates helplessness and banality out of it. Weigel's Courage bows low to her daughter's heroic corpse, but she bows lower to the weight of her cart. Now, in the final scene, Courage herself is only as good as her ability to pull her cart. Alienation reduces objects and people to their instrumental value: this is decathexis, in which capitalist fiscal values predominate, as – in extreme form – the human hair blankets and human skin lampshades of Auschwitz. Decathexis means a significant situation is rendered banal. Bond, in contrast, takes an object so banal as to be 'invisible' to us, and makes it significant: this is cathexis. Used in conjunction with deconstruction, it challenges our social value systems because it enables us to grasp that though society has us *all* bowing before Courage's valueless cart, humanity can value things differently. We identify with what we see on stage and so stay in society, thus gaining insight into ourselves socially. I hope to demonstrate how this is done in some detail by analysing Bond's new play *The Balancing Act* in the latter part of this chapter.

Story

To summarise: modernists realised that to extract ideology from story it was necessary to take story to pieces. Brecht begins what later, post-modern practices take up enthusiastically: the deconstruction of story. He theorises and develops a practice whereby story is *interrupted* temporally and spatially and fact is inserted in the gap. Thus actor comments on character, sound comments on image, image contradicts image and audience uses the sign systems of reality to judge the fallacious signs from the fiction or story. It is because *story* has been interrupted that reason and imagination are split so damagingly from each other so that reason wipes out imagination. Reason and imagination can work together in story: it's the whole purpose of story to enable humans to use fiction to reason imaginatively and imagine reasonably. Story gives us novelty and depth that might be lacking, or might be too familiar or too dangerous to our psyche, for us to 'see' in real life. The separation of reason and imagination is the interruption of story: post-modern schizoid alienation results.

For Bond then it is imperative *not* to interrupt the story: that is why his plays might sometimes look, superficially, as though they were realist in style. Time and space may be stretched in a Bond play (his plays are interestingly now often set in the future), but they are not voguishly chopped about. For Bond, the political is the social, the cultural, not the scientific and purely rational: he is interested in humanity, in *social* constructs. Bond's imperative as an artist is to enable the audience to see the *self* operating in society so he cannot alienate what he shows as Brecht does: the story must be kept intact for reason and imagination to function together. How then can he expose that to which familiarity blinds us: the hidden plot, the invisible ideology? Interrupting and deconstructing the story may separate reason from imagination but at least along the way you get a sense of our social ills before you settle into the rightist emotional denial of a feckless Courage, or the leftist, helplessly rational, hoarse frustration of a sterile Cassandra who accurately predicts the future but is heard by nobody: these are the bipolar options available to us if we use alienation.

Alienation From Within the Act

To expose the social and ideological, the drama now has to semi-deconstruct or *dislodge*, though on no account sever, the relationship between reason and imagination: we have to find a means of analysis which does not disrupt the integrity of the fictional art form. That means analysing from *within* the action. Bond does this with cathexis, by putting emotional commitment into objects rather than people, avoiding Stanislavskian trance-like sentimentality *and* the Brechtian double bind. By putting the argument into an object, as I hope to demonstrate, all the sign systems of the stage open up for creative interrogation, yet the integrity of the fiction is not compromised. As the French director, Alain Francon, noted when directing Bond's plays, if the small things are right the bigger things fall into place.

The Balancing Act
Cathexis

What happens when an object becomes cathexed? Look at a moment from Bond's new play *The Balancing Act*. The first draft of the play was written by Bond in April 2003 and was being toured by Big Brum Theatre in Education at the time of writing this chapter: it has since been redrafted, but is not yet published. In Act 1 we see Viv, who is a young woman, clearly very disturbed, living rough in an abandoned house. Her boyfriend visits her to bring her food and finds her unaccountably 'defending' a 'spot' on the floor of the derelict house. He persuades her to explain what is the matter and she tells him about her sense that things are changing so fast that the world is becoming unbalanced: she sees the world like a ship whose passengers dance on the decks without noticing its dangerous instability. If the 'spot' on the floorboards were to be disturbed, the world would sink like a ship hit from a great height with a grain of sand: the passengers would still feel they were dancing but they would be dead, just corpses pushed by water. She describes humanity, realising its demise too late to act, howling inarticulately like the wind, and she spills a packet of crisps on the floor to illustrate:

> They wouldn't scream – their tongues 'Id be pull out. The wind makes that sound. It'd be terrible. (She spills a packet) They'd go like that. Be dead and silent like the crisps. (*The Balancing Act*, Act 1)

The crisps stay on the floor while she describes her obsession: presently, Nelson her boyfriend concludes, 'Yer potty.' To teach her a lesson, make her see sense, he threatens to demonstrate her insanity by jumping on the spot to prove that the world will not end. This sends her into a panic followed by the calm resolution that if the world does not end it just means she has got the wrong spot. And so, realising the futility of his threat, he picks up the 'scattered crisps and puts them back into the packet' before 'carefully' putting 'the bag of crisps on the spot', which would destroy the world.

> Yer get away with this lark 'cause I feed yer. I ain anymore. Somethin' 'as t' knock some sense in t' yer. (Crisps) If you wan' t' eat yer'll 'ave 't take it from there. (*The Balancing Act,* Act 1)

So the argument between sanity and madness is invested in the crisps: imaginatively, (madly?), they signify dismembered bodies; rationally they signify food. Viv uses them emotionally, Nelson instrumentally. Because they are central to the argument, the stage, the whole currency of the play, Viv and Nelson focus on them and so do we in the audience. Every word and action is *delivered in relation to those crisps*, so that the argument, the play's centre, is made visually, semiotically, clear. We all care what happens to the crisps, whether we view them reasonably or imaginatively, because we define ourselves in relation to them. They have become cathexed, that is to say, it matters to the audience what happens to them. We are engaged in the emotional logic that they give to people's actions. Alienation would force us to view them rationally, but cathexis allows us the emotional *as well* as the rational dimension in the same moment. Now, *how* Nelson picks up the crisps and how Viv reacts to his handling of them becomes a very important 'live' event – a Theatre Event in fact. Time slows because the action is loaded with responsibility for the audience. The decision about how to view the crisps, and its significance, is open to us: whether we laugh or cry depends on whether we are being reasonable or imaginative: Both are acceptable. Nothing dictates to us how to conceptualise what we see: we can think, 'It's a crisp!' (it's worth nothing) or 'It's a corpse!' (it's worth everything). We may laugh if Nelson playfully eats one to prove his point: we may recoil in horror with Viv at the same act. We may both laugh and recoil. We are free to value this live, because genuinely open, event as we need to.

The Theatre Event
In a Theatre Event, which occurs when you use cathexis, time slows down almost automatically. This is a temporal distortion, like Brecht's modernist 'not... but', in a sense, but with crucial differences. Like the 'not... but', the integrity of the story is not broken, but crucially, unlike the 'not... but', there is no 'right' way to respond. As Grusha hesitates over risking her life to rescue the baby in Act Two of Brecht's *The Caucasian Chalk Circle*, it is obvious to the audience what is the human and 'right' action for her to take.

Here, in Bond's TE we are genuinely provoked; emotionally we may side with Viv, sympathise with her in her psychosis; rationally we know that Nelson is right – *they are just crisps.* We see Viv's delusion and can sympathise with it: Mother Courage's delusion is what alienates us. So we are taken to the play's 'centre': is it sane to be mad? Or mad to be sane? Compare this with Barthes' interpretation of Brecht's central question, tinged with morality – how to be 'good' in a 'bad' world? Brecht does not make us responsible for the 'badness': we can blame someone else, stupid Mother Courage for instance, for it. The TE makes us responsible and yet it does not moralise because morality alienates us from ourselves: if we see something as 'wrong', it is difficult for us to own it. We cannot dodge the issue because the question is inherent in how we see those crisps, yet morality, the stultifying sense of a 'right' and 'wrong' response is noticeably absent. Every action, every object on stage, becomes caught in what Bond calls a 'vortex', in relation to which the crisps sit 'innocently', inanimate and still in the eye of the storm. In the storm swirl different possibilities for value for the audience to piece together creatively. The centre of the play is thus re-iterated in different ways in every image concerning the crisps; when these Theatre Events occur, the play shifts from what Bond calls description to analysis, without compromising the story, without using signs from outside the play to reveal the hidden ideologies. How exactly is this done?

Partial Deconstruction and Cathexis

If alienation uses a significant situation to create banality, the Theatre Event, in stark contrast, takes a *banal* object and uses it to create enormous *significance.* What is the grammatical structure of a packet of crisps? We can see this fascinatingly explored in *The Balancing Act.*

From the very beginning of the play, Nelson's crisps are invested with human concern: he has bought the food to keep Viv going in her three-day vigil in the derelict house. They undergo a fascinating trajectory. Nelson is concerned for Viv so he brings her crisps to eat. Viv is concerned about the world so she spills the crisps to show Nelson how people are in crisis. Then the crisps become, as we have seen, the centre of a debate about how they should be valued: as foodstuff, or as humanity. Nelson picks them up off the floor and places them carefully on the 'spot' at the end of Act One: if Viv wants to eat she has to risk 'ending the world' or admit that she is mad. Viv, who hides underneath the floorboards, dies in the demolition, but the crisps are rescued by Nelson: he walks innocently over Viv's hiding place, risks treading on the 'spot' and ending the world to get the packet. By Act

Three the crisps are referred to by the DSS Officer as 'life-threatening consumables', a trite statement which adds authority's social take on the crisps,
which is ironic in the light of their previous incarnations as life-givers and
'existential utensils' illustrating the plight of humanity! In Act Four Nelson
goes guiltily to eat one crisp, from sheer hunger. The Thief scoffs them 'fun-
nelling the crumbs in the packet into his mouth' before persuading Nelson
to get him a bag of 'Provencal Olive n' Tomato' flavour. Nelson returns from
the shop at the end of the scene with a replacement bag of the more prosaic
'Liver n' Bacon' flavour: it's 'all they 'ad!'. They resurface at the end of the
play as the DSS Officer '(*Takes the crisps packet from Nelson's pocket and
gives it to the Foreman*) Your wedding present!' (*The Balancing Act*, Act 6).

What we see here is the *partial* deconstruction of the crisps: the social
values inherent in the crisps can be wrung out of them and explored. Few
things can be instrumentally cheaper for us than a bag of crisps. Authority
tells us they are 'life-threatening'. The crisp manufacturing industry invents
ludicrous gourmet-sounding 'flavours'; they sell a 'Provencal Olive n'
Tomato' dream in a crisp packet to those of us who are stuck in 'Liver n'
Bacon' Britain. Our society is recognisably sent-up: we see ourselves and
laugh at ourselves. It's very recognisably British. So the crisps are used to
explore our social values. We know our society has these mad contradictions: things that are physically bad for us, such as crisps and cigarettes, are
packaged and alluringly marketed for huge profit. Our imaginations are hijacked in the process. If you eat too many crisps, because advertising has
hijacked your imagination or because they are all you can afford to buy,
you'll get a heart attack: if we don't care about the world, and why would we
if we don't care about ourselves, we'll destroy it. Separating reason from
imagination in this cultural double bind seems to have become a capitalist
media imperative. It makes us spend our bodies, our world, recklessly to
feed the markets: it is as if we have become the consumables in our consumer democracy. Crisps consume people as it were. In this sense the
crisps can be shown to contain society in all its dimensions, as does any
manufactured object which has gone through the production process
identified by Marx; the manufacture, the marketing, the generation of
profit for shareholders, and the ripping off (fiscally and imaginatively) of
the consumer (Grady, 2003).

But the crisps remain crisps in the play. They still *function* as crisps – at the
end of the play it is still reasonable, logical even, for hungry people (the
Demolition Expert) to want to eat them: they have not been destroyed in
the process. The relationship between the signifier and the thing it signifies

is not destroyed in the process of revealing ideology as it would be if they were completely deconstructed. They can still be used, seen by the audience, as crisps, as well as society. It is cathexis which structurally allows this layering of the significance of an object to take place: all the meanings coexist and are not functioning to cancel each other out as in alienation's double-bind of 'do not read this sign!' It is just that the relationship between structure (the crisp-signifier) and ideology (the social-signified), reason and imagination, has been loosened. The crisps, if used in this way, show us our social site, and the fact that it still seems reasonable to want to eat them means we are still *inhabiting* our social site, we are not alienated. This means that the paradox of wanting to do something that will kill you, willingly being consumed by consumables, is personally available to us and that central paradox of the play, *joie de mourir*, of living in our society, is starkly revealed. The relationship between reason and imagination has not been *split* but it has been *loosened*. The fiction is still intact, the crisps are still crisps, the story is still a story, the play is still a play but society, and by implication we ourselves in all its (our) very real ideological madness is simultaneously available to us.

Revaluing the Object: The Tragic

More than this, the crisps are 'recathexed'. The social meaning has been wrung out of them, allowing us a rational interpretation of our society but the opportunity is given for them to acquire new, imaginatively created meanings in their social context. The reasoned analysis is part of our social grammar, a recognised facet of our social set-up. So much so that 'provencal olive n' tomato flavour' versus 'liver n' bacon' gets a laugh from the audience: we recognise our social selves. Class values are wryly and banally represented as 'taste'. What could be more British? But beneath the wry laughter of helpless self-recognition there is always a tragic dimension at work for Bond, an attempt to get right beneath ideology and revalue the object completely. As he prepares to barge into the derelict room where Viv is in the process of burying herself alive under the floorboards, with the crisp packet as her epitaph above her, the Foreman tells us of his dog who was also called Viv: at the end of her life she wouldn't eat – you could 'practice arithmetic on her ribs' (*The Balancing Act*, Scene 2). We are invited to juxtapose the instrumental (arithmetic) with the tragic (the ontological mystery of dying). From now on in the play, the banal is to be juxtaposed with the tragic: the banal is to *become* tragic. The girl vanishes, entombed in a condemned house beneath the floor and all we can see is a packet of crisps.

The Site of Radical Innocence

So the crisps, humble, instrumental little earners of profit and cardiac disease, become associated with the tragic, with the great, unanswered questions of philosophy. Because this is culturally unheard of, semiotically unexpected, the crisps have now escaped from their usual ideological or semantic field. This is what Bond calls the 'site of radical innocence'. Here, language, all socially constructed meaning, is insufficient because culture / society cannot provide the answers. It is the function of ideology to answer questions but here on the site of radical innocence there are no answers because the questions are ontological (Bond, 2000:114). The site of radical innocence is the place where an object is so dislocated from its usual, habitual place in the world (it is usually so insignificant as to be invisible, like a crisp packet blowing down a street) that in its new position it is as if we 'see' it for the first time. Like a child having an elemental experience, we have to conceptualise and value it on our own terms because society, ideology, language cannot place it for us. '*What* are *crisps* doing there?' we ask in surprise. Who would think of using *crisps* as an epitaph for a girl? Where the object is placed in the world, in relation to what, affects how we think about it, as Eisenstein and the Russian Formalists knew.

Radical Innocence, Accident Time, and facing the Blank Canvas

Radical innocence itself is the mind set of the pre-speech child who has not yet learned to name and value objects. To this child the world of objects, their situations and configurations, is not yet either habitual or expected. Neural pathways in the mind, connecting and forming associations, have not yet been forged. Language, and so social meanings and values for things, has not yet been learnt. We all go back to the site of radical innocence when we are confronted with the blindingly unexpected. I say blindingly unexpected because when this happens we cannot see the situation through our usual channels. We find it hard to accept, to place what we see. Words cannot describe it, nor can society ascribe value to it. Radical innocence is as inarticulate as the wind that Viv describes.

Bond calls part of this process Accident Time (Bond, 2000:48). A combination of slowness and shock as in a car crash, it is the sudden perception of a conjunction of things we have never seen in relation to each other before, things we cannot yet understand, name or rationalise. By exploring that in the theatre, we can experience our own radical innocence through the eyes of an Oedipus or a Lear.

In *Eleven Vests* (Bond, 1997), we see it through the eyes of the Student. He is a British soldier in the last gasp of an unspecified war. He has callously bayoneted an 'Enemy' soldier in revenge because the Enemy accidentally shot and killed his colleague. Imagining the Enemy soldier to be dead, the Student watches with horror as the dying Enemy sits up and wipes clean the blade that has killed him on his own vest. If Radical Innocence is the question '*what* is it doing *there*?', in the invisible object moment we ask '*what* is he doing with *that*?'. The invisible object is usually so much a part of our daily lives that we do not 'see' it. In such dramatic moments the object is used in such an unusual way that it becomes cathexed: it is as if we see it for the first time. This enables us to make connections we would not normally make. The eleventh vest is used by the dying Enemy soldier to clean his own messy blood off the blade that killed him. Why does he do it? Technically, cleaning up is not the responsibility of the corpse. The question makes us, and the Student who has killed the Enemy, put ourselves imaginatively into his situation. Why would anyone – why would I – do that? While it may have seemed rational for the Student to take revenge for his dead colleague, now that he has engaged with his victim imaginatively it is as if he stabbed himself to death. It is the novel use of the *object* that puts us, our imaginative processes, into the situation we are shown on stage: rather than engaging with or being alienated from the *character's* emotions, we engage with the scenario directly ourselves. This is what makes the Theatre Event live and exciting. We create our humanity in the theatre confronting the tragic as we consider our mortality. When imagination seeks reasons for things hitherto unexplained, we are free from ideology and able to become truly creative: it is creativity, rather than Brechtian value judgment, that induces change socially and imaginatively. It is a frightening process: Bond calls it facing the 'blank canvas' upon which society has written nothing. But its very blankness enables us to shake off the instrumental and create *human* values.

The Tragic and Instrumental Values Juxtaposed: Bathetic Tragi-Comedy

As with the vest in *Eleven Vests*, the crisps in *The Balancing Act* become tragic by association with death, and yet they avoid sentimentality by still being crisps as we see in the following exchange from *The Balancing Act* (Scene Four):

> THIEF: Give us a crisp.
> NELSON: They ain' mine.
> THIEF: Whose is they?

NELSON: Me girl's.
THIEF: (looks around) Arst 'er if I can 'ave one.
NELSON: Can't.
THIEF: Why not?
NELSON: She's dead.
THIEF: That would make it difficult. I'll soon join 'er if I don't eat. Give us a crisp.

The crisps still function instrumentally as well as tragically: the combination of the rational and the imaginative generates a macabre tragic-comic effect. Tragedy juxtaposed with instrumental values gives repeated bathos: bathos can be defined as tragedy we laugh at.

The Stage: the Imagined Universe

The stage contains a room with a door, a table, floorboards. The medieval stage on the back of a cart, represented the culturally imagined dimensions of the universe. Heaven was there in a raised place, later a balcony, here in *The Balancing Act* a table. Hell was under the floorboards, later a trapdoor, here beneath the floorboards again. The living world was represented by the floor of the cart, later the boards of the stage itself. To us in post-modernity these moral spaces are no longer imagined. No God means no Heaven; no Devil means no Hell; only the world exists and once *that* has been deconstructed, imaginatively prized apart from reality, its very existence is debatable. Of course Bond's whole project is to reconnect the mind with reality. Bond's stage shows these spaces as they were and as they are now: the set represents a kind of history of the imagination, the mind in relation to the world, as it was and as it is. We not only look at ourselves in the present as we look at a Bond set but our selves culturally as we have been, as we have imagined (Bond, 2000:51). In the last act of *The Balancing Act* we see the Demolition Expert, formerly the Foreman, (his career has clearly developed since Act 2), dancing in 'heaven': a Fandango, a dance of abandonment, of *joie de vivre* – on top of a table. Our post-modern Romeo has made it onto the balcony. But in the process it has transformed into a coffin image. His wife, stuck with a butter knife like a Spanish bull, is 'buried', sitting opposite Nelson, who is gagged and swaddled in Viv's blanket like a baby, beneath it. In post-modernity heaven is a coffin; hell is a coffin under the floorboards; the boards of the stage itself at the end of the play, a sarcophagus, represent our envisioned cultural future. The stage is set for the last dance, a literal reiteration of Viv's image of the boat from Scene 1: people dancing joyously on, and finally in, their coffins. Our social site is unequivocally represented.

The Invisible Object

Re-enter the crisps, snatched from Nelson's hand by the DSS officer, Mr. Pringle, who has also enjoyed a career-driven change of identity since we first saw her. Taking rapid advantage of The Demolition Expert's marital hiatus, she gives the crisps as a wedding present to him: he becomes her new fiancée, before they dance deliriously, trip up, fall onto the 'spot' and end the world. What does he DO with them? What would you do? The crisps can now dictate their partially deconstructed, cathexed logic to the scene: an emblem of British social inequality, the plight of the planet, they still function as 'life threatening consumables', and he and we are hungry for them. It is logical for the Demolition Expert, wifeless and so bathetically tea-less, to want to eat them. Whatever he does with them, if he follows this logic, we in the audience are not alienated: we can engage with the Demolition Expert's hunger for the crisps and so we are present inside the white heat of the satire, responding to the crisps ourselves, as we engage with the Demolition Expert. We are not alienated but socially *united* by our desire to eat 'life threatening consumables': it is tantamount to wanting to dance on our own graves, so metaphorically we are dancing with the Demolition Expert. The comic, the banal, the tragic, all are accessible to us as the actor enacts the logic of the crisps in their situation at the end of the world. As individuals we can laugh, cry, feel numb, but we can see ourselves in our society, so we are *all* made responsible for this ludicrous tragedy!

Structure and Value

Marx described how ideology interferes with the act of perceiving the world, Saussure asserted that perception consisted of the superimposition of sign systems and Einstein theorised that one's position relative to phenomena dictated what one saw (Counsell 1996:109). The modernists responded: if reality is *by definition* other than as it appears, then realism cannot work effectively as art. If stories, images and manufactured objects have values embedded in them, disturbing time, space, structure will disturb the values. But post-modern *dismantling* of structure by the same token dismantles value: the tragic becomes banal. As Bond puts it:

> Deconstruction... exposes false meanings, the elisions and seemingly impenetrable gaps which hold things together. It can expose empty effects that make false meanings plausible or compelling. But it does not create new meanings. (Bond, 2000: 38)

Bond's dramaturgy, as we have seen, deconstructs and cathexes objects: it alienates and engages us in the same moment, reanimating as it dissects.

By disturbing the normal relationship between an object and its meaning, cathexis makes the images available to us on stage appear familiar *and different*. When the banal becomes tragic, the resulting dialectical relationship between understanding (seeing) and conceptualising (revaluing) works in a way our minds can structurally handle.

The Theatre Event: Expressing and Signifying

If you 'express' how the world is, you offer an interpretation which will have your ideological stance embedded in the story: if you 'signify' the world, you offer objects which *invite* an interpretation from the *audience*, a process in which they may create their own values. It could be argued that Brecht *tried* to do both of these things but the structures he used subtly split the two discourses. His audience is held in a double bind in which *individuals* either reason or emote. For Bond the split exists *socially*: our society since the enlightenment, and particularly now in post-modernity, has trouble connecting the rational with the imaginative. Bond's plays *illustrate* the social split or double bind, and invite us to reconnect rational analysis with human values. We see rationally where our society is heading in the images of people dancing on coffins: at the same time, we are invited completely to recreate our values by seeing ordinary objects, crisps in this instance, in a new and tragic light. It is the *interrelationship* between the two live and simultaneous processes, deconstruction and cathexis, which essentially comprise a Theatre Event, which is so innovative and powerful in Bond's dramaturgy. Perhaps because it echoes the way the mind sequences and values events, perhaps it is because it allows the self and society to be viewed holistically. Neither deconstruction nor cathexis have been invented by Bond – his genius lies in the *conflation* of the two in the Theatre Event.

Theatre Event: Self, Society and Political Potency

What makes this such a significant innovation for us in post-modernity? The deconstructed, cathexed object gives the power to signify, to create value to the audience's imagination but it does so in the *social context* of the object: creativity is thus rooted firmly in our social reality and cannot take off irresponsibly in a post-modern flight of fancy. In this way the individual imagination values and so takes responsibility for the social world: The process makes us engage politically: we cannot rise above or stand outside society but are firmly in it, of it and *responsible* for it. This means that we do not get sidetracked into blaming others' actions and values for the state of society but recognise our own actions and values for what they are: we have to be scrupulously honest with ourselves. When we view the self and society as a holism, as in the TE, we cannot indulge in the dangerous tendency, usually prompted by political or religious morality, to hive off and destroy those aspects of the self and, by extension, of society, of which we do not politically approve. Thus the puritan and rather paranoid tendency of the left, in the twentieth century, to form mutually destructive factions, each more 'pure' than the other, is mercifully avoided, leaving us free to grasp and tackle our grave, and blatantly obvious, social problems. It is as if the theatre is a space in society where our *responses* to society are on show to ourselves: the real stage is the auditorium.

If reason, represented by deconstruction and alienation, predominates in the structure of the drama, the audience feels omniscient and lonely: we hate and try to kill off those emotional aspects of ourselves (of society) which we cannot rationalise. This is the pitiless 'theatre of Auschwitz': if emotion predominates, the audience is emotionally connected but socially myopic; both eventualities generate helplessness. The rationally deconstructed but imaginatively cathexed *object* sets up a balanced process in which we gain identity, we see ourselves in our society, *and* gain potency: we can recreate human value in the face of its cultural absence. The play, says Bond, is about YOU (Bond, 2003).

References

Barthes, R (1996) 'The Tasks of Brechtian Criticism (1956)' in Eagleton and Milne (Eds) *Marxist Literary Theory* Oxford: Blackwells

Bateson, G, Jackson, D, Hayley, J, and Weakland, J, (1956) 'Towards a Theory of Schizophrenia' in *Behavioral Science 1*

Brecht, B (1964) *Brecht on Theatre* London: Methuen

Brecht, B (1983) *Mother Courage* London: Methuen

Bond, E (1997) *Eleven Vests* London: Methuen

Bond, E (2000) *The Hidden Plot* London: Methuen

Bond, E (2003) an unpublished discussion with Edward Bond, which took place with the contributors to this book at Newman College of Higher Education, Birmingham, recorded on video

Bond, E *The Balancing Act* A draft of Bond's play performed in schools in 2003 by Big Brum theatre in Education Company unpublished at the time of writing

Counsell, C (1996) *Signs of Performance: an introduction to twentieth century theatre* London: Routledge

Derrida, J (1967) *On Grammatology* Baltimore: John Hopkins University Press

Derrida, J (1988) 'Structure, sign and play in the discourse of the human sciences' in Lodge, D *Modern Criticism and Theory* (Second Edition) London: Longman

Eisenstein, S (1999) ' From Film Form: Beyond the Shot (the cinematographic principle and the ideogram)' in Braudy and Cohen (Eds) *Film Theory and Criticism* (Fifth Edition) Oxford: OUP

Fortier, M (1997) *Theory/Theatre: an introduction* London: Routledge

Grady (2003) from various conversations with my colleague Tony Grady, who tragically died before he had finished his chapter for this book

Hawkes, T (1977) *Structuralism and Semiotics* London: Routledge

Lenin, V (1996) 'Leo Tolstoy and His Epoch (1911)' in Eagleton and Milne (Eds) *Marxist Literary Theory* Oxford: Blackwells

Toller, E (1995) 'From Post-war German Drama 1928' in Drain, R (Ed.) *Twentieth Century Theatre: a sourcebook* London: Routledge

4

Edward Bond and the Big Brum plays

Chris Cooper

One
Edward Bond and Theatre in Education (TIE)

> TIE lets children come to know themselves and their world and their relation to it. That is the only way that they can know who they are and accept responsibility for themselves. TIE is carrying out the injunction of the Greeks who founded our democracy and our theatre: they said know yourself – otherwise you are a mere consumer of time, space, air and fodder.
> (Bond, 1994:37)

The working relationship between Big Brum and Edward Bond began in 1995 but its roots lie in the Second World War. Bond's childhood experience of the war and the fragile post-war peace have been transformed into the blistering imagery of one brilliant play after another. Theatre in Education (TIE) also grew out of the devastation of that war and the defeat of fascism, a child of the welfare state. The Belgrade TIE Company, the first of its kind in the world, was formed in September 1965 the same year that *Saved* was first performed at the Royal Court. Belgrade TIE provided a free public service and a new art form for young people in Coventry schools. This example was soon being followed by theatres, funding bodies and local authorities throughout the UK.

This growing movement naturally required a theoretically guided method and in 1973 The Standing Conference of Young People's Theatre (SCYPT) was founded. The history of this organisation and its significance for theatre and drama has yet to be written, but the body of knowledge developed within SCYPT defined Theatre in Education. It is worth briefly outlining the distinctive components of this definition for the uninitiated.

TIE Methodology

The basis of the work is the use of theatre as a tool for learning. TIE companies employ actor-teachers working with *one* class at a time. This is critical to our work which is highly participative, requiring the highest teacher-student ratio possible, and it distinguishes TIE from any other form of theatre, including Young People's Theatre.

In TIE learning is not instrumental but conceptual, using the power of theatre to resonate with our own lives in order to reach new social understandings about the world we inhabit, to explore the human condition and behaviour so that it can be integrated into young people's minds and make them more human by, as Bond says, allowing them to know themselves.

> And, because such things concern the **processes** of **social** and human **interaction**, the domain particularly of drama and theatre in education, real understanding is a process of coming to understand: we cannot 'give' someone our understanding. Real understanding is felt. Only if the understanding is felt can it be integrated into children's minds, or anyone's. Resonance is the starting point of the integration process. The resonance of something engages us powerfully; that is, affectively. But, significantly, it also engages us indirectly with that which it resonates. Resonance is not authoritarian; yet it's an offer you cannot refuse! (Gillham, 1994:5)

Gillham's understanding that resonance is not authoritarian but 'an offer you cannot refuse' connects directly with how the plays of Edward Bond work with their audience.

A distinctive feature of theatre is the distance it provides. In theatre we do not encounter real life but reality through a fiction. TIE utilises this to draw young people in. The fictional context means that the learning material is subject to the child's control, s/he can engage with the absolute guts of the situation in safety.

However, the most distinctive feature of TIE is participation. In all of our work the theatre or performance element is a part of a whole programme. There is often work before a performance, in between scenes and episodes and, or, after. The participatory element is sometimes integrated even further into the structure, with a much more fluid boundary between the two different modes of audience and active participant. Participation will often relate to the use of a role and there is an always a task, a purpose to it for the class. For example, the play element of the programme concerns the death of people in a village as a result of contaminated water. The children are in role as investigators for the UN, whose task is to produce a report which will bring those responsible for contaminating the water to account and set up a more accountable and efficient means of water purification. The task is a way of encoding their learning. Being able to engage in this way enables the participant to bring their whole selves to the TIE programme: it matters to them and they are not watching it but are in it. But by utilising the distance that fiction provides, the participants are protected into the world of the fiction. The physical manipulation of the TIE programme has all the characteristics of learning in real life.

The plays of Edward Bond also seek to place the whole self in the site of the plays that he writes. In many ways the process is the same and demands giving the situations over to the audience/participants.

The Shift to Theatre Practice

As SCYPT struggled to define and develop the methodology of TIE it was inevitable that it would seek to build a relationship with a writer like Edward Bond, who shared SCYPT's interest in and concern for young people. A great deal of the dialogue between the two rested on the mutual respect between Edward Bond and Geoff Gillham. A closer collaboration developed in response to the first Gulf War in 1991, during which he wrote a seminal article, *The Culture of the Child* (Bond 1991), in the *Theatre and Education Journal*.

Throughout the 1990s Edward Bond was called upon to write in support of TIE Companies as theatres, arts funders and LEAs throughout Britain cut funding to company after company, including of course the Belgrade TIE in 1995. Like all aspects of the welfare state, TIE is under threat of extinction and today, out of all those companies steeped in the practice of SCYPT, there are only two remaining in existence, Big Brum and Theatr Powys in Wales.

It was Bond's decision to respond positively to overtures from Big Brum and write a play for the Company that finally transformed the collaboration into a theatre practice. The decision came at a critical time for the Company, who had just lost all its LEA funding in one fell swoop and was on the verge of closing. The Company is in no doubt that this decision was one of the most important factors in helping Big Brum survive the cuts in funding and re-establish itself with the relative stability it now enjoys.

Today, we no longer have a movement but we are perhaps at the beginning of a new phase in the development of TIE, at the heart of which is the creation of a new form of theatre and the challenges to TIE that Edward Bond's writing poses for us all.

Two
The Big Brum Plays 1995 – 2000
At the Inland Sea was the first play in what has become the Big Brum Quartet: *At The Inland Sea*, 1995, *Eleven Vests*, 1997, *Have I None*, 2000, *The Balancing Act*, 2003.

What follows is an attempt to look at some of the pivotal questions the plays posed to the Company.

At the Inland Sea
Boy: The Soldiers have guns! How will a story stop them?
Woman: It only has to stop them for a moment. So that they look down at the stones – for a moment – or look at each other.
(*At the Inland Sea*, Scene Two)

The Play
It is the day of a Boy's exams. His Mother frets over the importance of them for his future. A Woman carrying a baby appears from his bed. She explains that there are soldiers who are going to kill her baby. The Boy wants to help, the Woman thinks he can by his telling a story. The Boy asks his Mother who cannot see the Woman to tell a story. She telephones the doctor.

Later we see the Boy recuperating in bed. The Woman reappears, she is at the doors of the gas chamber. The Boy finds a story to tell but the baby stops listening when the doors are opened and they walk in.

Months later, when the Boy has passed his exams the woman reappears. She has lost her baby in the crowded gas chamber and wants the Boy to help her. He enters the chamber. He finds the baby. The Woman, and all the people around her, beg him for a story. He takes the baby out of the chamber to save it and the people in the gas chamber are frozen in time.

The Mother is waiting for the Boy when he returns. An Old Woman enters. He gives the baby to his Mother and tries to tell her and the Old Woman the story of the baby. The Old Woman laughs at the suffering he describes. She carries all of humanity's suffering under her smock. The Old Woman helps the Mother to tell her story – it is the story of her life and her love for her son. The Boy realises that he will have to take the baby back to die. The Old Woman is not dead, she is not yet born.

The Boy re-enters the gas chamber. He gives the Woman the baby and time starts. Between them, the Woman and the Boy tell the story that the Woman tried to tell her baby as they were dying. The Woman dies. As she dies the baby unravels cocooning the Boy. He finishes the story. He is born. He describes the dead in the chamber and the guards dragging out the corpses. The Boy drags the Woman out.

He returns to his home and his Mother. He tells her his story about how he will live his life. The Mother won't listen to it. He makes her some tea.

This description does little service to the complexity of the storyability of Edward's play but it does highlight for the reader the kind of situations that Edward puts before young audiences.

Working in the Imagination

At the Inland Sea is about the imagination. Edward wrote his *Rough Notes on Theatre* at around the same time as he was writing this play. The Company used them extensively in rehearsal:

> The imagination is the mode in which subjectivity knows itself. It does not express the ego but the ego's relationship to the world. Whatever is in the imagination is learnt. Imagination combines reason and emotion. When imagination is invoked reason and emotion cannot be separated. When imagination is invoked it is in a critical state. Anything may become critical in imagination. In some aspects of life we can use reason and emotion (especially logic and feeling) in isolation (though even then imagination is residually present, and may even be dominant in a disguised form). The ability to analyse and calculate is characteristic of isolated reason: when it is combined with emotion, to produce imagination, it becomes 'story-ness' (storyability etc). Imagination is essentially storyability. Imagination needs to relate experience as story or potentially storyable. When experience becomes overwhelming or chaotic radical stories are told. (Bond, 1996a:8)

Edward's theory of the imagination, similar to the concept of 'felt understanding' developed in TIE, is extensively expanded in *Notes on the Imagination* published with *Coffee* which was written in the same year as *At the Inland Sea*. Here the storyability of the imagination incorporates the notion of mapping the self, 'A child's world is a map. It learns to live in the world by mapping it. Its map of the world is its means of being. A child could not think or move without its map of the world. Nothing may be unmapped. Anything unmapped would be like a hole in nothingness.' (Bond, 1995a: vii)

In *At the Inland Sea* the Boy needs the knowledge of a map to live in the world, rather than the knowledge he uses to pass exams. The Woman's and the Old Woman's story are vital to this process. Without the stories of others he cannot make his map.

Performing the Play

In approaching the rehearsal process the Company were forced to address two immediate concerns; how exactly to produce and perform this play, and what is its relationship to the audience? The central concern of all theatre is, or at least should be, its relationship to the audience. But the point here is given added emphasis because of the *active* engagement of the audience in TIE through participation and in Edward's plays through the use of the imagination.

Furthermore, it became apparent as the production developed from the first tour to the re-tour in 1996, that Edward was demanding a different approach to theatre from that with which the actors in the Company were familiar. This relates to the question of use: 'It's a way of involving the audience in a situation. I do not find it useful to talk about empathy or non-empathy. It is necessary to find ways of making an audience accept responsibility for a situation.' (Bond, 1996b:14)

At the Inland Sea is an extraordinary play, and an extraordinarily difficult play to perform. Bobby Colvill describes the play, the process of engaging with it, as a shock. It wasn't like anything else he had ever encountered as an actor. Mandy Finney, one of the actor-teachers, describes how Geoff Gillham, the director, had structured exercises on geste to open up the text. Bobby feels that this approach hampered the acting of the play throughout, resulting in the first tour in an approach that closed down meaning. Every act of significance was emphasised in performance to the extent that it resulted in insignificance. He recalls Edward remarking to the Company that they weren't '...doing *Kabuki*. You don't have to alienate the moment. You don't have to ring a bell.' In contrast, Edward's input into rehearsals for the first tour was focussed almost entirely on the text. 'One of the first things he pointed us to, was paying attention to how the text is written – the language, the construction, the punctuation, how one image follows on from another, the form of it.' (Finney, 1996: 22)

In a letter to the Company following his visit to rehearsal, Edward re-inforced the point that the imagination cannot be dragooned. For the Woman's story to penetrate ideology, which justifies the inhuman and the unjust, it must present the site of the story. Edward's drama is not con-cerned with the story itself as much as the site of the story, similarly, not the character but the site of the character. In this way, the social, in which the personal is situated, invokes the audience's imagination, through which they gain access to the site of the story. The audience is responding through the logic of the imagination, which is the logic of value: their humanity. The logic of the imagination seeks justice in the face of an unjust world justified by ideology. This is the purpose of modern drama, because the imagination can then penetrate reality, the audience can take responsibility and create the connections through the site of the self in its total situation: self and society, psychology and politics.

> The text does not say that Auschwitz, the holocaust, the brutality, waste are horrible, inhuman, cruel. The text contains no 'ahs' or groans. If it did it would be doing the work of the audience. The audience must condemn Auschwitz – not be told it is being or has been condemned. (Bond, 1995b)

In a final remark on emotion in relation to 'use', he begins to explain a fundamental theoretical proposition that in a variety of ways and different formulations each play has posed and the Company has tussled with relentlessly. Brechtian theatre demands we alienate the audience in order to enable them to de-construct the emotion through reason. This defines meaning for the audience and therefore removes them from the situation. Neither is Edward seeking a Stanislavskian use of emotion, which allows the actor to retreat into individual psychology. He is interested in the social-psyche and he wants the audience fully in the site of the play. Hence the emphasis on an appropriate use of emotion which is redirected towards 'use' – handing responsibility to the audience.

> The play then is not less emotional than Stanislavski – but, instead its emotion is redirected into the area of use. Emotion is usually (in Stanis-lavski) an expression of the situation; after its redirection the play itself be-comes the situation, the situation of the audience – and a new form of theatre becomes possible. (Bond, 1995c)

The gap between what *At the Inland Sea* demanded in performance and the tools the Company was equipped with to do it was a productive contra-diction. Edward was insisting that the Company create the site, the unity of the social-self, and the socio-political. The experience of the first tour, how-ever, was invaluable and the Company's work developed in quantum leaps when reworking for the second tour. Big Brum was busily equipping itself with the right tools.

The workshop

The TIE programme that toured schools was structured so that the pupils were working with the Company for a whole day. The morning was taken up by a workshop to prepare them to watch the play in the afternoon. Nothing followed the play; the audience's imaginations were left to do its work. The workshop itself was a triumph of simplicity skilfully executed.[1] It is worth making a few observations about it here.

The workshop began with a gentle discussion about the imagination, how and when it is used in everyday life. The class was then split into pairs and asked to share stories with each other that they were told as younger children, and where they were when the stories were told. These experiences were shared as a whole group before moving on to stories told by adults. The pupils were then asked individually to imagine, in a space of their own, that they were in an art gallery, not as visitors but cleaners. Gradually a picture of the gallery and their relationship to it as cleaners was created socially, including their relationship to specific works of art and the tool they most use as cleaners. Soon they were working as a group of cleaners maintaining the gallery. They were then introduced to a new role, that of an artist creating an installation. She is using materials she has brought to the gallery: a dirty bundled sheet suggestive of a baby; a piece of board resonant of a grave; a sack of dry earth; a plank of wood; a picture of flowers; and a grey concrete block. She invites the public to change it as they see fit: the drama focussed round the cleaners taking up the invitation of manipulating the exhibit into how they would like others to see it. This required a very complex process of exploring the meaning of the artist's work, in particular the relationship between birth and death. An intervention in role by one of the Company as a security guard, who pointed out that they were paid to clean not mess around with public art, created a conflict with the cleaners. The dramatic situation drove them to defend their actions, their imaginative response to the exhibit. Through this the class was able to explore further and share their understandings of their individual and collective response to the installation.

The most important point is the existential drama mode of the workshop. The relationship of the workshop to the play was oblique, in that it didn't directly deal with the play by focusing on history for example, or concentration camps or indeed Auschwitz. The students were gaining practical experience of the site of the play by working in the imagination, by being in role as cleaners and working creatively with the installation.

It was playful and adolescents are still at a stage where they can, just, reach back into earlier childhood and remember/experience play as it should be remembered /experienced – as real. In the TIE programme as a whole the collaboration between Edward and Big Brum really forged a connection for the creative strategies of a playwright and the art form of Theatre in Education to come together to explore humanness dramatically in the most profound way.

In many respects Edward had given the Company a play it felt it couldn't do, not least technically and in terms of resources, but it was also a play that only those particular people in that particular SCYPT Theatre in Education Company were able to do.

Eleven Vests

Head: I didn't make the world what it is. I hoped that when the time came for you to leave some of you would go out and make it a better place. That's why I became a teacher. There! – I've confessed something about my life. Can't you confess about a book? Just say you regret what you've done. You don't even have to mean it. Just make the gesture to what decent civilised people do. (*Eleven Vests*)

In 1997 Edward delivered the script of his next play for Big Brum. Again it is worth identifying the situations the play presents the audience with.

The Play

Book: A Student is accused by a Head teacher of slashing the pages of a book. The Student does not speak.

Jacket: Another Student's school blazer is slashed. The Head accuses the Student. The Student remains silent. The Head instructs the Student to help the Other Student take the jacket off. The Student tears another strip off it. The Head expels the Student and calls the police.

Gate: The Student who has been living rough returns to the school gates. The Head appears telling the Student that the police are on their way. The Student stabs the Head, the Head staggers away to die. The Student throws the knife into the school yard before fleeing.

Lesson: The Student is in the army. The Instructor is giving him a lesson in firing the rifle. The lesson shifts to bayonet practice. The Student is unable to carry this out until a sack is provided for him to practice on. The Instructor demands that the Student scream as he charges. The Instructor terrorises the Student until he gets tangled up with the sack and falls in a heap.

Reccy: The Student is in combat on reconnaissance with a fellow Soldier. They are watching a hunting lodge that is quartering enemy soldiers. They report back to HQ by intercom. The enemy is surrendering by hanging out their white vests from a window. They count the vests, 10. HQ instructs them to take the surrender.

Roof: Inside the roof of the tower where the soldiers are surrendering an Enemy Soldier sits alone. There is a shout from below. He ignores it and starts to play with a toy train left behind by the previous occupants. The Enemy decides to go further up into the roof to sleep.

Tower: The Student and the Other Soldier take the surrender and instruct the prisoners to come out of the tower and gather down in the dip. A shot kills the Other Soldier. The Enemy is unaware his comrades have surrendered. The Enemy surrenders. The Student interrogates him but they cannot speak the same language. The Enemy takes off his vest. The Student decides to kill the Enemy. A Prisoner who can translate pleads on the Enemy's behalf. The Student bayonets the Enemy, and cleans the blood off it with the Enemy's vest. The Enemy is still alive. The Enemy starts to talk to him, picks up his vest and begins to clean the bayonet with it. The Student bayonets the Enemy dead. He instructs the Prisoner to take the body away. The Student wants to know what the Enemy was saying and he tries to speak the foreign language. The Student picks up the rifles and the Enemy's vest. He tugs down the vests that were hung in surrender and leaves carrying them.

Like *At the in Inland Sea, Eleven Vests* had two tours. The first, a TIE tour, took place in 1997. The second was toured to theatre venues nationally in 1999. *Eleven Vests* was the first Big Brum/Bond production that I worked on, in the first as an actor-teacher and in the second as actor and director.

Fortunately for Big Brum the first process was directed once more by Geoff Gillham who brought an enormous amount of developed understanding of Edward as a writer from the production of *At the Inland Sea* to this. Geoff died in 2001, he is sorely missed. Geoff's contribution to the development of TIE and his skill as a theatre practitioner in bringing Edward's plays to life was second to none.

Exploring 'self'

The rehearsal process propelled us straight into a painstaking examination of the text in order to map the play's site, particularly through the concept of 'self'. In school the Student is silent. He is unable to speak. He rejects authority, the Head, who does not know how to engage with the young people he is meant to teach. The Head fills the silence between himself and the Student with ideology. The Student is excluded from the school but returns to the gates because, like every child he wants justice, to belong in the school, to feel at home in the world. The Head is also incapable of questioning his own self as he stands in the gate. The stabbing of the Head by the Student is a tragic act of self-defence.

In *Lesson*, the play's pivotal episode, the Instructor teaches the Student about the relationship between history, science and technology in the first part of the lesson. But the Instructor teaches the lesson not for the purposes of understanding and freedom, but to further imprison the Student's self. His scream is the first breath of a being newborn. In the sack he is confronted by his ghost. Dramatically the sack demands that we reassess our reaction to the stabbing of the Head. When we see the Student in a new uniform, that of the soldier, the scream has become a new language, the language of the army, which is the language of authority that controls them. *Roof* is like an interior of the mind. The Enemy we watch is like a mirror of the Student. It is a sharp contrast to how the sack was used for the Student.

The bayoneting of the Enemy is infinitely more insane than the violence we have already seen. The Enemy is not his enemy, and vice versa. The anger the Student expresses at the loss of his mate is not the cause of killing the Enemy, it is the effect of the barbarism he has learned. In a sense he is killing himself. It is only after he has committed the act that the Student begins to sense this and struggles to find himself in response. The cries of the watching prisoners are in the language of humanness, unlike those of the watchers when the Head is killed, and he is confronted by the enormity of what has happened and the need to take responsibility for himself and his actions.

Opening the site for the audience

The play begins with a question. Why? In many ways this expresses the core principle of the theatre of Edward Bond. His plays always ask 'why?' The audience needs to be able to see themselves in the site of each character, including figures like the Head and hear the 'whys' he asks, however unjust his actions. The first production failed to achieve this. I speak from the experience of playing the Head. The drive to explain the Head, rather than show him, to the audience still tended to dominate. In the second production Edward wanted to focus on *how* the Head asks 'why?', the objective being to ask a real question that required a real response from the audience. I had been consistently failing to do this because I, the actor, had determined the meaning of the Head's actions for the audience. This is of course wrong. The Head *has* condemned the Student but he still needs, his humanness demands, to know why anyone should do something so destructive. The destruction of the book is a destruction of the Head's values: his question is a question to the world. As a result of Edward's prompting I think that the second production was much more contradictory and demanding of the audiences.

To be useful the performance must maintain the logic of the site. Every situation, however extreme, has a logic in which the acting must be rooted, otherwise the acting shuts the audience out. Edward helped us to address this problem in performing the Head but also in other situations the play creates for the audience. After the first ever performance of *Eleven Vests*, Edward suggested we rework Tower from the point that the Enemy was bayoneted for the first time. It was blocked so that the Enemy rose up from lying on his back to a sitting up position, the Student confronted by himself. But Edward pointed out that while this was true, the audience could not read our intention and we were mystifying the action: the Enemy rising ghoul-like merely obscured the logic of the site. Edward got us to focus on the actions of a dying man who has not been bayoneted efficiently because of the anxiety of the Student. The rework was very 'material' and focussed the audience on the action (a Theatre Event) of a dying man using the vest he had surrendered with, to wipe his own blood from the bayonet that had been used to kill him. Human beings create their minds in relation to specific situations. Each experience becomes layered into the psyche or self like 'strata in a cliff.' Authority can make use of these strata in order to maintain control as much as individuals draw on that experience: soldiers are often children in uniform, and authority utilises the experience of infants in the military structures it creates.

This is why acting that searches for the 'soul' is generalised and ultimately empty. When emotion drives the play, the acting becomes static. People enter into particular strata in response to particular situations. Actors need to create living contradictions, and conflicts between the different strata become critical and show how the individual negotiates this in the face of a given situation. We can explore this through objects. The enemy's behaviour is not generalised fear, begging for his life and wiping the bayonet for his killer. He is tapping into different strata of experience, appealing as a soldier, as a fellow human being, as a child who fears the dark. We must ask, when is he obeying authority? When is he creating his freedom? Through the objects they:

> become speaking mirrors – we use them to talk. The object is in social space – but it is also lodged in a particular stratum or in several strata of the mind. So various languages will attach to the object – and these come from our psyches, the strata that provide us with imaginative insight and imaginative need – and so the ability to create: to judge and understand and use the real world. In this sense they are like living maps – maps of the real world. (Bond, 1997)

Objects become psycho-social, what Edward calls a modern form of soliloquy that combines the psychology of the user of the object with the social situation.

The Use of Objects

The significance of objects has been at the centre of our work in TIE. But Edward is offering a deeper understanding of the use of objects in theatre and drama and providing a new theoretical framework to assess what we do in TIE. Geoff was the first to draw our attention to this.

> His [Edward's] comments about objects are v. sound. (Based on Marx and Freud). Marx understood that products (man-made-processed-objects) contain (literally, actually) 'congealed labour power'– *value* is first given to the object by the exercise of labour-power. Therefore every object *first* contains the worker's life, dying, death. Then it is circulated/consumed in society – used in specific situations and by specific people undergoing further transformations in value (use-values). Freud then explores this role of objects from a psychological point of view in his work on fetishism. (Interesting that Marx refers also to fetishism, in the economic sphere). EB's use of 'cathecting' derives from Freud – where an object becomes imbued (by the fetishist – we're *all* fetishists to some extent) with special significance which does not belong to the object-in-itself. To draw on Vygotski's terms: 'the meaning (object-for-me) dominates over the in-itself-object.' This psychological operation is 'cathexis'– a meaning becomes attached *to* the object by the 'user' greater than the object's original use. Freud of course focused upon the sexual aspect of this. For Vygotski, it's significant for the development of symbolic thought. Edward is closer to Marx because he is probing the *social* significance of the object, and asking us to be conscious of this when we act, or use an object in the theatre (the work

it does, and that we need to be conscious of). DH [Dorothy Heathcote] and TIE is conscious of this – look how we use objects in so much of our work. But Edward is bringing yet more insight into this, at the 'deep' (Marxist) level. 'Layers of Meaning'![2] (Gillham, 1997) [Emphasis in original]

The workshop

Focusing on the objects in the play rather than the characters, provided the basis of the TIE programme as a whole. The day began with an exploration of the set, which was a wall. We asked the class what it was made of and then began to share common phrases about walls, stone and stone walls: 'walls have ears', 'I feel walled in', 'backs to the wall' *et cetera.* We often discussed the historical use of walls and shared our knowledge of them. We then named this wall, 'the wall of .....' and recorded the names the groups had given it on a whiteboard for everyone to see.

We then moved into the play. After *Gate* we paused to look at the knife that had just been used to stab the Head and asked the class to give voice to it, as if it could speak, and then literally place it in the wall where it belonged. This required careful negotiation before we could move on to the next episode of the play.

After the play we recreated the final image of the Student as we had him, carrying his and the Enemy's arms and vest, the intercom dangling from his pack and trailing the tied vests of the surrendered soldiers behind him. '*If we had to place him in the stone-wall how would he appear at the time we left him at the end of the play?*' This was a whole group activity that could take a long time because we had only one image to create using Bobby Colvill, the actor playing the Student, as a living model, and we had to be sure that the whole class was satisfied with what it revealed to us. In order to find this we had to undergo an excavation of the Student's life, his historical origins and development. Together with the class we explored his actions in the play primarily by looking at the objects in order to explore these concepts:

Self, society, authority, ownership, owned society
Owned self, owning yourself
Responsibility (to society)
Responsibility (to self)
Responsibility (for self)
Responsibility (for society)

For example, intense debate would occur over whether the Student owned his school jacket or whether it owned him. The Student's silence at the beginning of the play and his attempt to speak a foreign language at the end were contrasted through image, lines of text, the voices of the knife and of the bayonet, provided by both the actor-teachers and the participants, to explore his responsibility to society and to and for himself. The final image was often a really complex palimpsest, showing him emerging from the wall or sinking into it as if being absorbed by it. This obviously related to what they had named the wall in the first place. Or he was shown wearing his school jacket under his army jacket, carrying the train rather than the rifle, the bayonet lodged in the dictionary *et cetera*. The possibilities were enormous and the work the students created was the most intensely concentrated I have ever been privileged to work on.

> Their image of the student in the wall, was of him being born out of it. They spent a lot of time over it – developing their birth image in all its complexity and contradiction. …I think the students have sometimes been surprising themselves with what they are saying and discovering. A couple of times there has been a 'confusion' around the Roof scene – where they have re-ferred to the time the student talked to the train. They then realise and are embarrassed about their 'mistake'. But, of course, they have sub-con-sciously made deep connections. So, each time that's happened, we've swiftly gone and got the train, and tried to make sure the connections aren't lost. (Finney, 1997)

The important lesson we were learning was that the connection would be forged through the train, the object.

The task of the young people was to record 'notes on your father' for the as yet unborn child of the Student which would help the child understand his orher father. They were fashioned as we were working on the image by recording things of significance agreed upon by the group.

On the day when the group built the image of the Student being born out of the wall at the end of the play, they recoded the following 'notes on your father' to accompany the image.

NOTES ON YOUR FATHER
– He didn't do well at school. He didn't believe in himself and no one be-lieved in him.

– He didn't speak at school – but in the army he spoke a lot.

– He was silent because he was always being pinpointed as trouble.

– At school he was never asked if he'd done the things he was accused of.

- At school, language was garbage to him.

- Language could be used against him.

- In the army he was taught all over again, and at first he was hesitant. He learnt the language of aggression and combat.

- He had to report the death of his friend as if he wasn't bothered.

- He couldn't express himself clearly – his enemy could, and he could hear that.

- When he killed the enemy he began to see him as a person, as a friend.

- When he killed the enemy there was no one to hold him back.

- He has never had anyone who cared enough to give him something like the toy train – a sense of security.

Have I None

Jams: (slight pause) Let me get this right. You hear a knock – open the door- no-one's there?
Sara: Yes.
Jams: You're going potty.
(*Have I None*, Sc1)

Have I None looks at the present through the future. The play is set on 18 July 2077 in a living space.

The Play

One: Sara sits at the table, there is a repeated knocking on the door. When she goes to answer the door there is nothing on the other side. Jams arrives home from his patrol. He begins to tell a tale about what happened when the patrol found an old woman hanging a picture in a derelict house in the ruins. He does not hear the knocking. Jams gets angry when he realises that Sara is not listening. She explains that someone is knocking on the door and that there is never anyone there. He tells her she's going potty, and storms out of the door to eat in the canteen.

Two: There is a knock. Jams goes opens the door to a stranger, Grit. Grit has come to see Sara. Jams invites him in. Grit explains that he is Sara's brother. He walked from the North because he was unable to get a travel pass due to staff throwing themselves off the roof. Jams says that it must be a suicide outbreak. Grit explains he came because he found a photograph of him and his sister as children. Jams retorts that all papers, including photographs, were destroyed when they abolished the past.

Sara returns. She denies that Grit is her brother. Grit sits in Sara's chair and falls asleep. Sara is horrified that Grit has taken her chair and a huge row erupts between her and Jams. Sara rips up the photograph. Sara and Jams continue to row ferociously. Grit wakes up. He moves Sara's chair over to the door thus interrupting the argument. 'He's ruining the home.'Jams grabs the table and hugs it to him while Sara hugs the other chair – they are glaring from behind the furniture at each other from opposing corners of the room. When the situation calms, the furniture is reset and Grit is sent to the toilet. While he is gone Jams decides that they have no choice but to kill Grit. Sara goes out to buy poison.

Three: Grit is alone. The knocking on the door resumes. There is no one there. Sara enters wearing a coat of sky blue covered in metal spoons. She has been gone for 4 days. Sara tells Grit a story about when they were children. Grit, satisfied that he has found his sister, lies down to sleep. Sara turns her coat inside out – it is black and covered in bones. Jams enters, he cannot see Sara who leaves. He is worried that if Sara's body turns up he will be censured for not reporting her missing. He is angry at Grit for sleeping when he should have been watching and ties him up in one of the chairs.

Sara enters. She has been to the ruins, the site of Jams' story. A row breaks out because Jams has tied Grit to her chair. Grit awakes and struggles to get out of the chair. The argument rages until Grit sneezes and brings the focus back onto him. Sara has bought the poison. Jams goes to the kitchen to prepare the soup. Sara tells Grit about the ruins. She tells him that she has never seen him before, that it's all in his head. Jams brings the poisoned soup for Grit, but Sara deliberately drinks it. She asks to be taken outside because she doesn't want to die in the house. Jams slashes Grit's ropes and lets him help her out. Jams shouts down the street after them telling them to get round the corner before anyone sees. There is a knock at the door, Jams turns towards the door and shouts 'bugger off' before going off in to the kitchen howling.

Unlocking the play

The play, in many respects a black comedy, is about life, death and community.

In a discussion prior to the rehearsal process, Edward talked of how the state feeds people in order to deny their murder. Authority provides Jams and Sara with all they need to survive, including pre-packaged food, all of which serves to obscure the fact that their lives are killing them. In the play people are not childlike but their behaviour is infantile. They argue about chairs because in this world there is nothing else to argue about. They have no other experience to map or territory to own, they do not own themselves. Jams' story belongs to authority, Sara has lost her story. The world outside the door of their hermetically sealed living quarters is crumbling and dysfunctional, a world of mass hallucinations and mass suicides. These silent deaths contrast with the suicide of Sara at the end of the play. Her death is full of humanity. Sarah can no longer live with the pain of the world but by killing herself she creates the opportunity for Grit to escape his own death. She can only have her humanity by giving Grit his, thus reversing the action of the story from their childhood when she dragged a dying Grit towards the window and the outside world.

The key to unlocking the play lies in following the knock. It is the play's metaphor, its dialectic, and is cathected from one moment to another. To be able to create the knock is to create the site of the play. This was the hardest part of the production. The knocking is like the conductor that orchestrates the stories that converge, commingle and separate throughout the play. The knocking moves through every moment. The story that Jams tells about the woman in the ruins starts to tell him and the details of it become more and more obsessive and minute, specific and cathected. As Edward remarked in a letter after seeing a performance:

> It's as if the story is 'knocking him'. Its useful to say throughout work on the play, at any moment: where is the knocking now – what is knocking now – as if the knock were constantly moving about and hiding in various 'sites' in people and in the room. The knocking seems to represent what authority cannot explain, control or repress – and it breaks out in various ways. The audience need not be especially aware of this – but it's the actors' guide to what they are doing at any moment. (Bond, 2000a)

The Rehearsal Process

How does Sara approach the door in scene one? We struggled to convert 'comment' to 'use'. Early on it was very much a case of the character in this situation rather than the situation in the character. At that stage the acting was still essentially Stanislavskian. In the opening of the play in rehearsal we were demonstrating generalised fear. What we needed to do was define specifically what Sara feared was behind the door in order to know how to particularise the acting. After Edward's visit to rehearsal I think we were finally able to do this, in order to play the knocking at the beginning and it was remarkable to watch. The workshop element of the TIE programme after the play, began by specifying with the students what Sara feared about the knock at the beginning of the play. Our mistake was then to follow Sara's journey into the ruins which, while productive, was in hindsight not as rich as staying in the site of the room and following the journey of the knock through Grit and Jams. Yet because we hadn't really grasped the meaning of the knock and the need to follow its movement in the site, we were never able to realise the potential of the knock throughout the rest of the play.

Forcing the situation too soon, trying to fix our understanding, charac-terised the rehearsal process throughout: it was fuelled with anxiety about being ready in time. Trying to do too much too soon results in generalisa-tion. The process was tough, at times gruelling, and the more we tried to determine things before we had explored them fully, the more we became lost and the more we collectively resisted the play.

This was a consequence of our collective confusion around the play and my own inexperience as a director of Edward's plays. We no longer had Geoff, and while I had directed the second tour of *Eleven Vests*, it stood very much on the shoulders of the first. While I tried to use the *Hidden Plot* in rehearsal, the results would often be sterile. During Edward's visits to rehearsal I had attempted to TE Jams hanging up his jacket having returned from patrol. I directed Richard Holmes, the actor playing Jams, to hold it up in such a way that we immediately cathected the hanger into a gibbet. His arm was ex-tended almost like a Nazi salute, the jacket obscuring his face, making him faceless as he talked. I was rather pleased with myself and Richard executed it beautifully. Edward wrote to me that what was intended to be a TE that was social and political, was in fact aesthetic because:

> We nod and say 'yes, how clever, how true' – we understand it and so we stop thinking. We stop thinking because we are presented with a complete explanation. But why doesn't he hang his trousers on the coathanger? – and instead of showing this (holding up the jacket as if it were crucified on that coathanger: it's a good image, of course) how can we enact it and put the imagination in movement? (Bond, 2000b)

Edward wanted to provoke us to explore more, to shift from showing to enactment, to find the important questions, like why does this man who is obsessive about hygiene and tidiness throw the coat hanger on the floor? It is an apparent cliché in argument but what lies behind it? The coat hanger is cathected for Jams in the way the picture is cathected for the old woman in the story he tells. This requires real exploration for the actors before they play the character.

It is interesting that the question had arisen 'are G[rit] and S[ara] really [brother and sister]? – because it is a Stanislavskian question. Of course you'd realised that it wasn't important – but all the same it had to be asked because of our training. We didn't ask: what happens when you hang the coat hanger on the door handle? Now that is an investigation of the objects on the site. I think I would probably be precious and arty to actually hang it there in performance – but there is a connection between the two objects. And the door isn't locked. It's as if we know a whole lot of things – but we put them on one side when we rehearse because we don't know how to use them. We know how to use Stanislavski and Brecht – but not how to enact and use *our* world. (Bond, 2000c)

Design

Edward notes in the *Hidden Plot* 'design is at the centre of my plays and if the design isn't right the play can't work.' (Bond, 2000d:51) We could add that if the design isn't right we cannot locate the site. In the end, the design for *Have I None* was absolutely right and marked a real development in our approach to producing Edward's plays, and fundamentally changed the way the Company approaches any production. This was the first production in which we really engaged with the question of design in relation to the site of the play. Initially it was born out of a crisis when we realised, following an exchange of letters between the designer Ceri Townsend and Edward, that the first design would not work.

The essential component of the design was a long blank wall with the door built into it. Edward described it as 'Like seeing the white screen in an empty cinema when the cleaners are vacuuming the place.' (Bond, 2000e) This blankness, painted a sickly pallid green colour and framed with a skirting board, provided the backdrop to the rest of the room, the utilitarian table and chairs on a plain beige industrial-strength carpet. These were familiar surroundings but distorted principally by the design of the door and the absence of a window. It also gave the audience's imagination a blank canvas to project onto: the extraordinary images of the action of the play, their own images of the outside world referred to, the old woman in the ruins, the faceless people jumping to their deaths from roofs and bridges, and the images of childhood brought into the room by the story which Sara tells Jams.

Where the original design suggested a futuristic prison, which would be far more comfortable for the audience because once more it provided a complete answer and would have made the play more remote, the final design incorporated authority in the room, and in the audience's own living spaces, through the viciously utilitarian black table and chairs and the absence of all other human effects, pictures, photos and ornaments.

As I write, I now recognise that my experience of *At the Inland Sea* as an audience member was seriously hampered by the design in that production. The Boy's bedroom was simply marked out on the school hall floor with tape and his bedroom wall was a large black flat. The design owed much to epic theatre. I now realise that it alienated me in the sense that it propelled me away from the play site, it put a barrier between me and the play. I needed to be drawn into the Boy's bedroom. Then I begin to think about having *Eleven Vests* written into the wall in the design of the first production to remind the audience they are watching a play and wonder...

Unanswered Questions

As pointed out earlier, the issue of whether Grit and Sara are brother or sister inevitably became a question. It still lingers because I remain unconvinced whether the question is entirely Stanislavskian because it relates to the logic of the site. I realise that I am still unable to distinguish clearly between what are the important and unimportant questions to be addressed in making the play useful for an audience. And although I still don't really know how the site worked for the audience, I sense it resonated for them in a different way. The incident between Sara in the blue spoon/ bone coat and Grit upon the adolescents watching seemed to penetrate very deeply, although very few wanted to talk about it. I suspect it was because it had entered a very private space, the trauma of lost childhood. Their response was something we never wished to trespass on unless invited to. While the programme as a whole worked extremely well, because of our uncertainty about how to use the experience of the play with young people, it was never wholly satisfactory for the Company. In many ways *Have I None* is a play that young people will grow into. Edward took a radical step in writing this play. We were not yet ready to take that step with him.

Three
A Case Study: *The Balancing Act* – 2003

Viv: There's a huge ship on this flat sea that lasts forever. When the ship goes through the sea it crunches it like bones. The passengers don't 'ear. They're all dancing. High up in the sky there is a grain of sand. It falls on the ship. The ship sinks. Straightaway. Goes straight t' the bottom. The people don't notice. They go on moving-the water pushes 'em. They think they're dancing. They don't know they're dead. (*The Balancing Act,* Scene One)

The play

It is worth noting for the reader that the original version of the play that Big Brum performed was in five parts. The published version of the play will include a new scene five, thus extending the piece to six parts.

One: Viv is alone with a blanket in an empty windowless room. She is frightened to move. Nelson her boyfriend brings her food. We learn that she is fearful because she is safeguarding a spot that is keeping the whole world in balance. The slightest movement could upset it and end the world. She will not let him near it. Nelson tries to reason with her but in frustration decides that he'll jump on the spot to prove she is potty. Viv becomes hysterical. Nelson gathers in all the food he has brought her. He scrapes up a bag of crisps that she has spilled to illustrate what the end of the world would be like, back into the bag and carefully puts the packet on the spot and then leaves.

Two: Three days later Viv is still in the room covered by the blanket. The crisp packet is still on the spot. Nelson returns. The door is locked. Men have come to knock the house down. The Foreman arrives. While the Foreman talks Viv quietly lifts a floorboard – she has already prepared a hiding place. She climbs in just as the Foreman breaks the door in. It appears she has gone. The Foreman goes leaving a stunned Nelson staring at the crisps on the spot. He picks them up and is about to stamp on the spot but thinks better of it. He picks up the blanket. Suddenly Nelson turns, runs to the spot, jumps on it and dashes out.

Three: Nelson is in the DSS Office. He carries the blanket and the packet of crisps. The Officer begins to talk at him. Nelson cannot answer. The Officer wants to know about the death of Viv. The Officer wants to know why this girl with everything to live for is dead. Nelson is unable to answer. The Officer attempts both to cajole and abuse Nelson into speaking, eventually the silence is filled with her own paranoia and she vents her spleen at all those she holds responsible for the weaknesses of the world and her own loneliness in it. Defeated by his silence she judges and condemns Nelson for Viv's death before dismissing him.

Four: Nelson is begging in an empty street draped in the blanket. Desperate he takes out the packet of crisps and goes to eat one. He is stopped by the wail of a police siren. A One Legged Thief (OLT) using a crutch and wearing a top hat appears. He asks Nelson to hide him. The Thief gives Nelson the crutch and the hat and hides from the police under the blanket. When the police have gone the OTL explains that an old woman had accused him of snatching her handbag, he points with a handbag to indicate the scene of a crime. The OLT is hungry and wants some crisps. The OLT says, 'I'll eat 'em for yer n' yer'll be free.' He devours them as Nelson weeps. The Thief introduces himself – 'I'm Bernard the one-legged dancer.' The OLT dances and in doing so finds his other leg. Unbalanced by this the Thief gives Nelson some loose change from the handbag and sends him to buy more crisps to get over the shock. The OLT having examined and rejected the blanket gathers his props and leaves just as the police screech after him. Nelson returns with some crisps. The police car returns: 'We caught the one-legged thief with the top hat. He fell over his crutch and broke his neck.' Nelson bawls after the OLT 'Liver 'n bacon! 'S all they 'ad!' He leaves with the blanket and a new bag of liver and bacon flavoured crisps.

Five: In the Foreman's home his Wife is setting the table for dinner. There is a pile of dust in the corner of the dinette that keeps drawing her attention. The Foreman enters. He carries a parcel, which he puts down. His voice has undergone an affected change that compliments the bow-tie he now wears with his overalls. The Wife tells him her Mother is coming. The laying of the table becomes a crisis between them that escalates. The Wife armed with a dust pan and brush demands an explanation for the pile of dust in her dinette. He is eventually forced to tell her the truth. The dust he explains is the balancing point of the world – a hair could trigger it. He tells the Wife about Viv, about how she had picked the wrong spot. He unwraps the parcel. It is a rope barrier he got from a monastery that is closing down. He stops the Wife from advancing on the dust by performing a tremendous flamenco. She goes to clean the spot. He stabs her with a butter knife. He buries his Wife under the floorboards. Nelson arrives in the blanket carrying the crisps and a newspaper. The Foreman cleans his nails with the now bent butter knife as Nelson tries to explain why Viv believed in the spot. Nelson uses the newspaper as a map of the world. On every page there is a catastrophe. She was right but you can't change the world on your own. The spots are everywhere.... The Wife crawls out from under the floorboards. The Foreman knocks Nelson out with the frying pan to stop him getting help, using the blanket to tie him to a chair, and a napkin to gag him. The Foreman snatches the dust pan and brush from his Wife just as she reaches the barrier. She dies. Exhausted and hungry the Foreman decides to let the toss of a coin decide the fate of the world. Tails – the world must end. He performs a fantastic flamenco, and is about to stamp on the spot when there is a knock at the door. It is their neighbour Mr Pringle. He is in fact the DSS Officer, who now pretends to be a man in order to get on in the world. Mr Pringle explains that she has comes to compliment him on his virile flamenco. Pringle proposes to the hungry Foreman and hands him Nelson's crisps as a wedding present. They dance a furious Tango. As they crash through the barrier Pringle falls onto the dust and the world ends.

I would be a liar if I did not admit that upon reading it my first response to *The Balancing Act* was to hide it under my bed. I was still very much in my own zone of proximal development regarding *Have I None* and not ready to make the leap with this play.

My disturbance centred on form, particularly the surreal farce Edward chose for the play. I now understand, having formed a much clearer understanding of the relationship between the comic and tragic, that the form and the structure of such a superbly crafted play is hugely advantageous for exploring this most serious and disturbing content.

At the first read-through before rehearsals began, I suggested that the Company just try to respond to the images in the play that most resonated for them:

> One legged thief with the top hat and crutch
> Viv flattened against the back wall of the room
> Viv under the blanket
> One legged thief finding his other leg
> Dance of the one legged thief
> The foreman's second dance with the foot poised over the spot, about to end the world.

I would argue that these initial responses go right to the centre of the play. It is when we begin to think about the significance of imagery that ideology intervenes. We can reason ourselves *away* from the site, become incredibly sceptical about what we know, and in seeking to explain/justify this or that, in stepping back from the radical creativity of the first intuitive response, ideology fills the gap for us. This is not an argument for being a slave to spontaneity, but for recognition of the need to develop our reason through imagination. Reflecting here, I can already see how more of the rehearsal process could have come out of those responses.

A Discussion with the playwright

Two weeks after the read-through, I met Edward to discuss the play. The US and British invasion of Iraq was over and the war against the occupation was beginning. The impact of the war had certainly affected my initial response to what Edward had written. Uppermost in my mind was how to speak clearly to young people and make a difference to their lives in these most disastrous of times. In *The Balancing Act* the young people are crushed by calamity: Viv is buried alive, Nelson, at the point of understanding his situation, is bound and gagged. All the adults in the play are corrupt.

This is the bleak reality of our times: *The Balancing Act* shows what will happen to the world unless we intervene to take control of it, take it back from the rule of those dominated by irrational ideas, obsession and fanaticism. I knew that this play was exploring the most deadly serious questions about humanness but I also knew I needed to understand more about how the play was going to work.

The Balancing Act is full of those creative choices for the audience, indeed they are necessary in order to make sense of it: whether we categorise Viv as insane, sane, or as both simultaneously, is a choice that fundamentally effects the self-site of the audience. It is the audience, not the actors, who have to solve Nelson's problems. Edward chose a form that rigorously asks us what, or who, we believe. And despite the outer chaos of the farce, at the centre of the play is a stillness that is rock-like in its consistency. This is provided largely by the presence throughout, in some form or other, of Viv and Nelson who are so close to the lived experience of the audience. It is their powerful engagement with Viv and Nelson that drives them into the site of play.

Edward compared Racine and Shakespeare, showing how the former obeyed all the rules and in doing so became a religious fanatic, whereas the latter broke them all. In many ways *The Balancing Act* does this too: words of wisdom come from the DSS Officer, the OLT speaks honestly. Most importantly, we are invited to laugh: even in the face of Nelson's desperation at the end, we can laugh. This is critical because it gives us, the audience, some control of the situation. Laughter objectifies things for us, which is why comedy is very dangerous.

In many ways the play is a celebration of the actor, which Edward also described as the skill of the audience. The problems it creates for the actor are necessary for the energy of the drama and for the imagination of the audience. The play gives energy *to the audience*.

> The audience has to be as creative as the actors – otherwise what is transmitted? (this isn't necessarily true of spectators at sports.) But the skills mustn't be deadened. You often see actors doing clever things when they put a letter in an envelope or shut a drawer etc and I shudder when I see this. The skills really have to be life skills – to have an object other than being exhibitions of skills. (I take it that a tight-rope walker is teaching you not to fall over in the street and a juggler not to drop a plate in the kitchen: but circus skills are in a particular sub-class: the clown makes you laugh but he is also teaching you how to cry.) Max Miller – and other MH [musical hall] stars – talked about their audiences lives – in a way *grilled* them about the

reality of their lives – modern 'celebs' give interviews about their own lives and encourage the audience to escape-dream about *their* own lives. So there is a particular skill about a one-legged dancer dancing. But also, in what sense is the foreman a crippled dancer? – because he has learned to flamenco so skilfully? It would probably be crass to make him awkward – the disturbing thing is he is good: but in the audience's imagination there will still be the one-legged thief's dance – and it's this that comments on the Foreman's dance. The TBA [The Balancing Act] uses series of movements to gain its effects – like transparent slides being slid over transparent slides... (Bond, 2003a)

In the *The Balancing Act* everything is defined with absolute clarity: the problem for the actor is to find the ways of enacting the site. This requires great skill but then so does building a bridge. Drama has to go beyond this – it has to be beyond the skill itself:

So the energy has always to be tied to an object(ive) in situ – and mustn't be 'for itself'. And then it's the objective that releases the energy: usually rehearsals reverse this process. The object of energy is clarity – so that mere rush/gush can't substitute for it. (I think the stillness [referring back to Max Miller] and the fact that this was 'aimed' shows his intention, his object(ive) – I aim at you. He would also often pick out some one in the audience to address directly – 'missus' or 'gal', and the audience knew that this really addressed all of them. For me it was as if instead of being dazzled by the light I could see the hand holding and aiming the torch.) Filmic 'slow motion' is an empty way of trying to achieve this: it reifies instead of releases. But this is the whole problem of modern acting: it becomes mannered because there is a desire to show things without examining them. (Bond, 2003b)

This discussion set clear parameters for the rehearsal process, which I decided should focus on the releasing of energy in the site.

Preparing to rehearse the text

Geoff Gillham once described Edward as the Shakespeare of our times because of their shared understanding of what theatre must do: explore the society in which we live, its mechanisms and dynamics, its problems and its ideology and simultaneously to explore the human psyche in it *and* the inter-relationship between the two. This is very important because he does not focus on psychology, which is what the vast majority of acting is about, in the sense of specific characteristics of the personality, but the human psyche which is at any given time/epoch/situation, the interior world of us all. This is a question of dialectics, which is at the heart of Edward's writing, dealing with the movement of the inner and the outer, the passage of each into the other, and their reciprocal interaction.

The method of Edward's plays is one of dramatising the problems of humanness so that they connect to the layers of our psyche (of the pre-ideologised self) that demand justice, which is the residue from the child's need to be at home in world. Although the site has a highly coherent and powerful logic, *The Balancing Act*, like all Edward's plays, does not have a message to be rationally understood. The audience is brought into the centre of the problem posed by the plays, which function as a metaphor. Through the metaphors of *The Balancing Act our imagination*, where feeling and thought are united, becomes the site of re-defining what it is to be human in *this* (drama site) world.

I felt the need to revisit *Hidden Plot* and more recent writings but to find practical ways of exploring the ideas in rehearsal without resorting to handing out photocopies for discussion. I was able to use *Modern Drama and the Invisible Object* to do this. Edward explains that while theatre event (TE) is a quasi-directorial tool, the problems for modern acting need to be explored by the actor through acting the invisible object (IO), the means by which the energy and emotion of the performer is re-directed and brings the audience into the play-site.

Rehearsals

Drama does not place every object on the site of the IO. But placing objects on it creates its form of acting and *mise en scene*. It is in general realistic. There is also another use of the word site which has a wider meaning: the play's site. This is the site of the total economic and social relations and the immediate situation. Character is still important but in modern drama site in this sense is more important than character. This is because of the extremity of change in modern society. This also changes the use of metaphor. Theatre observes the metaphor from outside, in drama the actor enters the metaphor. In the actor's training, Medea becomes the blade with which she makes the wound. She enters the wound, it fills the rehearsal room. The wound may contain many things. Medea may meet someone in it. In extremity the conventional parameters of space and time go, as they do in a serious accident (in 'accident time'). For the mature actor, entering the metaphor becomes part of the creative sense. In drama the play must also enter the metaphor; it is the source of its language and action. Inhabiting the metaphor is a definition of poetry. In the day-to-day world we use objects, it is the technological process. Drama reverses the process – objects use us by taking us into their metaphors. We learn to think with the eyes. Theatre acts, drama enacts. (Bond, 2003c)

Our task was to help Katie Baxter, the actor playing Viv, like Medea, enter the metaphor, to step *into* Viv's spot. We explored 'accident time' through the use of the blanket, which appears throughout the play. In order to understand how the blanket is cathected in part one, for it to take us into its metaphor and therefore the play site, we broke the action of the blanket in part one down into nine titled depictions. The depictions gave us a useful tool for working on part one and we decided to follow the journey of the blanket and the crisps throughout the rest of the play, titling every moment when they are cathected and de-cathected. On reflection, we did not spend as much time exploring this cathexis as the production actually requires.

Viv explains her experience of maintaining the world's balance through her dream. The imagery in this speech provides an extraordinary tool for the audience and we realised that it provided the centre of the play for our production. Other interpretations could of course be useful.

> A play consists of one speech which is repeated in increasingly searching ways. Each character takes the speech and reworks it. This speech is the central speech (CS) – it contains the basic theme of the play and also – in its utterance – the way the characters relate to the theme. At each occasion a character will take the speech and then push it as far as he can in exploration of the theme. It will search for the truths the play wishes to tell. Usually in the speech there will come a line which is the furthest that character can take the speech – for himself – at that time. Often the speech will continue for a while. It will then reflect on what it has discovered in the central line of the central speech....as the play progresses the CS and the CL [central line] will develop, becoming more clarified, revealing and definite. The speaking of the speech will define the characters: for some the CL will become more human, in others more inhuman. (Bond, 1996c: 161)

We identified the dream as the central speech of the play explaining the imbalance of the world. It is repeated by Viv and others in different ways throughout the play, its meaning becoming more and more defined by the situation. The central line for us was 'They think they're dancing. They don't know they're dead.' The dancing Foreman appropriates Viv's words, which in his mouth make him more inhuman. The Foreman's dancing in relation to the stillness of Viv, and Nelson after Viv's death, is one of the most important contrasts in the play.

The writer in rehearsal
Edward's contributions to the rehearsal process are instructive, not just because he is both generous and careful in his work but because his interventions always reap qualitative development.

When Edward works on his own text he is having a dialogue with it. He constantly asks questions about it, 'Why does he do that?' What does that mean?' It never gets you anywhere to respond with, 'I don't know, you wrote it.' He is exploring the site too and while, as the writer, he is ahead of us, you can only really know the site when you enact it: writers can write, directors direct but to know the site you need the actors to create it, which is why Edward has such belief in the creativity of the actor. He creates the problems as the writer, but he wants the actor to solve them. The truth, like the imagination, is concrete.

A good example of Edward's approach to dramatic problems was illustrated when we were really struggling to capture Viv's response to Nelson as he counts down before stamping on the spot.

VIV: (*Looks from under the blanket*) Monster! Cruel!
Children! Old people! Sufferin! Cruel! Cruel!
NELSON: Four.
VIV: (*Throws the blanket open*) Come t' me! Quick!
Come! Come! Children! All of yer! I cover yer in me blanket!
Come t' me!
(*The Balancing Act,* Scene One)

We were finding the throwing open of the blanket particularly problematic. I knew we were flooding the audience with a sea of emotion. We hadn't found a way of doing it. Edward found the way to unlock the problem by using objects to take us into the metaphor, to 'think with the eyes.'

He placed the shopping that Nelson brings around Viv's room and added other objects to it that were lying round the rehearsal room. He told Katie that these things, the cheesebiks, drinks *et cetera*, were all the children and old people that Viv was seeking to bring under the protection of the blanket. He wanted her to speak to them and gather them into the blanket and repeat the lines as often as necessary until the job was done. The physicality of doing this slowed time right down. The work became very precise and defined. Above all it had a great simplicity. Eventually Katie was able to work without the objects: she was making the Invisible Object visible The image provided by the blanket for the stage direction 'she throws the blanket open' was extraordinary, an action that the audience could project themselves onto.

While working on the DSS Officer he made me very conscious of something I often forget as a director, and suspect that directors often forget. When an actor plays any part they have to be allowed to find their 'self' in it. As a director it is very easy to get an image in your head of how it should be done, how something should be said *et cetera*. Edward wasn't offering practical solutions to difficult problems in general; he was offering specific solutions to problems for those actors in that production. Working with another Company would have required different solutions. Naturally the actors respond very well to this. They appreciate the care of this approach and are much more creative as a result. It is an approach that makes use of the actor for the audience.

Edward came into rehearsal for a second time after we had finished blocking part five. Although our understanding was clear in a general sense, we were still finding the particularity of the meaning of the site. The timing of Edward's visit was ideal. His response to a run of part five was to point out that we were trying to make the play work rather than allowing the play to work for us by playing the illogicality of the site. Farce is not farce if it is funny to those who are in it. It is deadly serious to the people in it. We were commenting on the action, which then undermined the illogicality. Humour comes out of playing the situation. The world of the Foreman is absolutely crazy but he believes in it absolutely, so we have to enact its normality. Where there is madness it has to be particular. The key to part five is the opening sequence when the Wife is laying the table and the Foreman enters. We are confronted with the Foreman's and the Wife's obsessions: the table is her world, the spot is his, and they are very territorial. This is a house of secrets and it is all about to fall apart.

We then have a contrast with Nelson's arrival. Nelson brings reality into the room with him. We were allowing Nelson to be drawn into the Foreman's world. Edward worked with Richard Holmes, the actor playing Nelson, on how Nelson brings reality into the midst of this insanity. What began as Nelson standing in the door introducing himself, was transformed into one of the most powerful images of the production. Nelson came into the room by half-staggering, half-falling backwards, swathed in Viv's blanket. Richard had created a birth image, knocking on the door was as if he had been pushing against it, pushing against a membrane. Richard used the newspaper literally to make a map. In performance, it created an incredible stillness in the midst of the noisy mess of the Foreman's contorted reality, a hush would fall over the young people still giddy from the murder and burial of the Wife and the assault with the frying pan, watching as they listened to Nelson explaining Viv's reason to them. The slowing down of time directed the energy of the site to the audience and took us into 'accident time'.

The TIE Programme

The play was the centre piece of the TIE programme, designed for fourteen to sixteen year olds. Our audience was largely working-class, a majority of them were third or fourth generation immigrants to Britain and a sizeable minority of them were asylum seekers and refugees.

In creating a TIE programme out of *The Balancing Act* we understood that reconstructing images was an essential activity for the minds of the audience. We wanted to make that process socially conscious. We need to reconstruct the images for what they mean in the world of the play and what they mean in the world of our society. The play opens up, and exists in, a gap in the mind of the audience between their understanding of the world and their consciousness of themselves. In this gap they define themselves in relation to the world.

The Programme Structure

We decided that we wanted to prepare the class to watch the play. We began by identifying a learning zone for exploration:

> Young people (the age of the audiences we are performing to) do not feel at home in the world. The relationship between adults (authority) and the young is being corrupted. Young people feel alone in the world, without the freedom to change it – while adults (who have matured into their loneliness) are destroying the world.

The programme began by working in the imagination on a simple task with the same blanket we used in the show. Jo Underwood, who facilitated the programme, asked the class what she was holding: a blanket. She then shaped it into a bundle, cradling and rocking it before asking 'what do you see now?' The task developed by asking the actor/teachers and volunteers from the class to place it on, or in relation to Richard, without thinking about it.

> No one could look at Richard and the blanket without imagining what they could be, depending on how the blanket was draped or shaped: it could be a picnic blanket, he could be a Mexican bandit, a religious man, an African princess, a king, a stone, someone who's cold, someone who's ill, a child hiding under a blanket, someone who is lonely, someone looking at the blanket that their dead baby played on, fear, it was also a barrier, a tomb, a river....the possibilities were endless and playfully explored. (Colvill, 2004)

Following this exercise Jo would spend a few moments reflecting on the use of the imagination and its relationship to dreams. For the rest of the session, using sugar paper and pastels, the class worked in groups detailing four images from dreams they had had, which was then shared on the set. Jo offered that the empty room was like a mind, we filled it with their dreams as we shared the work.

Following a break, Jo lay the blanket on the set, as it is at the beginning of the play, 'an empty room and a blanket' and the Company performed parts one to four of *The Balancing Act*, which took us through to lunch.

To refocus after the break the class was invited to read an image of Nelson after his encounter with the One Legged Thief, to read his state of being, and to interrogate the crisps and the blanket in terms of what he is carrying with him at this point in the play. Sometimes Jo would ask the class to imagine Nelson's dream that night and get them to build the dream on the set. This was followed by part five of the play.

At the end of the play the class was asked to survey the wreckage of the 'end of the world in the play'. She placed a question: 'Although we know that Vivian died when they demolished the flats she was watching her spot in, if she was in this room when the world ended, where would she be?' Placing Viv often involved exploring the crisps and the blanket or any other object that was significant in the image created. It was put to the class that everyone in the play was seeking something (Often, at a later point, we would explore this in relation to the other characters by building images). The process often involved the exploration of Viv's dream. Finally, the class was asked to place Nelson in relation to Viv, physically, in terms of what they were *both* seeking.

For the final task the students worked in their groups, a specific audience was designated to each: 'the young people of our world', 'those with power and authority in our world', 'the parents of our world' and 'the teachers of our world'. They were asked to select a moment from the world of the play which best explains the world of our society today to their designated audience. The final sharing of this work marked a moment, a shared understanding held by the Company and the young people they were working with, of *The Balancing Act*; a shared understanding of our lives.

During the tour we returned to some schools to continue with more follow-up work. We asked the students, 'Since our day together has anything made you think of the play?'

'News about suicide bombers'
'World news about terrorists'

'I was asked a personal question about whether I thought power or religion
was more important. Made me think of Viv's decisions'
'Yes life generally. Just talking to people, and my crazy friend'
'How people ignore the tragedies of the world'
'A child falling from his bike made me remember the imbalance from
balance'
'I saw a candle and it reminded me of the world'
'Yes, I thought I saw a man on the bus waving his hand like Viv, just as if he
was calming the air around the spot'

One of the tasks of the follow-up work we had planned was to repeat one of
the first tasks of our rehearsal process. The class was asked to choose someone from the play to write to, explaining to them what they did and didn't
understand about their situation. Some examples were:

Dear Viv
I am writing to explain to you what Nelson could not before you died. You
were under the impression that the balance of the world lay in one spot.
Many thought you were mad, I know there were times when you thought
this yourself. Hopefully I can convince you that you were not crazy, merely
confused... It is everyone's collective responsibility to maintain this balance
and that is why everyone has to take responsibility for the state of the
world. If you are unclear as to what I mean by 'spots all over the world',
look at a newspaper, it is a map of the spots where the balance of the world
is threatened; as you may notice, these spots change from day to day; from
moment to moment.

Dear One-Legged Man
.... In a way you could be related to the devil when he tempted Jesus, however whether you had good intentions or bad intentions is irrelevant. You
strongly affected and to some extent helped Nelson in his thoughts, and for
this I give credit where credit is due. Good luck in the search for what you
truly seek.

Dear Nelson
I was truly touched by the affection that you had for your girlfriend. ...In a
way she was right to do what she did since the 'balance-point' of the world
could have been anywhere and with Viv's dedication and loyalty to what
she believed in, she would have made a wonderful guardian. In my point
of view the people that you encountered after Viv's death seemed to be
'curses' on your own life. ... The person that I thought was conveying this
the most towards you was the One-Legged Thief. He made you give up a
long term memory of Viv (the packet of crisps) for short term satisfaction
(his hunger). At that moment I felt rage on your behalf. ....

A short postscript

In February 2004 Edward completed a revised version of *The Balancing Act*. There are many changes, many small but significant. It is worth pointing to two of the changes in the hope that they will resonate with what I have attempted to outline.

There is now a new scene after part four. Edward got the idea for this from watching the play in rehearsal. This inclusion defines the play more usefully for the audience. Nelson now meets a Woman with her own blanket claiming to be his long lost mother. Nelson tries to explain to her that she is confusing him with the One Legged Thief. Once again the crisps are cathected when she produces a bag of her own which she sits and eats; a packet of liver n' bacon crisps, to get over the disappointment of bringing a complicated son into the world. When Nelson tries to explain to her that the world is in a bad way she tells him that it's worse than bad, it doesn't exist. She is transcendentalism gone mad. 'We are but playthings in the 'ands a' destiny.' The Woman has been waiting for years for a bus that never comes. When she is gone Nelson tells Viv that he won't give up until people understand. At that moment a bus careers past and piles into the bus stop killing the Woman. He leaves with her blood-drenched blanket.

When he arrives at the Foreman's house Nelson, wrapped in his own blanket and the blood-drenched blanket of the woman, is bringing a forceful material reality into the insanity of the Foreman's reality. For me, it completes the birth image Richard created in rehearsals and makes Nelson a stronger presence in the melee that goes on around him. I believe that our production managed to avoid the easy option of cloaking Nelson in mysticism. This version of the play makes that possibility so much more remote, and I think it is much the better for it.

Conclusion

The Balancing Act represents another stage in the developing relationship between Edward Bond and the Company. The next play, for we both wish there to be one, will undoubtedly be very different again. *The Balancing Act* is a brilliant piece of modern drama. It is theatre that understands that the imagination gives value to the human mind and the choices it makes; that the use of modern theatre is to give the creativity of choice over to the audience by dramatising the problems of our humanity through the comic tragic. And, above all, this modern drama places the audience at the centre of the site. It is a theatre for our times which recognises that drama and theatre is not a lesson but a tool, and a tool must create something. Edward Bond offers us the choice between creating either our humanness or our inhumanness.

References

Bond, E (1991) 'The Culture of the Child', *Theatre and Education Journal* 4, pp 4-12

Bond, E (1994) 'The Importance of Belgrade TIE' in *SCYPT Journal* 27, pp 36-38

Bond, E (1995a) 'Notes on the Imagination' published with *Coffee*, London: Methuen

Bond E (1995b) unpublished letter to Big Brum, April 24

Bond, E (1995c) unpublished letter to Big Brum April 24

Bond, E (1996a) 'Rough Notes on Theatre' in *SCYPT Journal* 31, pp 8-17

Bond, E (1996b) 'Rough Notes on Theatre' in *SCYPT Journal* 31, pp 8-17

Bond, E (1996c) *Letters Volume III*, Amsterdam: Harwood Academic

Bond, E (1997) unpublished letter to Big Brum November 12

Bond, E (2000a) unpublished letter to Chris Cooper October 5

Bond, E (2000b) unpublished letter to Chris Cooper October 5

Bond, E (2000c) unpublished letter to Chris Cooper October 5

Bond, E (2000d) *The Hidden Plot*, Methuen:London

Bond, E (2000e) unpublished letter to Ceri Townsend, September 26

Bond, E (2003a) unpublished letter to Chris Cooper, May 24

Bond, E (2003b) unpublished letter to Chris Cooper, May 24

Bond, E (2003c) Modern Drama and the Invisible Object, (unpublished paper)

Colvill, B (2004) 'Evoking the Imagination to Seek Reason' in *The Journal for Drama in Education* 20:2

Finney, M (1996) 'Making Theatre for Knowing', in *SCYPT Journal* 31, pp 18-26

Finney, M (1997) unpublished letter to Geoff Gillham, October 27

Gillham, G (1994) The Value of Theatre in Education in *SCYPT Journal* 27, pp 4-11

Gillham, G (1997) unpublished letter to Chris Cooper, November 30

Big Brum TIE Company for the Edward Bond plays
At The Inland Sea 1995 and 1996, *Eleven Vests* 1997 and 1999, *Have I None* 2000, T*he Balancing Act* 2003

Actor-teachers:

Bobby Colvill (1995,1996, 2000, 2003)	Amanda Finney (1995, 1997, 1999, 2000)
Terina Talbot (1995, 1996)	Chris Cooper (1997, 1999)
Richard Holmes (1999, 2000, 2003)	Jo Underwood (2003)
Katie Baxter (2003)	

Directors:

Geoff Gillham (1995, 1997)	Chris Cooper (1999, 2000, 2003)
Design/Touring Company Member:	Ceri Townsend (1999, 2000, 2003)
Administration:	Jane Woddis (1995 – 2003)
Outreach and Development:	Maria Gee (1995- 2003)

Notes

1 For a full account of Big Brum's collaboration with Edward Bond on ATIS see Tony Coult's notes and commentary in *At the Inland Sea*, Methuen Modern plays.

2 'Layers of Meaning' is a reference to Dorothy Heathcote's theory of there being five layers of meaning or five levels of explanation in an action, see Gillham, G. (1998) 'What Life is For', *SCYPT Journal*, 34

Drama Devices

Edward Bond

[This description of Drama Devices that are intrinsic to Bond's theatre was specially written for this publication. They are written in note form to act as a guide for actors, directors and for all those who want to use Edward Bond's plays. Ed.]

The drama devices are used individually or in combinations. Their use is covered by the general notion of TE (Theatre Event). TE drama proceeds by constantly recreating the meaning of its events. The devices are used to this end. TE drama contrasts with other forms of contemporary drama. The TEs must be picked out and dramatised, not swamped in generalised dramatisation of expected and conventional crises. If this is not done, a TE play 'ceases to be' because it cannot be reduced to the conventional. The text may exactly describe the setting-up of a TE but this does not restrict the way it is played. On the contrary, TEs make greater demand on creativity than conventional theatrics. All forms of theatre have equivalents to TEs, and for many of them the instructions are far more restrictive than for TEs. This is unnoticed because they have become conventional effects. Any play which has meaning (which not all plays do) may be TEd. In TE drama the TEs may be marked in the text but any critical point may be TEd. Character is important in all theatre, but TEs are used to elucidate the character's meaning – the meaning does not come from character alone. Theatre such as Stanislavsky's based on character can be compared to filling a bucket with water. When the play begins there is a little water in the bottom of the bucket. During the play the bucket is filled till it overflows in the climax. But, as it were, bucket and water do not change. Theatre based on self-validating stories may be compared to a gadget made from a kit of prefabricated bits. As the play proceeds the bits are assembled to make the completed gadget. The meaning exists before the play begins. The audience's responsibility is limited to watching and emoting. TE involves the audience in the creation of meaning.

The whole play is not TEd but TEs create the style of playing the whole play. They make spurious effects redundant. In contemporary theatre violence, sentimentality and pessimism are taken to have meaning in themselves and are used to give meaning to a play's events. That is decadence. It is not possible in TE drama and this is another argument in its favour.

TEs are analytic, not stylistic. They are the play's backbone. They close the gap of empty effects and aesthetics between drama and life. They make drama *radical* in a time of show-biz, reductive entertainment, TV drama and 'show productions'. TE restores to the Tragic and the Comic their formidable power. It opens up vast new areas of meaning and drama and places it back at the centre of our lives.

TE (Theatre event)

TE invalidates received and ideological meanings and establishes new meanings in their place. The audience are aware of the TE's outcome but the characters need not be.

MO (Misplaced object)

Many meanings are attached to objects or situations. Objects and situations are then cathexed with meaning: things such as religious symbols, clothes, common utensils.

Examples: The cup in *Olly's Prison* – the daughter is murdered because she will not drink the tea. In *The Children* the youngsters are murdered with a brick and towel. These are common building or domestic articles. It is sometimes suggested that a dagger should be used instead. At the beginning of *Have I None* the policeman is deeply disturbed at seeing an old woman hanging a picture in ruins. During the play his wife in a sense enters the picture. In *Great Peace* a cigarette packet in the wrong place becomes a mutinous act.

RP (Repeated pattern)

Patterns of events are repeated. Each time they may be TEd in new ways. Later TEs relate to meanings created in earlier TEs.

Examples: In *At the Inland Sea*, the scene in a crowded gas chamber. Later it's as if the scene were turned over like a page. The reverse scene is an empty hut in a forest. In the gas chamber only two characters are seen but they are buffeted about in the roaring invisible crowd. This takes place in a character's imagination. At one moment he freezes the action – stillness and silence. Later, beautiful singing draws him to the forest hut. He enters and the singing stops – stillness and silence. But in the empty hut are signs of life. The contrast between death chamber and forest hut is an extended TE. Some directors stage the gas chamber by making the two visible characters pose like spectators at the front. The double-TE is not dramatised so its meaning is not enacted. In *Eleven Vests* TEs use tearing, cutting, slashing, knives and bayonets. A parallel series of aural TEs uses silence, screams, chat, a soldier's imitation of a child's 'choo', mechanical-intercom, a totally new language. In the end the two series come together. The student is silent throughout the first scene. The text says he moves twice: once to look at the sky, then almost immediately at the floor. In these two looks the actor may TE the play's centre. If the student fidgets it may be naturalistically effective (though in reality the student probably wouldn't fidget) but it destroys the TE and limits its subsequent effect throughout the play. Another series of TEs uses mess and cleaning-up, sweeping *etc*. This leads to a penultimate TE which comes straight from the play's centre. A dying soldier uses his vest to wipe his blood from the bayonet used to kill him. The complex meaning of many TEs cannot be put and certainly not enacted in other ways.

CO (Contrasted objects)

Many objects have assigned relationships: cup and saucer. Meaning changes if the relationship is broken or a new relationship established. Someone in danger of frostbite puts their gloves on their feet. This conveys not just cold but its insidious destructive effect. The small displays the large.

Examples: In *Restoration* the aristocrat is less disturbed by the murder than that it takes place at the breakfast table. The play contrasts polite convention and legal barbarity. In *The Balancing Act* a packet of crisps and a blanket form parallel extended TEs. The variety of crisps repeatedly changes yet the meaning of 'crisps' is constant in itself: it is changed by being put in new situations. The blanket is not constant, it becomes bloody: this changes the meaning of situations in which it is put. *The Crime of the Twenty-first Century* uses bricks and ordinary stones. They are thrown in half-play, anger, used to make a map, placed in a dead woman's hand to scare off dogs. In the last scene they turn into the geometrical perfection of a classical pedestal to contrast with the dereliction of the survivor. CO is a form of MO. TEs are not static but used creatively.

SS (Site and Situation)

Site and situation replace the *reduction* to character. The site is everything to hand in the play 's subject (theoretically this is everything). This gives great facility because anything on site can be used to create meaning. Simple objects may be decathexed and recathexed. When meaning changes, the situation on the whole site changes. It is a social event not limited to change in character. Concentration on *characteristics* obscures the wider situation on site. A dosser in a Park Lane hotel changes the situation on site but the site reacts in a determined way. A burglar in a middle-class house alters the situation on site. But justice is also on site. Justice is not predetermined. It does not exist in the way courts and prisons exist. When the burglar changes the situation on the site he brings into contention the meaning of justice. All meanings which are merely *assumed* become sites of violence. Violence holds ideology together.

Examples: The entry of the Rat Wife into the conventional household in Ibsen's *Little Eyolf*. In a concentration camp one prisoner's theft of another prisoner's spoon is a capital offence because both spoon and prisoners belong to Authority.

Use

All objects and situations have human use. Ideology burdens the sun with meanings and counter meanings to carry the use made of it: Apollo is a god and a rocket, sun spots interfere with communications. Use of a domestic object may comment on its usual use, or its usual use comment on another activity.

Examples: In *The Children* the use of towel and brick (MO) activates hidden domestic stress. In *Have I None* Sara drinks poison. The text does not name the poison. A director said the actress must know what poison so that she can reproduce the effects. The point is irrelevant. What do you want to use the effect for? A TE might show society as poisoning, destroying itself. Instead of realistic contortions, perhaps a rigid confrontation with the object containing the poison or with nothingness? A martyr deliberately put his hand into the fire first because it had signed a heretical document. In Seppuku you should show no emotion.

Palimpsest

The layers of a person's character and habitual self. They are formed at different ages and in different situations. The layers need not be thought of as Freudian. They may exists contiguously. This explains the socially important problem of why in some situations people behave out of character.

Examples: In *Have I None* the policeman behaves to his wife as a criminal-conspirator or policeman according to what danger he sees himself in. In the same play the two dresses TE an earlier stage of his wife's life. The TE is extended (spoons and bones) to bring the parameters of human life into the living room. In *The Crime of the Twenty-first Century* Sweden sings a nursery rhyme immediately after killing Hoxton. In *Coffee* the soldiers are enraged not by orders to commit massacres but by interruption of their coffee-break (a historical event).

Centre

The central problem of all drama is justice (not all plays have a centre). Particular plays deal with the centre in relation to specific situations. The play's main metaphors and similes reflect its centre. Its patterns are based on structures extended from the centre. In *Born* Luke is in turn in the situation of all the other characters he relates to. In *In the Company of Men* Leonard repeatedly changes his character (heir, drunkard, criminal, saint, waif, businessman, assassin, suicide) in his attempts to express the centre. Bartley and Wilbraham are aspects of Luke also related to the centre.

Examples: In *The Balancing Act* the play's centre is literally staged as a spot on the floor. In the play it becomes buried under dirt. The character's relation to the spot literally TEs each character's responsibility for the world.

Barrier

It marks the division between acting and enactment. If a play has no centre then usually it is only acted. Acting is style or self-referential expression (rite, performance art *etc*). Meaning is unexamined. The barrier is what Van Gogh understood as the anxiety and terror of the white canvas: it is without ideological or conventional markings. On this side of the barrier there is skilful repetition, on the other the creation of human meaning. There the removal of the barrier between drama and life may be absolute.

Examples: As the objective of TE drama is to cross the barrier, all TE dramas provide examples. The Boy in *At the Inland Sea*, Sara in *Have I None*, Sweden in *The Crime of the Twenty-first Century*, Luke in *Born* – these are random examples. In *Existence* 'x' crosses the barrier downstairs in the hall after he leaves the room – he returns and barricades himself in.

Acting beyond the barrier involves **Extreme, IO, AT.**

Extreme

Need not be physical or violent. It may be (and must also be) extremity of meaning. In the extreme ordinary meanings break down. When a situation's extremity is faced the barrier is crossed. On this side of the barrier there may be pain and pleasure, on the other side there are the Tragic and the Comic. The latter two integrate meanings into emotion. They then become agents of justice. All change in history is a change in meaning. The violence that holds ideology together is hidden under platitudes and sentimentality – the extreme forces this violence to reveal itself.

Examples: The murder over a cup of tea in *Olly's Prison*. In the same play, the policeman's 'fake' violence blinds his victim. In an Ivory Coast production the male audience applauded the father's murder of his daughter, the women in the audience wept. An ideological split was revealed and discussed. A less extrovert European audience is confronted with the father's discovery of his innocence in the face of the violence ideologically installed in society. The scene in *Saved* in which a baby is stoned is built as a series of possible stopping points. At each of these the baby could be saved. The violence is not atavistic but ideologised in economic structures. For instance, one of the gang has a new expensive jacket for his 'night out'. Early in the scene it is ruined. It shocks to realise that if it had not been ruined the baby would not have been stoned. This does not excuse the act but explains it. I have never seen a production that TEd the violence to show how it is used to integrate society. The play asks, in the expression 'a night out', what is 'out'?

IO (Invisible Object)

Fundamental to TE drama. The difference is between acting and enactment. The actor finds the IO in the extreme on the far side of the barrier. The site is social but the self must express it individually. The IO is the actor-and-character in the specific situation. More than one actor may create the IO. It is called *Object* because it objectifies the situation on the site: it is its meaning. Before the IO is enacted it is hidden in ideology and convention. The actor enacts the meaning in the IO and makes it visible. It may be action, vocal, brief or ongoing – anything may be used. It relates to the centre. Only the actor may find the IO and make it visible. The writer and director assist by pointing to where it may be found in the SS. The IO involves the logic of imagination and the logic of humanness. On this side of the barrier they have no logic, on the other side they have logic because there they bring humanness into the situation. The IO creates the form of TE theatre and even before an IO is reached the performance leads to it.

Examples: In *Chair* Billy's appearances after he leaves the house is a series of IOs. In *Saved* Len's final poses on the chair are also IO. In *Have I None* Sara's IOs are drawn to their extreme expression when she poisons herself and leaves the room.

AT (Accident Time)

A biological effect. In emergencies such as a car crash the brain is flooded with chemicals as concentration increases. The effect is the apparent slowing down of time. More is seen and more actions become possible. Extreme drama creates this effect. The accident is not physical, it is a crisis in existential meanings. It exposes contradictions we accept in daily life in order to survive. The contradictions are historical limitations. For instance, slavery was necessary in the ancient world (it led to the glory that was Greece). When contradictions lose their historical purpose they are destructive, but they have become deeply interwoven into daily life. They are unjust and provoke injustice and are maintained through violence. The extreme reveals the contradictions in the form of paradoxes. This creates an 'accident in the *self*' just as a car accident occurs in the street. In the accident we must choose. The crises prevent withdrawal. If we close our eyes – literally or metaphorically – we still suffer the consequence. A choice must be made in the paradox. Refusal to choose is itself a choice with consequences. But in the deep creativity of human beings it is natural to want to choose. The choice we make redefines our self, we choose what we are. This is the reality of drama.

Note AT is not artificial slow-motion. The Audience not the actor are in AT. They enter it through the intensity of concentration created by what passes on the stage. Perhaps all creativity occurs in AT. If so, the audience's and the actor's AT are different. AT cannot be aesthetically faked.

DR (Drama Reality)

Drama is fiction used to create the truth. TE drama is not about life but in life. When Hamlet dies he is not dead but his death is real – real in the sense that it is not just one death but all deaths. It is the meaning of death *and we live meanings*. What can be said of significance about Hamlet's death can be said about our own. It is as if his death were our own. We feel fear when we watch a fright movie. We tell ourselves it isn't real but our fear is real. Our involvement in Tragedy is far deeper because it involves an idea. We do not feel ideas but live them, we live not our biology but the meaning we and our culture give us.

Emotion follows meaning. The Tragic and Comic involve the logic of imagination. Imagination must be fancy-free in order to have the possibility of logic. I see someone about to put their hand under the circular saw: I am free to imagine the hand won't be harmed or that it will be amputated. This situation is obvious, I may be said to 'know'. But the saw may suddenly be switched off. All important human truths involve some unknown. People have known that thunder was a bolt hurled by Zeus, others that saints have walked on water. These ideas are integrated into the cultures of people's daily lives. In a highly technological world they are increasingly matters of life and death. Extreme drama does not imitate reality, it creates it by changing its meaning. In our time the only drama that can do this is TE drama.

The Logic of Humanness

A scientific age understands human beings reductively. We are said to be determined by our biology. Literally, it is claimed that science knows more about us than we know about ourselves. This makes science the enactment of paranoia. It ignores the fact that we do not evolve as animals in their environment. Our environment is history and we create our own humanness in culture. Humanness is not a thing given to us, it is a relationship we create between other things: nature, society, economy, rationality, emotion, imagination, the search for justice and an imperative to be human which derives from radical innocence. These things forever change historically. The logic of humanness is always to achieve the balance between them which most increases our shared welfare and happiness, so that where there were enemies there are friends. If we get the balance wrong we will destroy ourselves. Drama is the logic of humanness.

5

The Sheet of Glass:
a drama project by Tameside schools on
an Edward Bond poem

John Doona

n the spring of 2001 a group of teachers in Tameside, on the eastern edge
of Manchester, began an experiment to explore the use of drama in the
delivery of an education which addresses the concerns of being human
in the modern world. The ideas of Edward Bond, his belief in both the
importance of drama and the imaginative potential of young people, were
our starting point.

The project draws from seven Tameside secondary schools and Tameside
FE College. In response to pieces offered by Edward Bond, staff and artists
met to create a challenging two-hour performance and workshop for
students. During the workshop the students from all schools worked
together. With the exception of the Tameside College students who were
studying BTEC Performing Arts, all students were in their first year of
studies in GCSE Drama and were fourteen or fifteen years old. Following
the launch event students worked with staff from their own school for
seven weeks before coming together to share. During this time they created
a response to the stimulus and drew this into a public performance.

This chapter will explore three episodes in the developing work. The experiments detailed are taken from the work of the Egerton Park group. Parallel
explorations took place in other institutions. The three areas explored are;
experiencing the imagination, working with image and narratives and
creating public theatre.

Section One: The Sheet of Glass

Our first act as a group was to approach Edward Bond. We posed this question: 'What does a young person need to think about or to know at this time?' *The Sheet of Glass* was his reply.

The Sheet of Glass

There is a sheet of glass.
You see through to what is beyond.
A window
It keeps out cold and rain.

You paint the back with silver
You see yourself.
The same glass but now it does a different thing
The opposite
You see yourself but not beyond.

At night you dream.
Can't remember who you are.
You go to the mirror to look for yourself.
All you see is the dark.
You can't see through it
... or anything in it.
You don't know who you are or what's beyond the mirror.
A dream is the opposite of being awake.
Or is it?
Is a dream a sort of mirror?

You wake and go to the mirror.
The dream's upset you.
You'd like a mirror which shows you who you are and at the same time
    lets you see what's beyond it.
So you break the mirror.
You cut your hand.
It bleeds.
But it works!
Through the broken gaps you see what's beyond the mirror
– you see other people there and what's happening.
And in the broken mirror still in place you see yourself.
But only bits of yourself.
For every bit you see of what's beyond the mirror you have to lose a bit
    of yourself.
It can't be otherwise.
It is the law of opposites.

Now
The mirror was magic.
Every morning when you washed your face you asked it
'Who's the best person in the world?'
The mirror looked you straight in the eye and said 'You'.

But the morning on which it was broken
...it didn't
– and it never did again.
Instead it said:

What are you for?
What are other people for?

The Sheet of Glass is difficult. It is probably at odds with the material we teachers might ordinarily offer young people in the classroom. Ordinarily, our instincts are for the direct. We present narratives that are accessible and immediate and pursue our 'humanising' goals through exploring the meanings of the situations that arise. Edward Bond gave us something different. He says, with regard to audiences, 'If we trust the audience they become artists... The audience's experience becomes part of the practice of their daily lives. It is the difference between a photograph and a ring at the door.' (Bond, 1998, p336) The same is true for young people encountering Bond's work as participants and performers. From his earliest plays he has *confronted* audiences. In *The Sheet of Glass* there is no compromise to its young audience. By presenting us with a piece that is fundamentally problematic, he gives authority to the young people.

During the Manchester leg of the Classworks' tour of Bond's *The Children*, a young cast member had commented in regard to Bond, 'He doesn't hide things from us. He knows we'll understand.' The comment was made at the end of a process which had allowed the young person to absorb Bond's creative work. It expressed a sympathy with the playwright which we had yet to win in the current project.

When *The Sheet of Glass* was offered to our young people we had to be ready for the possibility of flight from the expectation expressed by it. And we had to be prepared to counter this flight. It seems that there is no place in our culture for meaning. Our culture is dramatised but is dramatised meaninglessly. Our televisions endlessly tell us stories but they are stories which do not offer us any insight into our situation. The reaction of young people to Bond's deep questioning can be to turn away, to express impatience and a desire to stay within the restricted terms allowed by the parent culture.

In working with the Egerton Park group, I ease students into approaching Bond with:

> We do not live in a world that asks us to question. Indeed, we are told not to. But it is our ability to question that makes us human. We aren't just special kinds of objects in the world. We are human beings who think and need to understand. Each one of us is capable of asking the BIG questions... and answering them for ourselves. By believing that these problems are not beyond you Edward Bond is showing you great respect.

The countervailing response to the flight-response is the silence. The silence comes before the flight. It is as if the young people hear it and then leap to defend themselves from the danger. Bond says, 'A child asks what, why, how – the questions of the great philosophers.' (Bond 1998, p261) It is this conviction which compels him to offer such work as *The Sheet of Glass*. But in the same essay he says, '...innocence protects itself by being corrupt.' (Bond, 1998, p252). Young people have developed survival strategies for living in the world. These strategies, Bond says, corrupt the young. Their response to Bond's questioning is a symptom of this corruption.

The silence and the flight are a paradox. Bond's piece has 'rung the door-bell' but the young people seem to recognise the danger of engaging with the questions. The group needs to understand their responses before they can understand the piece. *The Sheet of Glass* leads us to the exploration of identity. It now becomes important for us to begin to untangle its questions: who are we and what is our place in the world? It is addressed to young people, standing, as they do, at the point of separation from the structures of authority which have thus far sought to contain their self-knowledge. To begin to allow the young people to understand themselves we look to Bond's concept of the imagination.

Section Two: Experiencing the Imagination

In the summer of 1985 Bond's trilogy of nuclear holocaust, *The War Plays* (Bond, 1998), was staged by the Royal Shakespeare Company. In the *Commentary on the War Plays* (Bond, 1998) that was to follow, Bond gives us his account of the theatre necessary to the modern world and begins to uncover the concept of imagination that has become the cornerstone of his thought. In the *Commentary* he writes,

> I devised a scheme for improvisation by students at Palermo University. A soldier returns home with orders to choose a baby from his street and kill it. Two babies live in his street: his mother's and his neighbour's (...) As I planned the improvisation I realised how it would end. I noted the end in my notebook.

> Next day the students improvised. I asked them to act honestly what the soldier would do. The soldier came home and was welcomed by his mother. She showed him her baby. He went next door. His neighbour welcomed him and gave him her baby to hold. The action became very slow. The soldier seemed to be staring into a watch as if he tried to tell the time from its workings. He gave the child back to the neighbour. The he went home and killed his mother's baby. In my notebook I had written that this is what he would do. He and the other students were surprised that he had done it. They were surprised when the next student to play the soldier also murdered the 'wrong' baby. All the students played the soldier and none of them could bring himself to kill the 'right' baby. It was a paradox. (Bond, 1998, p247)

What has become known as the Palermo Improvisation describes the uncovering of a paradox in which the human individual acts in a manner which, to the understanding of the world, should be impossible. We all know that 'blood is thicker than water' and that 'we look after our own'. Clearly the soldier will kill the neighbour's child in order to save his own sibling. But the paradox is unavoidable. If we are even surprised ourselves at the answer that we have given, what is the source of our answer?

Bond continues, 'The unconscious sees through us and our social corruption and sends us messages of our humanity, ingeniously and persistently trying to reconcile the divisive tensions in our lives. Our unconscious makes us sane.' (Bond, 1998, p250) Elsewhere he will re-shape this 'unconscious' as the imagination and make it the source of all human value.

The Palermo Improvisation is seminal. Its importance lies in identifying the moment at which an individual is able to recognise the extent to which his or her own thoughts are occupied by ideology. It is important that the paradox is revealed by an act of creativity. In Bond's framework it is the Imagination which supplies the surprising answer.

In our work with students we followed Bond's description above as a lesson plan. Students were invited to enact their own answers to Bond's situation. The responses noted by him fifteen years earlier proved remarkable consistent. Students' solutions are loaded with imagination: The soldier kills himself rather than harm another. The soldier kills his own brother to contain the suffering. The soldier accepts the court-martial. The soldier kills the officer. The solutions are simple but clearly not the expected. The soldier does not kill the 'right' child.

Immediately after the improvisations we begin to discuss the students' responses. In the workshop I go on to ask: 'Why has no-one done the 'obvious' thing? Were you just trying to be dramatic or original? This is a possibility and there is a use of the word 'imaginative' where we mean simply 'original' or 'unexpected'.'

At this point it is time to explain Edward Bond's concept of the Imagination. I continue by asking:

> Had I told you the soldier's story and simply *asked* you to *tell me* what he might do, or if we had spoken of it in an 'ordinary' way (i.e. in the site of the ideologised world) you may have given me the 'obvious' answer. Really, Edward Bond says, this is the *world's* answer. He tells us that many of the thoughts we think are our own are not. Because of how the world is organised, we carry thoughts around in our heads as if they were our own. If it were not true, for example, that 'we look after our own' we might not continue to compete to *own* more than other people, continue to be, as we might say, 'competitive consumers'. Without this our society, our economic system, could not work. BUT, Edward Bond's theory says, we can give another answer. We are not limited to the answers of the 'world-in-our-head'. We hold onto a 'deeper' place that is ourselves. Edward Bond calls this our Imagination. He says we understand the world, firstly as children, by telling ourselves stories about the world. When our imagination speaks, as in your creation of these scenes, it gives its own answers. It speaks 'humanly'. It doesn't say that 'we look after our own'; it says, 'we cannot create our own happiness on another's suffering.' If this is true, don't we have to start again to understand who we are? Don't we have to look very closely at what we believe, feel, understand, think?

In opening up such a discussion the first response can be hostility. You are asking students to consider that they do not 'know themselves', that what they think they believe may not be a valid belief at all. In the same way that the theatre establishment and Bond's own audiences can be hostile to the challenges of his work, students resist this apparent attack on their dignity and self-knowledge. Bond has always been the one to turn the lights on at the party.

Three things prevent the students from turning away. Firstly, their understanding of themselves is in flux. Bond says, 'From the beginning the child needs a total explanation of the world.' (Bond, 1995, pvii.) And at this point in their development young people are in the full grip of this need. As they move to adulthood the desire becomes urgent. But the explanation of the world is also under constant challenge. One student, Vicky Shelmerdine, commented in notes after the project, 'My understanding of the world is still confused, in the making.' It is this recognition of confusion and desire for clarity that creates the conditions for the challenge of Bond's work.

Secondly, in as much as Bond's theory of imagination implicates a pervasive, malign authority, for the young, the example of how authority can control a person's idea of themselves may be very close at hand; their own recent childhood. Parents project their own (Authority's) concept of 'The good child' onto their off-spring from birth. As young people emerge from the sphere of this authority and complete the rituals of rebellion they are willing to recognise the ferocity of Authority's control. In a written statement on the project Vicky Shelmerdine gives her assessment of authority as, 'Authority is lost in this world, messed up. People have authority, people who don't deserve it. I don't like it. It's wrong. Why should authority be given out? I think it's used wrongly, unfairly.' Of course, this is a statement of general understanding but the thought is expressed in response to her work with Bond. She has found an ally and feels supported in her felt response to her own life. It is in this way that we can consider Bond a 'popular' writer. His thoughts are rooted in a general experience.

The third reason that students do not run from Bond is that the experience of the Palermo Improvisation has occurred amongst us. It must be explained. The students are struck by what their own creative response has given out, and especially since there seems to be a consistency across the group. So, not only does Bond reflect a general experience, he also creates new experiences for participants in his work and his audiences which demand explanation.

Bond's theatre involves moments in which individuals face themselves in need of understanding. In my own experience of Bond's self-revelatory aesthetic, the profundity of the thought that you hold ideological beliefs as your own is uniquely troubling. But it is also the fundamental act of separation necessary for both creation and 'human' living. It makes possible the self-interrogation needed to understand the truth of your place within the world. In my work with young people it is sometimes possible to recognise the moment at which they begin to understand the occupation of their 'selves'. They begin to separate *themselves* from their 'occupied' selves. It is in the vitality with which they approach the next stages of the work, the trust they place in their imaginations and the depth of the resulting theatre product, which attest to their understanding.

Section Three: Image and Narrative
i. Finding the image

In a discussion of the urgency of theatre's task Bond says, 'Theatre finds images to reveal (the) hidden drama so that its reality may not drive us into extinction.' (Bond, 2000, p192) and refers to imagery as, 'The means by which situations are known.' (Bond, 2000, p185)

All of Bond's plays 'find the image'. It is the image created by Bond's stage pictures, held in gesture and word and situation, that carry meaning and impact, a moment where meaning is gathered like a knot. It is what Bond calls a Theatre Event (TE). Bond says, 'Drama is a complex intervention in reality to get at truths society obscures or denies.' (Bond, 1998, p300-301) It is at the moment of the Theatre Event that the meaning is revealed.

In the summer of 2000 a Manchester community theatre group, Bare Witness, staged the first performance on British soil of Bond's *The Crime of the Twenty-first Century*. As I directed the production I became strikingly aware of what Bond refers to as Theatre Events (TE). As the play opens Hoxton is alone in the vast empty wilderness beyond the city. It could be a scene from one of Bond's earlier post-nuclear holocaust plays, but the city has been systematically and painstakingly felled by lorries with chains: lorries sent by the city's own ruling authority. The wasteland separates the secure from the criminal; the suburb from the prison. To live in the wasteland is a crime in itself. Hoxton, trying to wash the dust from her faded clothes, hears a sound. In the Manchester production she raises a stick. She wheels around. She looks to the sky. Her breathing is shallow. She listens. Her pointless weapon raised. We do not hear the helicopter gun-ship. Hoxton does. She swipes at the authority that has laid waste to her home as she might swipe at flies. She is suddenly frail and old, a worn rag. Her head twists but her body cannot follow. In the swipe of her stick and the twist of her neck we see the terror of the individual caught at rest, the foolishness of believing in your own sense of security. Hoxton's gesture is a moment that reveals a social truth; a Theatre Event.

In the next stage of our work with our young people we begin to follow Bond's process and to 'find the image'. In the following sections I will attempt to both capture the workshop experience and provide an analysis of it. I trust the stylistic shifts will be accessible to the reader.

Speaking in images is important for another reason. Bond sees the fact of human language as the source of our desire for justice. He writes,

> It is the self-consciousness sustained by human language that promotes both change and our ability to change. It is a basic dynamic. It originates in the speaker's sense of his or her right to be, to exist, and that this right ought to be acknowledged by the listener. It is the origin of our desire for justice. (Bond, 2000, 6)

In this 'desire for justice' our language is human, but Bond considers it axiomatic that the world is owned and therefore unjust. One site of this owning-authority's control is the control of language. The degree to which we are able to understand our own situation is determined by the language we are 'given' to speak. That is, our form of life generates our language; the conditions of our existence give us the language we speak. When a central condition of our existence is the management of an unjust world our language finds its limits at the limits of the allowable truth. Our language has been bled of its full explanatory function. An aspect of Bond's work has been the attempt to put a language back in place that allows a fuller understanding of our situation.

Bond indicates that we cannot 'talk' or 'reason' our way out of ideology's control. He says, 'Reason alone cannot help us to understand our situation humanly, or even use ideology against ideology.' (Bond, 2000, 179) and continues, 'Reason may be corrupted but imagination cannot be because it has no ideas – and so drama may directly confront imagination without the distortions of corrupted self-consciousness (and reason in its service)' (Bond, 2000, 181) So for Bond there is no 'talking-cure' for the occupation of ourselves. We need to create acts of imagination.

As a part of the process we find the moment to expunge speech. We want the imagination to have a clear route into the world and as far as possible not to be mediated by a language that may have been bled of its descriptive power. The young people are invited to speak in images.

We return to the practical. The Egerton Park workshop progresses.

We stand against a wall. Looking into an empty space that is the stage. It calls us. The wall against our backs won't let us retreat. We have to fill the stage. We start with images. Theatre begins where our words fail.

We ask the mirror's blunt question. What are you for? What is your purpose in the world? Again, we're not afraid of the silence. Silence is what divides our work from the meaningless.

Then someone steps forward. When they enter the space they may not yet know what it is they will create. This is encouraged. We trust the imagination. They ask for as many people as they think they need to join them in the space. They begin to place their actors. They are following an imaginative hunch. The teacher may question the creator, to press them to be confident and clear. A picture builds. At this point the 'audience' may not offer ideas or interpret. It is our goal to preserve the clear channel of the creator's imagining. The picture is complete. In one case we see a group crouched, eyes averted, hands busy, heads bowed. They are under the dangerous, in-different eye of supervisors. Those of us not participating stand back. We repeat the question: 'What are you for?' We look at the stage. It is no longer empty. We have a new line in the conversation of our imaginations.

These are all simple things. What matters is the light in which we are able to see them. What matters is meaning. We can all make plays. The point is to make meaning.

When the originator determines that the image is clear and right we empty the space and repeat the process. The images mount. They build on each other, or they reflect an alternative, or they break new ground. As we pro-gress we catalogue each image. We have images of desperate work, of sell-ing, of dangerous streets, of isolated individuals in empty rooms, a strangely smiling face, an individual under the surveillance of their own family.

Now we need language.

The images are enacted in the order in which they were created. Now each 'creator' must give a title to their image. We hear each title with each image. In interview students observe,

> Stacey: We used images to give us ideas of what the play was going to be about. Each image had a subject and each subject had words that went with it.

> Carol: Each image was a piece of the puzzle so that we could put the jigsaw together.

The images quickly became suggestive of theme, character and situation. The images outlined above move us towards a story of the struggle to find rest and peace under an authority which would have us constantly stimulated and constantly active; a kind of forced and necessary sleep-lessness. So the group has an embryonic narrative. At this point we begin to talk about performance. The following conversation ensues:

I ask the group whether we are ready to create a piece of public theatre from the accumulating ideas. One student comments 'They won't know what we're talking about.' She is challenged by another, 'Why not? Are they stupid.?' 'No,' comes the reply, 'it's just difficult.' I press the group, asking whether it is possible for us to create a performance that does for the audience what *this* work of ours has done for us. What has it done for us so far? A student replies, 'It has done our head in. What does this mean?' I pursue 'does it mean that we have challenged what we thought of as our understanding of the world?' A student replies, 'Yes, it has, it makes me look at everything new.' 'Can we do that for our friends and family and teachers?' 'Yes.' 'What do we need?' 'We need a story.' 'What sort of story?', I ask finally. 'A hard one.'

ii. Finding the narrative

Bond talks of 'storyability'. He says,

> The ability to analyse and calculate is characteristic of isolated reason: when it is combined with emotion, to produce imagination, it becomes 'storyness' (Storyability etc.). Imagination is essentially storyability. Imagination needs to relate experience as story or as potentially storyable. When experience becomes overwhelming or chaotic stories are told. (Bond, 1996:8)

In the account he gives of the self, the world is 'inscribed' in the imagination in the form of story. Indeed Bond says, 'The self is a story. The story relates experience to the real world.' (Bond, 2000, p118) And it is certainly true that when a person is asked to tell of who they are they will quickly resort to story. Our identities are largely the collection of stories we tell about ourselves. Bond goes further saying, 'When we introspect we ask: Tell me a story. ' (Bond, 2000, p117) For Bond, in the development of our understanding of the world and ourselves the story carries the load of meaning. When it comes to the communication of meaning in drama the process is reversed. We gain an understanding and the imagination drives out meaning as story. Storyability is the bridge from idea to theatre.

In the process we are engaged in our young people wish to move towards a public performance and, therefore, need 'story'. The process for the group mirrors the act of creation of the dramatist. Bond quotes a letter from Van Gogh to his brother,

> You don't know how paralysing that is, the stare of the blank canvas, which says to the painter 'you can't do anything'. Many painters are terrified of the blank canvas, but the blank canvas is terrified of the really passionate painter who dares – and who once and for all has broken the spell of 'you can't' (Bond, unpublished paper, no date.)

The moment of terror at the 'blank canvas' does not last long with young people. Perhaps this is because, as Bond says, 'Young people are still close to the practical use of imagination. ... Their imagination is critical. They are open to theatre.' (Bond, 1996, p15,) Perhaps, as observed in our projects, it is because the force of the new self-knowledge gained has created a sense of their own potency as creators. A professional actor employed to work with the project in our third year, a woman who had entered the profession at sixty, reported being very struck by the young people's serious approach, by the silence that seemed to attend the important moments of the work. It forced a change in her attitude to the young.

To return to the process. The work continues. The group assemble to create their story: Images, 'headlines', thoughts are accumulated onto a blank board. The board isn't blank any longer. But the absence of story is staring back at us like the 'blank canvas'. The group stand and look at the board for a time, in silence. We look for the narrative on the wall. We listen to all contributions. We discuss. We refine. The point is not to draw in all the images lazily into a plot. The point is to capture the meaning we wish to present. We build a consensus. We are dealing now with a 'social mind'. We are writing by committee. But the committee is standing in the same space, looking out from a shared perspective, responding to the same questions, sharing the same understanding. Is it remarkable that a structure emerges so painlessly?

To return to the collection of images noted earlier. The narrative evolves into the following, as recounted to me in interview by students, but retold in my own words: We are in the near future, in a work place where the work is urgent but meaningless. The authorities constantly re-enforce the sense of urgency in the full knowledge of it's meaninglessness. A worker catches the supervisors unguarded eye and knows the truth. She walks out. On her way home she passes the non-working poor begging and wailing. She doesn't give to them and wonders why she doesn't. She passes the scream-ing market-traders and wonders why she is appalled. Suddenly she is being chased. Authority has got wind of her 'free-thinking'. We see that she is 'chipped': a biological implant which allows authority to direct her move-ments and inflict pain. She is stilled. Finally, she returns home. She is visited by her dead mother. Her mother isn't a ghost, she has been cloned and directed to come to her daughter to re-enforce authority's thought-plan. Can the individual survive?

In the same interview students' own analysis of their work came as,

> Stacey: The images told the story, not the people.

> Carol: The future had gone to the past. Like the factory, when you think of the future you don't think of people working in a factory, the machines do everything. But, in ours, everyone did everything manually, and they had no choice....

Stacey: ... because of the power aspect.

Teacher: So they made people work on machines even though they didn't need to, just to keep power over them?

Stacey: It's all about power and control.

At this point it may be worth pausing to consider the role of the teacher-adult in the work. It almost goes without saying that the teacher has no special claim upon the understanding that is growing. We have to abandon the role we have developed as an institutional survival strategy. Each individual is the centre of their own meaning-making. Students and teachers are equal in the sight of the imagination. In an interview with students after the project, Stacey Appleby was satisfied that, 'The teachers let us be in control. It wasn't a school situation any more. You (the teacher) said, 'Right, make some images.' But the images were our own.' By an act of group mind our narrative emerges from the wall. In each of the seven constituent institutions parallel work has been progressing with each group generating their own short collection of scenes.

Section Four: Into Public Performance
i. Performance

The Sheet of Glass has been seminal to all of the Tameside work and to each performance. It has set a tone for the nature of all our work. It challenges staff, students and audience. It seems to sit like a mountain on the landscape. Theatre flows from it in strange and unexpected ways. Bond says,

> Theatre dramatises imagination in small seemingly insignificant incidents and in incidents of obvious importance. Drama cannot instruct, it confronts, perplexes and intrigues imagination into recreating reality. (Bond, 1995, pxxxiv)

In an attempt to capture a sense of other work resulting from the Tameside projects what follows is a brief account of a selection of moments from the performances. The images here will be drawn from the work of the full range of participating groups. The details of the process in each institution may be different but the spirit and the experiment is the same.

- An inmate is locked in the role of Dr Mengele. He repeatedly drowns baby dolls in a metal bucket. We cannot escape and ignore the storms of history without repeating them. (Stamford High School)

- A starlet paints her face to meet the world. Her hands are angry. She hates the necessity of meaningless actions and her own compliance. (Two Trees High School)

- A Palestinian child sits on her front step after curfew. She holds her knees and rocks back and forth. She repeats over and again, 'I'm just sitting here, I'm just sitting here.' She expects to be at home in the world. This is her protest. (Egerton Park Arts College and Astley High School)

- A young person breaks into a shop to steal the object that will give his life value; a designer coat. That which we believe will fulfil our need for meaning, owned objects will actually destroy our humanness. (Tameside College)

- A young man has gained the technological elixir of life; he will live forever. Then he recklessly cripples himself. He cannot die. Image: he lies helplessly on the edge of a bed, his head is fallen backwards, his face upside down. He dribbles into his own eyes. We chase the wrong goal and damage our-selves. We create our own tragedies and we know it. (St Damiens' RC High School.)

- A child's pet dies. A new one is cloned. The pet dies. Clone another one. The pet dies. Clone another one. The child learns the disposability of life. A parent dies. Owned technology fools us about the real nature of life. (Longendale High School).

Earlier in the process we spoke about narrative. It was suggested by a student that the story should be 'hard'. In this the young person is showing an understanding of Bond's statement above. In the interview with students quoted earlier, a further discussion ensued regarding the distinction between *this* drama and the 'popular' school drama, typified for the students by *Oliver!* Stacey: 'Our theatre's not plastic. Our theatre's wood. It's like trees. It's grown from our imaginations. It's natural. Organic. It's not had lots of things put into it to make it fancy. It's just what it is.'

We are creating public theatre from individual acts of imagination. We are up against the embarrassment of meaningfulness. In our general culture drama that seeks meaning is an aberration. Bond says,

> Drama may lie. Most modern entertainments – films, TV, news programmes (now part of the entertainment industry) – degrade the human image. So does 'high art' (...) The human image is exploited and sold and integrated into the dynamic of the economy. (Bond, 2000, p191)

It is amidst the meaningless that the young people come to speak. They are not yet at ease with their own authority. They expect the adult world to respond with; 'We won't be lectured at, and certainly not by the young!'. It is necessary to reassure. In the interview with students it was said,

> Carol: It was scary because we thought no-one would understand.
>
> Teacher: But you carried on?
>
> Stacey: Because we knew it was ours. It was right.

The process of development has revealed to our young people the meaning of their activity. They have dared to speak and make sense. The comment above shows confidence in the clear line from question to imagination to the stage. This is the source of students' confidence in what they will offer. Students are willing to recognise that the performance for which they have responsibility may be tough. The audience will need to listen to its own response. In interview Carol said,

> Our play's not been through a machine, not manufactured for people to come and sit and think 'Ah, this is good, let's sing along! 'Ours was *about* something. They didn't 'understand' it, it made them think.

For students the important thing is that the performance should provoke: it should not just be effective, which is fairly easy, but provoke an imaginative response. Through being provoked themselves, students have come to value provocation.

These moments of provocation are evident in Bond's own plays. The headline view here is his use of violence. It has been the violence which seeks to cut through to the human response. The creation of this response is a profound moment of individual politicisation. Bond's own explorations of this moment of political aesthetic have, however, been much more diverse and much more sophisticated. Our project has been groping towards realising a corresponding aesthetic as much as it has sought to discover a process.

ii. Reflections on performance

There is a distinctive nature to 'Bondian' performance. It is true of his own plays, and I believe, of plays written under the influence of his concepts. He writes,

> In drama imagination seeks the extreme situations which will take us to the limits of meaning where humanness is defined. It takes us into the extremity of the self. It seeks to show how people must finally come to the ex-

treme situations in which they lose every illusion about themselves yet hold onto their humanness or suffer what follows when they know they have lost it *because* that is the only way they can hold onto it. (Bond, 2000, p190)

And there's something else to prepare for: silence. Pinter is spoken of as the master of silence. But his silences are functional and simply effective. The silence in a Bond experience is truly aesthetic. It flies in the face of the expectation of an audience trained in cheap tricks, loud bangs and sparkle. The silence is a moment of terror; the terror of the blank canvas. The audience seems to say; 'What you have shown me, scares me. It is outside of the site on which I stand. I have no words yet to deal with it. Please leave me.'

Bond's theatre attempts to lead the audience to this moment of super-understanding. In discussing the concept of the Theatre Event (TE) he says,

In TE time may be experienced as slower, as in a car accident. TE can be understood by comparing it to a whirlwind or cyclone. The centre of the storm is calm and quiet... In it everything is seen with great clarity. (Bond, 2000, p17)

In a post-show discussion after Big Brum's preview of *Eleven Vests*, Edward Bond responded to a question about the audience laughing when a teacher was stabbed. Part of his response was that he didn't care how his audience responded *in the theatre*. He may be right. Speaking of my own experience in 'Bond audiences', the work of his theatre is strangely private. An audience watches from the site of the ideologised world. Their responses are limited by the language they are given to speak in public. Their responses are circumscribed by the expectations of their peers; each polices the other. The silence is partly the result of being abandoned at the edge of the socially-possible; Bond leaves us at the edge of the world.

iii. Responses to performance

The Tameside performances have each had an impact. Post-show discussions always reveal surprise and sometimes shock. We have been challenged to justify involving students in such work. However, the abiding feeling has been a generous awe. In interview the students state;

Stacey: The audience learn something...

Kelly: .... Respect.

Carol Davis gives an account of her grandfather's response, in which he is determined to learn from his grand-daughter the meaning of her factory image; he keeps her up the same night, followed by a restless sleep and tenacious questioning throughout the next few days. Their relationship was altered. He was now willing to recognise her authority as a meaning-maker.

Julian Hill, a professional actor and writer, saw the second performance. He reported: 'I didn't know that such things were possible in a school. They've taught me about the theatre.'

Bond writes of the Tameside performances:

> Something that struck me when I saw it – and stays with me – is how detailed – and accurately detailed – the acting was. There weren't the generalisations which come from simply releasing energy to animate conventional formulae. I found it almost unnerving. It meant that the young people were examining themselves closely and not just others – they were making demands on themselves. Even if they were acting under the guidance of teachers, clearly they'd been encouraged to act under their own initiatives. An amount of the imagery came from the 'media' – which attempts to define their lives and against which they must inevitably measure themselves. This had another strange effect: I became aware of how profoundly society abuses and harries young people – how badly it treats them. Badly not in the sense of say the depression of the thirties, the Orwellian poverty – but how our present culture tears people's lives to bits.

> There was a real sense of oppression. I don't mean that the young people were oppressed or cowed! – but it was strikingly clear how little society offers them that can make them really happy and content. And so behind the intricate structures of the scenes – individually and collectively – there lurked something ominous. That we don't offer them much of a life.

> ... the detailed observation and enactment... made it clear – as they acted their 'fictions' – that society could not be a fiction to them, could not successfully deceive them.

> Drama is very important to the education of young people. And that now – as the contradictions declare themselves more drastically – it becomes more important. This imposes its burden, also, on teachers. It's easier to see what is wrong in the present state. But now we're also asked, as educators, what world are we asking young people to grow up into.

> I was very encouraged. (Bond, an unpublished letter to the author, no date.)

Conclusion

In an article for the Standing Conference of Young People's Theatre (SCYPT) in 1996 Edward Bond wrote,

> The aim of the theatre should be to allow the autonomy of the child to pass into the autonomy of the adult – to remain creative. (....) We need passion and dispassion, an adequate metaphorical language, skill in using the images which bind complex ideological assumptions together – sometimes by returning to meanings from which they were purloined. (....) A play must enable the audience to examine and understand the events that are staged – their society. It must also enable them to examine and understand themselves. Otherwise nothing can be changed. This means invoking the crisis of the imagination. (Bond, 1996, p15-16)

The work of the Tameside project is not complete. Our experiments are unsatisfactory in many ways. The reflection that the writing of the current chapter has engendered has moved us on. The processes above will be the starting point for our fourth year. Bond gives us unfinishable business. *The Sheet of Glass* is still our problem.

References

Bond, Edward (1995) 'Notes on Imagination' in *Coffee*, London: Methuen Drama

Bond, Edward (1996) 'Rough Notes on Theatre', *SCYPT Journal* No31, Spring 1996

Bond, Edward (1998) *Commentary on The War Plays, Edward Bond, Plays: 6*, Methuen Contemporary Dramatists, London: Methuen Drama

Bond, Edward (2000) *The Hidden Plot*, London:Methuen

Bond, Edward, Unpublished letter to the author, 16.10.01

Bond, Edward (Unpublished, no date), An Incident in Hedda Gabler and an Actor's Exercise, Extract from The Fourth Story: A short treatise on self, society and Modern Acting.

6

Arguments with authority – the making of 'Tuesday'

Tony Coult

FATHER: You're in a state of shock. Ill. That's why you've got to go to the authorities. If you cut your finger you go and get it bound up. That's what authority's for. (Bond, 1993)

Tuesday, a three-part television drama commissioned by BBC Education, was broadcast in 1993 and has not been seen since. However, like many Bond radio and TV plays, stage productions are also increasing, particularly in Europe. Fortunately, the published version includes excellent notes and variations for stage production and it makes for a rich and challenging play reading experience.

Tuesday is a play about authority. It not only takes issue with the concept of Authority, its production history is also an argument with authority.

The action at the heart of *Tuesday* pulses away inside a matrix of authority relations and systems. Just as in its companion piece *Olly's Prison*, a three-part drama, broadcast in the same year as *Tuesday* but on the national channel, BBC1, there is a troubled relationship between a father and his daughter, Irene. This is more than merely the cliché of a generation gap. Bond has sensibly avoided the superficial cultural signifiers that would rapidly date the piece. Indeed the daughter's name establishes a connection with Greek drama. Irene, the daughter, is the Greek Goddess of Peace. The Theban Herald in Euripides' *Suppliant Women* speaks of the world that Bond's young woman reaches for:

> How far peace outweighs war in benefits to man... Irene, the enemy of revenge, lover of families and children, patroness of wealth. Yet these blessings we viciously neglect, embrace wars; man with man, city with city fights, the strong enslaves the weak.

The basic situation and story is simple, although what 'happens' is quite extraordinary. A teenage girl does her homework. Her father, her sole guardian, isn't home yet. Her boyfriend, Brian, arrives unexpectedly. He is a junior soldier and has deserted from his unit. So far, this could be a conventional enough 'problem play' or a story line in a soap opera. The surface familiarity of the setting is deceptive. We are about to be led into a world where the most fundamental arbiters of power, the family and the military, are challenged and examined.

Brian has recently returned from serving in a Middle-East desert country. (The play was written in the aftermath of the first Iraq war, launched after the invasion of Kuwait.) He is a deserter but he is still a soldier, entering and desecrating the house of Peace. So this play is about a warrior who returns from the war to challenge the world of war and authority. John Arden's recently-revived *Serjeant Musgrave's Dance* makes a similar gesture: his military atrocities originated in 1950s Cyprus, whereas Bond's spring from 1990s Iraq.

When Irene's father arrives home, a disturbing sequence of events unfolds. As he attempts to incorporate Brian's act of disobedience into his own, military-trained, way of understanding the world, he falls back on old responses. These become more authoritarian, motivated by a fear of events getting out of his control. In the play's key, and most provocative scene, Irene turns her boyfriend's gun on her father. Not knowing it is unloaded, she pulls the trigger.

This is a moment of terrible clarity. It is also a moment that sets a stark, challenging puzzle in front of the audience, one that demands a clearing-out of simplistic, mechanistic explanations and leads to profound questioning. All the reasons why an unexceptional teenager should murder her father will swarm to the surface, inviting conventional, family melodrama explanations. Has he been a child abuser? Has he been violent to his child? Was he about to do something to threaten her life and she acted in self-defence? These are tested, especially in the thrashing around the Father has to do to find some explanation for this terrible act, but there is no direct evidence for any conventional horrors. If an answer is to be found, it has to be in the territory shared by the audience and the world of the play as a whole. For all the mild suburban blankness of the setting: 'a suburban pre-war house, converted to flats... in a light industrial suburb', this world that contains the house of Irene, the house of Peace, is highly militarised.

Men of Edward Bond's generational cohort of writers in England share a common experience of war and the military. These are men who were children during war and called up into National Service post-war. Arnold Wesker went into the RAF and wrote *Chips With Everything* out of that experience. Harold Pinter engaged with National service by refusing it and becoming a conscientious objector. Infantryman Edward Bond ended up in the army occupying post-war Austria, where he found himself billeted in recently vacated SS barracks, ('infinitely better than I was used to'). The military has been a constant source of political learning, imagery and imaginative stimulus ever since.

Tuesday draws that formative experience of his own, involuntary, 1950s Army career in front of the studio camera for contemporary, 1990s youth to consider in *its* context. There was a cliché bandied around in the post-war years that a spell in the Armed Services 'knocked the corners off' young men – young women, it seems, had no such dangerous corners in the 1950s. As various post-war moral panics about youthful misbehaviour gathered strength, National Service in the armed forces was seen as a possible container of these unruly energies. When National Service was abandoned in the late Fifties, by a Tory government seeking to rid itself of old colonial drains on the exchequer, there was a deal of right wing anxiety that the youth of the time, impatient for a stake in the gaudy consumerism being waved in the air, would now 'cause trouble'. And in so far as there was a new, more democratic energy released by the post-war baby boom, expressed culturally in rock'n'roll and other popular art forms, the old right had a point: their hegemony *was* threatened by the young. There was also a mirror image to this 'containment' model of National Service. This was the 'melting pot' idea, in which men – again, *sic* – of all classes mingled in uniform and under the shared absurdity of military discipline, with a resultant erosion, it was thought, of class ignorance and prejudice. Undoubtedly there was a point to this notion: the Labour victory of 1945 would not have happened in quite the same way without the service vote, and the enforced awareness of other cultures and classes did have a radicalising influence on many servicemen.

It is therefore legitimate to see National Service as an important educative experience. Certainly, for intelligent, creative working-class minds, such as Bond and Wesker's, National Service was an education, though as a project to contain their critical energies it plainly failed. On the contrary, both men learned a great deal about the class system's workings from their National Service experience. Bond in particular, found in the military experience a clearly symbolised dramatisation of a class society, with pettiness, violence and injustice. As he told Jim Mulligan in an interview published with the playtext:

> There was an atmosphere of violence and coercion. It was a very brutal society. Various ranks were given very unjust powers over other people and if you were an offender you could be publicly humiliated, degraded and brutalised. I saw in it an image of society outside the Army. (Bond, 1993)

The recurring imagery of killing with a bayonet in plays from *Saved* to *Eleven Vests*, and including *Tuesday*, attests to the powerful emotional impact of this staple of Army training. It is another facet of Bond's personal placing of himself into history: that he was the last generation with a direct connection to the world of Homer, a man who knew, from within his own living memory, of travel by horse, of the blacksmith's forge in the next village. So here is a man, generations of men, still being taught the skills of killing with which Homer would have been familiar, disembowelling with the small sword even a prospering Greek poet might have possessed.

The ending of National service in 1958 appeared to be part of a process of renewal as Britain ended its overseas colonial responsibilities. In the young generation of writers from the 1950s, the seed had been sown of an authoritarian social structure, partly imagined as a world of officers and men, a culture of brutalising violence, and a neo-colonial project exemplified in the Suez fiasco and messy engagements in Malaya and Aden. 'Shooting up the yeller-nigs', as Barry in *Saved* succinctly puts it. Looming over all this was the final dark Authority of global nuclear war, once more in the hands of an apparently unchallengeable officer class.

Father – he's 'Mr. Briggs' at one point but has no first name, only the role description – is authoritarian. His is the chippiness of a sergeant, committed to the officer-led class structure but forever excluded from it. Like Harry in *Saved*, he has fought in a war and been subtly corrupted by it. His self-esteem is fragile and the little there is is undermined by his shame at having become a casualty of the times in which the play was conceived and written. These were the years when the aggressive market driven economics of the Thatcher/Major period pitched many men out of jobs and into the newly created Job Centres. Mr. Briggs spends a lot of his time in these places. He even seems to use the Job Centre cafe as a substitute NAAFI. For Father, then, the military is a period in history. For Brian, it is his immediate experience.

The story of the play is created on the premise of a very contemporary military irrupting into the unlovely 'peace' of suburbia. The deserter Brian is a double challenge to the ordinary: he brings with him the hot memory of violence from his soldiering in a Middle-Eastern desert country, and the cold gunmetal of a service revolver. His presence in his girlfriend's home disrupts all the mean conventions of life: dole queues, school exam revision, food shopping. It is clear that in rejecting the Army, Brian is attempting to put himself beyond the military, to reject its values. The traumatising experiences of killing, and a Damascene encounter with a wandering child in the empty desert, convince Brian to desert but his decision alone is not enough to cleanse his hands of the virus of violence. Bringing the gun with him ends the possibility of innocence for anyone in the house and specifically for Irene.

Brian is not to know that his entry into the closed world of his girlfriend's suburban flat will infect it both with violence and with an intense moral honesty that lays bare the antagonism between authority-worshipping father and reality-seeking daughter. Irene's father, in his shocked response to the events that invade his small territory, displays the desperate authority of a weak man, or rather a man who senses his own lack of consequence in the world. His reaction to the defection of Brian from his army unit is superficially concerned and he seeks to put things right, but only within the parameters he understands. Authority must be placated because he too, like Brian, was in the military and therefore subject to the same dehumanising process that has worked on Brian. His solution is to get Brian to return to his unit and re-enter the world of military authority.

What is troublingly credible about the father's reaction to the crisis is that he is tormented and haunted by the failure of his parental authority. He is not an easy 'fascist' monster who offers himself up for glib judgement. Indeed, the offence done to conventional filial relations by Irene's attempt to kill her father, makes the incident more than a swift, comfortable moral tale that merely regrets the breakdown of family relations and the proliferation of guns. It poses a major problem about the nature of power and power's ownership. The action is both surprising and, moment by moment, psychologically truthful and credible. It works in a rich and un-clichéd way, and is hard to characterise neatly. Its very inability to fit into neat categories of drama invites an inevitable clash with the institutions of education and of broadcasting, where pigeon-holing is often a means to contain dissidence and challenge.

Edward Bond has always been instinctively suspicious of authority. His own experiences as a working-class kid in pre-war and wartime London, of evacuation, of conscript life, early sharpened his sense of outraged justice. From the mid 1960s, he began to establish a professional career and to negotiate the complex relationships with new forms of authority: the arts bureaucracies, the metropolitan critical power-bloc (an early and iconic instance) and the still class-bound bohemianism of theatre administrations. The almost surreal machinations of the Hollywood machine also pulled him in, Bond at one point having to work scripting bits of *Nicholas and Alexandra* for the myth-generating Sam Spiegel, a figure of capricious and dictatorial authority in the Dream Factory.

Given Bond's anti-authoritarian tendency, it was inevitable that tensions would develop with the institutions which now impinged on his writing – and upon which his writing began to impinge. One difficulty with civilian as opposed to military authority is that it is very good at disguising itself in relaxed clothing, collaborative gestures and comforting bureaucracy. From the 1960s onwards, some of the clothing and the gestures may have become wilder and more libertarian, but the essence of authority is to hold power to itself. This is what Bond increasingly found himself confronting.

Others of his cohort fought parallel battles. Arden and his writing partner d'Arcy famously formed a picket line outside the Royal Shakespeare Company because of issues concerned with the treatment and ownership of Arden's script, *The Island of the Mighty*. Wesker fought battles with the National Theatre over his play, *The Journalists*, and has sustained an ongoing polemic with authority in the British theatre ever since. A younger generation of Seventies playwrights and theatre workers attempted to deal with the crisis of authority by attempting a transformation of the power relations between funders, theatre owners, directors, actors and playwrights. This worked through experimental formations of left-ish administration ranging from the anarcho-syndicalist to the unashamedly Stalinist. However whacky some elements of this process, at its heart was a challenge to arts establishment, and perhaps more importantly, to state authority, that spread like a stain through the new, or alternative, theatre movement. At its heart was a project to work politically and to experiment with different formations of collectivity. One outcome was the convergence of Bond and the Theatre/Drama in Education movement. However, I want to focus on the relationship that Bond has enjoyed, and endured, with the single most powerful institution of cultural authority in late twentieth century Britain: the British Broadcasting Corporation.

From early in his writing career, Bond imagined works for radio and television. As in the theatre, there were pockets of creativity and bohemian-ism in the deeper interstices of the huge bureaucratic institution of the national broadcaster that allowed younger dramatists to find a niche. The BBC's Third Programme was an early home for Harold Pinter and Tom Stoppard, as well as nurturing maverick writers like Giles Cooper. Bond's own submissions to the BBC were five radio plays between 1957 and 1958 and one play for television, *The Broken Shepherdess*. None of these plays made it to the studio. There have been occasional single television versions of the stage plays, *The Sea* and *Bingo*, and some radio adaptations of stage works including *In The Company of Men*. The late 1990s also saw a line of commissioned original radio plays, instigated by Turan Ali's 1999 com-mission *Chair* for the Bona Lattie independent production company, con-tinuing with Ali's 2002 *Existence*.

Bond's original television dramas *Olly's Prison* and *Tuesday* were first trans-mitted in 1993, just as the BBC was going through a transforming turmoil. Under pressure from a Conservative administration which was consistently embarrassed by hostile journalism, the BBC was moving rapidly towards a more commercial, ratings-led ethos. This was the fulfilment of the project of recently ousted Conservative Prime Minister, Margaret Thatcher, whose policies had transformed political, industrial and cultural life around the notion of the Free Market. 1993 had seen the arrival of John Birt as Director-General, with a brief to complete the 'modernisation' of the institution. One of his most radical and resented organisational innovations was a system of internal accounting that priced every transaction, human and mechanical, in the corporation. It was called, ironically, 'producer's choice' and co-incided with the effective death of any chance for producers ever again be-ing able to commission someone like Edward Bond.

One man already finding the new pressures inimical was a BBC drama pro-ducer called Richard Langridge. Originally an actor and playwright, Lan-gridge championed, along with other colleagues in a rapidly changing BBC, the single play with its single and singular vision of a writer. This tradition, the 1950s heritage of Sidney Newman's Armchair Theatre, for ATV, and the Wednesday Play, for the BBC, put the medium of television on a par with the Royal Court Theatre and Littlewood's Theatre Workshop as essential breeding grounds for new drama. However, by the 1990s, this tradition was dying on its feet.

The moment in 1992 when Langridge chose to approach Bond was thus one of particular potency in relations between the state and broadcasting.

The Drama department of BBC Television at that point still maintained a core of individuals for whom mature, challenging drama was a priority and a possibility. However, the mood in the organisation as a whole was one of turmoil as political pressures to embrace the free market bore down on the BBC hierarchy. Langridge explains his move from mainstream to educational drama:

> I'd become a bit disillusioned with BBC Drama. There was this 'glamour-fest' happening and I just sort of fell out with the powers that be because I wasn't savvy enough to get on the film bandwagon . Perhaps because of my theatre background I really enjoyed doing plays. And plays were a declining artform. So the chance to do plays for kids in education came like a godsend. (Langridge, 2003)

Working with Barry Hanson, another champion of the single play, in mainstream drama, Langridge had already commissioned a three-part drama from Bond, *Olly's Prison*, which was in many ways a companion piece to *Tuesday*. When *Olly's Prison* was about to be commissioned, Bond offered a characteristic 'pitch': 'I want to write a play about a cup': a cup of tea being one of the most potent, meaning-rich, images in the whole three hours of the drama! Langridge is now clear that such a moment has passed in television. Commercial imperatives allow no significant space for individual voices like Bond.

> If I was a mainstream TV drama producer now I would be trying to take an idea from Edward to David Thompson at BBC Films and say I've got an idea from Edward. But I couldn't anymore get away with saying its about a cup. I'd need to ask him to write a 20 page treatment. (Langridge, 2003)

In commissioning *Olly's Prison* in the teeth of this wave of change, and in trying to fulfil Bond's wish that the three plays should be transmitted on consecutive nights, Langridge and Hanson were fighting not only the naturally bureaucratic nature of the BBC institution, but also its newly emerging commercial priorities. As Langridge remembers:

> Barry (Hanson) was sufficiently of the old-fashioned school that supported plays, as opposed to the trend that was becoming apparent in the BBC in the middle 90s which was to try to emulate Hollywood. Everyone wanted to make movies, everyone wanted to make films for TV. There were examples of one or two directors who'd made one or two films for TV and then gone off to Hollywood. And everyone was trying to copy Channel 4. The Play was seen as old-fashioned and redundant. (Langridge, 2003)

Langridge brought a sensibility honed by respect for the single play and for the voice of the individual writer to the commissioning of new material for

BBC Education. He quickly took a strand that mixed documentary and drama, called *Scene*, and turned it into a showcase of work by contemporary dramatists. The high-profile writers he attracted, including Willy Russell and Tom Stoppard, gave Educational Drama some of the drawing power that made experienced directors, actors and technicians wish to work in BBC Education, although it paid less well.

Bond's dissatisfaction with the production of *Olly's Prison* meant that he wanted to have much greater influence on the way that *Tuesday* was made. Langridge, realising that the technical demands of television directing were likely to overwhelm the writer, teamed him with a television director, Sharon Miller, who had worked on Bond's plays at university and knew her craft in the studio. What might have been a fraught working relationship of dual-directorship turned into something fruitful and mutually respectful. Miller was clear what her task was:

> I thought it was a very stark piece and I thought it was a piece that demanded more thought and contemplation than a television show which is necessarily on and then off would allow it. My main aim in working for Edward was to make it accessible and understandable... when you get right down to it what Edward seems to be saying are actually very simple basic things. My intention, my hope, was to get to those basic things. And to make those rise to the surface. (Miller, 2003)

Bond, in turn, appreciated the active engagement of Miller and recorded his thanks in a published letter to her which includes these comments on the institution in which they worked:

> People are there in the end to sustain the Institution and its there in order to use people to sustain itself. This isn't a natural thing at all, it only happens because a human purpose is involved. In nature it would be as if fish created the sea. (Bond, 1996)

If the turbulence over the future direction and control of the BBC failed to impact immediately upon the production of *Tuesday*, it was part of an ideological wave that certainly affected the way that the play was used. The increasing pressure towards conformity and a narrow, instrumental ethos in education was embodied in the various education 'reforms', and gathered up into the National Curriculum. Because the play was relatively long and not an established text, increasing pressure on teachers' time meant that the kind of space required to use the play effectively was hard to find. *Tuesday* undoubtedly presented a challenge to all sorts of conventions of reception and use. Its refusal to make the experience of watching comfortable and conventional, even though it has some of the superficial characteristics of the 'troubled teen' genre, may have created problems of expectation in the staff room.

In the Miller-Bond co-direction, there is no comforting, genre-cocooning familiarity to tell an audience how to respond. External, suggestive sound is minimal. There is no mood music. When we look at BBC Education's Field-work Reports that evaluate teacher and student responses, the degree of challenge offered by the ambition of *Tuesday* and its unsweetened style is clear. The ambition is laid out at the beginning of the report:

> *Tuesday* was designed to provide an alternative to well-used and 'tired' GCSE plays. Teachers frequently indicate that this is an area of need. It was also intended to offer challenging and thought-provoking theatre to students whose sole experience of Drama is naturalistic feature-films. (*BBC*, 1993)

There is a small but significant error in the Fieldwork Report's plot summary. It states:

> Thinking he is armed, the police shoot Brian, and his death opens an unbridgeable divide between Irene and her father. (*BBC*, 1993)

It is Irene's attempted shooting of her father that opens the 'unbridgeable divide', rather than Brian's death. Arguably the divide is there anyway and the attempted shooting merely a confirmation of it. The plot summary tends to the conventional, focusing on the obvious act of violence, whereas the play demands that we question the whole context of a society's violence, in which a damaged young man cannot reject violence when he wants to. The gun he carries may be unloaded but it is still a gun, potent with symbolic power.

Clearly, the sheer size of this work is going to demand time and preparation to make it useful. Langridge evaluates the difficulties posed by the broad-cast in the light of the then recently introduced National Curriculum.

> Already the climate was changing, already I seem to remember that teachers were saying that with the new curriculum coming in we can't give so much attention to a 90 minute play. Half an hour we can do in PSE [Personal and Social Education] but 90 minutes of a new complex play by one of Britain's leading playwrights – we don't have the space in the curriculum any more. So I think, less than the worth of the play, the curriculum changes undermined the impact of the play. (Langridge, 2003)

It is plain that, intentionally or not, the National Curriculum was effectively excluding work such as Bond's from young people's experience. The challenge this poses is multi-faceted. *Tuesday* fits into no convenient category of the educational curriculum, yet it is concerned with matters which are absolutely central to young people's learning and growth.

The feedback from schools in the Fieldwork Reports was that:

1.1 The play was not found to be accessible by the majority of students in the age group. Students of lower ability found the play impenetrable, and more able pupils needed a highly structured approach before they felt able to articulate their responses. The play actually had the effect of subduing and slightly intimidating less able and less articulate youngsters.

1.2 Older, more confident, students were far more at ease discussing the play. It was also clear that if initial negative reactions could be overcome, re-examination of the text was rewarded. When parts of the drama were re-played and discussed with small groups of more motivated students, responses were markedly more positive.

1.3 There was strong evidence that the text would be appropriate for A-level students. (*BBC*, 1993)

At first glance these criticisms and responses appear to reflect real problems with the way *Tuesday* was received. However, they are really only criticisms of the institutional and bureaucratic framework within which the play was transmitted, criticisms of forms of authority. Authority in the shape of the new, commercial, ratings-led BBC is challenged by this play, as is the utilitarian model of education which shapes the state school system. That these are not conscious challenges from the play's creator makes them no less significant. They are, however, the results – accidental but significant – of the drama and its representation of authority. In a published letter to Richard Langridge taking up the issue of the Fieldwork Report's difficulties, Bond isolates the problem:

...what people retrospectively recall about their education – and in which they recognise their adult value – are the times when the barriers were breached and they were confronted with themselves by recognising the other's awareness. ...Obviously the value I have on occasions such as these is to take young people to the barrier, to the place where they don't know where they are... (Bond,1998)

Bond reflects on the teacher-student relationship and pinpoints the crisis of authority involved. Teachers are inhibited in their ability to use the play productively by institutional authority:

The teachers – and young people – find the film 'strange' or even 'bizarre' because it doesn't conform to what they are usually shown...Yet somehow, the report suggests at any rate, the teachers regard this as a difficulty – they don't seem to see it as an open door, they merely share the young people's 'estrangement'...They seem to want to make the film the same as all the others so that they can go through a form of education which explores only within strictly confined boundaries and does not transgress those boundaries – but doing the latter is essential to education. (Bond, 1998)

Tuesday grew in part from Bond's own knowledge of the army as a national serviceman. The experience was crucial in his formation of ideas and images of authority, and plainly left a reservoir of feeling and understanding into which he has dipped many times since in his writing. Later, his engagement is with other, superficially more benign authorities: the institutions of art, education, commerce and culture with which he has engaged with, often not simply on his own behalf but on behalf of other writers and theatre workers. The very presence of the work that became the broadcast *Tuesday* challenged – and still challenges – those institutions to adapt and orient themselves to the real needs of those they serve: young people.

In spite of the difficulties of accessing it in 1993, *Tuesday* is not a play that fails, either as education or as television drama. It is arguable that the institution of television, as it was constituted in 1992/3, failed *Tuesday*. If so-called 'students of lower ability' are reported to have difficulties with the play, it is equally probable that the circumstances of an ordinary, unsympathetic timetable will create those difficulties, rather than the students' 'ability' or the play. There's an echo here of Bond's work in relation to the major producing companies. In the latest phase of his work his best work is achieved in by-passing the institutions. *Tuesday's* themes and objectives make it a deep well of learning possibilities. Whether as classroom reading, or as a performance script, the play serves teachers and students. Indeed, with its simple domestic setting, the relatively easy availability of digital camcorders and editing software, the exciting possibility today is for a thousand films of *Tuesdays* to bloom...

Sharon Miller, who helped Bond to create the play as it was broadcast, makes the unassailable case for why *Tuesday* is so important:

Edward raises huge topics that begin and end with how on earth can we stop the way we treat each other so badly. Its a global question. And it leads to a very profound discussion – or it can... (Miller, 2003)

That 'profound discussion' is begun in Irene's shocked clawing at reason after the ambulances go:

I've been so confused. They teach you this and that. I try to understand. Their confusion.[...] They say it's a map. It's nothing, blank. Then I looked down – and the paper turned over – I saw – suddenly – clearly – the map's on the other side. I understood. There is a right and wrong, some things shouldn't be. (Bond, 1993)

And the play ends with a categorical demand as Irene, Peace, sinks into sleep:

Let me live. Let me live. (Bond, 1993)

References

BBC (1993) – BBC Education Policy Unit Fieldwork Reports, Autumn 1993, English File: *Tuesday* by Edward Bond

Bond, E (1993) *Tuesday* London, Methuen

Bond, E (1996) *Edward Bond Letters Vols. 3* ed. Ian Stuart, Amsterdam, Harwood, 1998

Bond E (1998) *Edward Bond Letters Vols. 4* ed. Ian Stuart, Amsterdam, Harwood, 1998

Mulligan, J (1993) in Bond, E. *Tuesday* London, Methuen 1995

Langridge (2003) Interview with Tony Coult, unpublished 2003

Miller, S (2003) Interview with Tony Coult, unpublished 2003

Referred to but not quoted from: Horrie and Clarke *Fuzzy Monsters – Fear and Loathing at the BBC* London, Mandarin Paperbacks,1994

7

Imagination and Self in Edward Bond's work*

Bill Roper

1. Analyst of audience and theatre

Over 40 years Edward Bond has consistently sought to engage imaginatively and often provoke the person, as audience of his work as a playwright. As part of this enterprise that aims to change the audience and which is political in its nature, he has sought to understand this person or self, focusing particularly on the mind and its relationship to the physical and social world. This theoretical project has been constantly returned to and gradually advanced in numerous published papers, letters, commentaries and notebooks, in which he has sought to trace the origins and nature of the human person in society. The scope of this has involved an increasingly detailed account of the human species, the development of the child, and the nature and history of theatre and society. In the last fifteen years, this has taken the form of an intense series of papers in which radical innocence, imagination and self are perhaps the central members of a cluster of broadly psychological concepts, which are the hub around which the possibilities, pitfalls and dangers of work in the theatre are examined.

Psychological and philosophical questions are a necessary part of Bond's practice of writing and directing plays that explore a whole set of issues around the politics of the present and the future. In working for a contemporary theatre that is vital and central to its historical and ideological context, he has, for example, analysed the theatre and the audience's responses to it, from classical Greek drama to the present (*Modern Drama* in Bond, 2000a). The prevalent forms of modern theatre are all analysed as being inadequate, particularly in the relationship that the audience is able to enter into with what occurs on stage. Therefore, in his own plays, he is seeking to use the relationship with the audience in new ways (see the chapter by Kate Katafiasz in this volume), and to facilitate this, complex psychological areas need to be explored

Bond has a focused and distinctive approach to understanding the human mind, redolent with associations to the history of ideas over 2,500 years. Most centrally, reason and imagination are essential to the mind and to the way we understand the world. In evolutionary terms, reason is what we share to some extent with some non-human species in our relationship to the world. In contrast, imagination is a uniquely human process that involves value and opens the person in society to critical possibilities and dangers. However, unlike most previous accounts of the relationship of reason and imagination, the processes of human reason are not dominant, imagination is not seen as being some added luxury that indulges in fiction and fantasy and is thus inessential, nor is reason's role necessarily that of orienting and controlling imagination to instrumental and technological ends and purposes. In human understanding of the material and social world *both* reason and imagination are needed. Imagination, through its relationship with value, seeks and uses reason, in a way that reason, because it has no human value, could not *use* imagination. Importantly, human value, not fiction, is at the heart of the mind's use of imagination to understand the world and society; imagination and reason together construct the human self and open the routes of corruption and innocence, through which the self is continually being created. Crucially, the initial state of value in the emerging mind of the newborn is one of radical innocence and it is this that Bond, the playwright, seeks to find and engage with in his audience. This radical innocence is what experience, habit and social corruption may bury in each of us as we get older. It tends to be nearer the surface in children and young people, hence the importance Bond attaches to drama and theatre for the young.

It is this account of the mind that we seek to open up and explore here. This chapter attempts to clarify these core concepts, to outline some of the inferences made, to look at the evidence for, and to assess the implications of, such an account. In keeping with Bond's own approach, we will attempt to lay out, explore and examine the key concepts with a minimum of reference to the history of ideas and thus stress the role the ideas play in the playwright's work as dramatist.

2. The context of the self: basic structures

The long essay *The Reason for Theatre* (Bond, 2000a) gives one of the most recent and radical accounts of the emergence of the human mind and self in Edward Bond's work. In it the main ideas of other papers over the previous ten or more years are reworked, sharpened and their implications examined. It is a text that anyone wanting to access Edward Bond's account of self and imagination needs to tackle and it is this text that we will constantly return to in this exposition.

It is impossible to present Bond's account of human psychology as a clear and simple mechanical edifice. The separateness and reduction of the ideas required for such a project would be inimical to the subtleties and range of purposes of the human mind as it actually exists in the world and society. So, whilst Bond's concepts and the relationships between them can appear relatively stable, what is designated by them in life or in drama constantly changes. The paradoxical, conflictual and dialectical nature of the mind – world relationship is what he wants you to enter into and think about, particularly where it involves the margin between freedom and necessity. This is one of the constants in Bond's work; that the world and society are a *dynamic and inter-connected set of processes*. He sums up the processes as, 'the logic of humanness'. A second set of constants can be inferred; that, at an *abstract* level, there are *basic elements and structures* involved in this mind – world relationship. In the early part of this paper we will schematically simplify these elements and structures to make them clear. Later, we will return to them to see the complexities of their relationship in the self and society.

Bond is consistent. Over more than 40 years, beginning in entries from 1959, collected in *Volume 1 of the Notebooks* (Bond, 2000b), to the recent *Modern Drama and the Invisible Object* (Bond, 2003b), common aims, processes and structures can be identified. What changes is the language: how processes are captured in words, but the underlying structure that it appears Bond is trying to make accessible to us seems to be remarkably similar during this time.

There are five reference points or areas on a map, that, whilst the language used changes, remain identifiable positions across the intervening 45 years. These are

- the self
- the potentially corrupting or creative group or society
- the void, the boundary, the gap or nothingness

- the natural world of matter
- the mind as essentially dramatising

These seem to be common elements in Bond's account of human psychology and theatre. Two points are worth noting. Firstly, the self and the mind are very closely related. The complexities of this relationship between self and mind will be explored in section four. Secondly, the invariant description that Bond gives is one where the elements circulate around the third of these elements, often referred to as nothingness. Because of its abstract nature and the central role it plays, this element needs some introduction. Bond has recently explained it as follows:

> Animals evolve in their natural environment. Humans develop in history. They share the animals' environment but to it they add 'nothingness'. Obviously animals have no concept of nothing. But the human mind is totalising and confronts everything. All humans have always asked what is before and behind the natural world, and how will whatever this is relate to the future. So nothingness becomes the site of the unknown and apparently inexplicable. It isn't only over the edge of the horizon, we go into nothingness when we die. It may also be used to explain other existential phenomena. Nothingness becomes a place of anxiety and fear. A moment's reflection shows how astonishingly our lives are involved with nothingness. It becomes the holy source of morality and judgement, is present in myth and the daily horoscope. It creates the transcendental as a corruption of material reality. Societies produce gurus and rulers who claim to represent and speak for nothingness. This gives ideology extraordinary power, especially when it is combined with control of existential necessities. It combines the existential and the ontological in one extraordinary structure, so that history zooms far out beyond nature. Whoever owns nothingness owns you. The self is penetrated deeply because of its anxiety before nothingness. But paradoxically it is also the origin of freedom. As the world's meaning has been inscribed in nothingness, so throughout history the meaning is contested – prompted by change in our material relations. This leads to the idea of the 'gap'– a sort of mini-nothingness between each self and the world. Animals have no gap, their contact with reality is direct, not mediated through culture. The gap is the site of a two-way interaction between the self and society-world. It's the way we establish our volatile relationship with material reality. In effect, you can say we create ourselves in the gap. We are the total meaning we produce in the gap. This explains cultural antagonisms. The gap is like the site of a self-theatre. We do not live our biology – in a merely animalistic way – but the meaning we create in the gap. This gives us the possibility of freedom, within the limits of material necessity. But humanness isn't arbitrary. The meaning in the gap conforms to the logic of humanness. This is why I talk of the logic of

imagination – it must be freewheeling, it can't be predetermined to imagine humanness because humanness doesn't exist, we create it. If we abuse the logic (briefly, the imperative to produce our common happiness) we destroy ourselves – and it would be no good praying to nothingness for help. We are the masters of nothingness.

I sometimes use the word 'void' instead of nothingness when I want to stress the structure rather than its ideological colouring of dread, coercion and resistance. The 'boundary' is between material reality and nothingness. I sometimes say Authority writes its ideology on the boundary – like a No Trespass notice which lists laws and penalties for disobedience. Ironically I call this sacro-legal script the graffiti on the boundary. The boundary doesn't just exist out there, it exists in you because of the way ideology penetrates the gap. The boundary becomes a site of contention. (Bond, 2004)

In summary, Bond sees self, the world and society oriented, through the question of meaning, around nothingness. Nothingness is an absence of meaning, value and justice in a particular place or time, which provokes humans to ask questions; often this place is a contested site, such as the future, where different sources instate different meanings, values and interpretations of justice in answer to the questions asked. Nothingness is therefore the place or site where the most important events, conflicts and human enquiries are played out.

Though there are dangers in simplifying Bond's ideas for the sake of exposition, the way that the five elements enter into inter-relationship to form a *structure* displays a consistency of a topographical kind that can be presented diagrammatically. Given that the mind and self can be regarded as one at this stage, a broad structure seems to be mapped out in Bond's writing. This is shown in figure 1 on page 130.

Society/ideology encompasses the institutions of society; the law, the church, education *et cetera*, but also, and importantly, the theatre. This model therefore allows Bond to consider the role of the theatre, actual and possible, across history to the present day. This involves not only its relationship to other institutions and ideology, but also to the human self and to nothingness. The relationship of society, institutions and ideology to the human self is centred in the problem of what makes humans human, what humanises people in society, and in what ways and with what consequences processes of humanisation can fail. Bond's answer to the first question is that the nature of the human self in society is not intrinsic, something inside, inhering or innate. Rather it is *extrinsic*, outside, in the

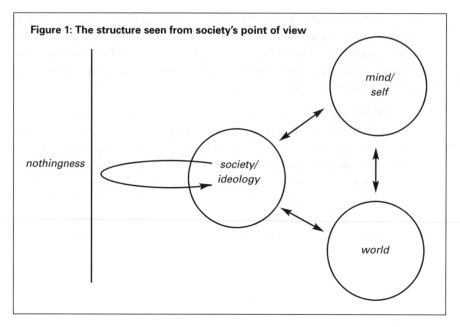

Figure 1: The structure seen from society's point of view

form of its relationship to human culture, beliefs, rituals, stories, art *et cetera*. It is also not static but historically changing, in a dialectic, as in Marx's writings, with technology and the class or ownership structure of society. Bond summarises these relationships as the working out of the logic of humanness. So, figure 1 can be redrawn from the self's point of view, with the gap as the mini-nothingness in which meaning is created, as in figure 2.

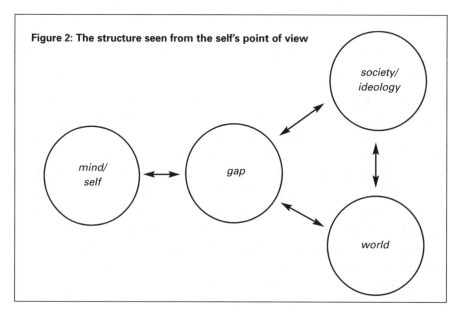

Figure 2: The structure seen from the self's point of view

In Bond's 1989 Address to the National Association for the Teaching of Drama (NATD) Conference (Bond, 1989), these points are captured anew in different words; we now have:

Station 1, the Subject (self)
Station 2, the Administration (society/ideology)
Station 3, the Boundary (nothingness).

Here, the Boundary is shown as the relational term, denoting a border between the ordinarily known and meaningful and the unknown and lacking in meaning. The human Subject has various needs: some of them are for food, shelter, clothing and so on. The organisation of the meeting of these is handled by the Administration. But also the Subject needs meaning in answer to the countless why and what questions about the world, others and itself that occur at the Boundary. The Administration seeks to speak for these also, through its ideology.

Bond's motivation for this new way of describing the five positions is very important for his theatre and indicates the problems of literal diagrammatic representations of his ideas. What is happening here is that one of the positions, the Boundary, is the position both of the physical world *and* of nothingness/the void and that the Administration, being the most powerful source, is seeking to speak for it. It is, in turn, a position that other sources, for example religion, politics, education and the theatre, can attempt to speak for and explore. Bond would see many of these as, in fact, expressive of ideology. The Boundary is therefore a contested site to which the Subject, as a self, brings his or her mind, with its reason, imagination, character and other features. We can now think of the Boundary as it is ideologically installed in the gap. The gap then contains within it, in conflictual forms, the elements of theatre and dramatisation. That is, places, physical objects, human beings, events and their meanings and rationalisations are dramatised in the gap. Within this, Bond's theatrical devices such as theatre events and acting the invisible object operate (see Glossary). The self becomes the site of drama.

The condensation of the initial elements that occurs in the gap can take numerous forms, and has implications for the processes of the mind. Reason and imagination are not complementary opposites, each with their own sphere of operation: reason on one side with the material world, and imagination on the other side with society and ideology. Rather *both* are engaged with *both* contents; imagination using reason and reason directing imagination. Thus, material reality and physical objects come into relationship with both reason and imagination. The same object can have a meaning, derived from means-ends reason *and* from value-imparting imagination: the cup can contain a drink *and* a dying man's blood, and the latter can be mistaken for the former, as in the example in *Pearl White* (Bond, 2000a). Bond calls this a TE (theatre event). This is a major area of Bond's theatre: his use of physical objects, such as cups, tables, windows, blankets, crisps, to unsettle habitual ideologised understandings and perhaps allow new meaning to enter our understanding. The hitherto taken for granted, instrumentalised and ideologised object is worked with in the drama, to allow it to relate to parts of the self and its meanings which run counter to habit, with its unthinking prudence or convenience. The relationship of reason and imagination is addressed in the next section, following an overview of Bond's account.

In the slightly later *Notes on Post-modernism* (Bond, 1990), the basic structure is developed and such features as technology and theatre are further differentiated and integrated into the picture:

> The threefold model of people, authority and the boundary can be used to understand the history and ... present state of the relationship between people, technology and authority: and the way in which theatre and the other arts are part of that relationship. (Bond, 1990: 213-4)

This allows articulation of the complexities of the history of societies and the theatre in their relationship to the self. The history and creation of societies cannot be divided from the history and creation of the self. A crucial historical change occurs in the recent past when, as a result of technology, the dominant societies change their function from being a means to meet human needs to being based, in consumer capitalism, in satisfying wants (Bond, 1989).

As he puts it in *The Dramatic Child*:

> Western societies are the first human societies that have dispensed with the making of culture. They depend not on their ability to humanise and legitimate authority – but on providing goods. They are societies of means without ends. (Bond, 1993: 46)

For Bond these postmodern societies, of means without ends, throw all the relationships into a perilous crisis. There is a situation of great complexity, change and contestation in which processes at least partly humanising (the Truth-lie) are now not only inoperative but positively corrupting (the Lie-lie). For example within the theatre, dominant forms, such as what he calls the theatre of Stanislavsky, Performance and Brecht are inadequate to deal with this contemporary crisis. (*Modern Drama*, Bond, 2000a)

In the recent *The Cap* (Bond, 2001/2003a) the position of Nothingness is again explored and the battle of unjust society is described as that for the 'ownership of nothingness'.

> We are not simply embodiments of Someness, we carry Nothingness with us in our mortality and vulnerability. Nothingness gives us the possibility of creativeness, of choice and freedom. (Bond, 2003a:xix)

In other recent writings, the closeness of society/ideology and the world/ nature is explored and described as 'the meeting of tectonic plates' (Bond 2000a:175). This emphasises the ill fit between capitalist society and the natural world. In the same paper Bond explains aspects of the gap.

> The gap is the site of the meaning we give to reality and our self. This meaning is our 'being' (and the meaning of our 'being'). We are the gap, it is our consciousness and self-consciousness because 'being' is its meaning to us. (Bond, 2000a:176)

Two points need to be explained here. First, whereas nothingness and the void are seemingly abstract and freestanding, the gap suggests a more complex feature which is a *relationship* between things; the gap *between* x, y and perhaps z, suggests different topographies. In this case the gap is *between* society/ideology and the world/material reality on the one hand and the self on the other; it is a void region of the map in which we ask questions and build meanings and our being. Secondly, the self enters the gap when it is seen as the meaning created in the gap. Bond says, it 'is necessary to humanness that we live our meaning not our biology. It is also important to drama.' (Bond, 2004). As self has its meanings partly from ideology and partly from material reality, along with consciousness and self-consciousness, it is thus contested and indeterminate and hence is in the gap and has the gap's creativity. Thus we can now say that the theatre and dramatisation are a place where not only objects events and places, but also selves, can have their meaning dramatised and recreated.

Having begun in this exposition with a rather simplistic articulation of mind, self, nothingness, society and the world as separate and distanced positions, increasingly, Bond forces us to see the failings of overly literal readings. That one part of the structure can be the position of, and in some sense contain or hold the other parts is crucial to the dialectical mode of operation here. The stage is, *par excellence*, the place that can do this, and in conjunction with dramatisation, this opens up a very powerful place where change in meaning and selves might occur. Recently, Bond has used the notion of *the site* in several papers that have elaborated and developed this idea:

> Theatre can only be understood by understanding its sites. The self and the world are sites. They are also the sites of each other. They meet critically in the freedom-tragic. The stage is a site – it is the exact topographical analogue of the self-site. When we stand on the stage we stand on ourselves and the world. The play's story comes from its centre. (*Modern Drama*, Bond, 2000a:18)

This notion of the freedom-tragic is crucial to the linking of audience and stage. It is the place where, from the earliest days of the child's life, humanness has been created in the confrontation between the emerging (conscious, choosing, innocent or corrupt) self and the extreme situations of pain and pleasure of oneself and others. This leads us to explore, in section 3, the psychological grounding of this humanness and then, in section 4, the development of the self.

3. Radical innocence, reason and imagination

Within these underlying themes of the elements, structures and the dynamic nature of the processes at work, Bond's theoretical and dramatic work has attached enormous importance to the psychology of the human mind and person. Thus the concern with the subjective and the psychological, particularly the processes of imagination and the self, are at the heart of his approach. It would be wrong to say that the psychological and subjective come to exclude the other parts of the picture or that they are used reductively. Bond's analysis always depends on the mind's and self's *relationship* with the other elements, in order creatively to understand the self in society and the audience – stage processes.

In the early 1990s, Bond introduced a seemingly major new concept to psychological understanding: radical innocence. Later in the 1990s, he re-worked the pair of fundamental concepts that derive from Greek philosophy: reason and imagination. This was not only to restate their importance as a pair but also to rehabilitate imagination and to assert its importance in a time of linear, technological thought.

From the *Notes on Post-modernism* (Bond, 1990) and particularly in *Commentary on the War Plays* (Bond, 1991) and *The Dramatic Child* (Bond, 1993) the idea of radical innocence or the child's 'right to be in the world', 'to be at home in the world' and 'for the world to be its home' is explored:

> We are born radically innocent, and neither animal nor human; we create our humanness as our minds begin to think our instincts. (Bond, 1991:251)

This is a fundamental aspect of the human, something the child brings to the world and is the developmental origin of value and meaning which, as the child grows and enters into the larger society, comes to be elaborated into the concept of justice. This becomes the baseline or starting point of human becoming, well before language is formed. It therefore ventures into dealing with a concept which is before words and probably untranslatable into words. It points towards the idea that there is a basic orientation of the newborn human towards the world, and of the world towards it. Intrinsic to this new centre of awareness is its right to be; this is gradually articulated into its right to be at home, to make the world its home and for the world to be its home, which in time is articulated into the right of itself and others to be at home in the world. This is the positive site on which self, understanding and character will come to be constructed. It is also simultaneously the same site as the Tragic and the Comic, and the site on which drama and self-dramatisation can occur, and, in which, the right to be and the need for justice can go violently wrong, or fall laughably short, or in time be accomplished.

This is the argument in Bond's own words. It is not arbitrary but based on analysis and careful inference:

> There is a pre-self state of unfocused but burgeoning awareness. The pre-self is subject to pleasure and pain. The self begins to cohere from these affects. And there is a singularity: self-consciousness differs from all other things, it is *sui generis*. Functionally it must express its own 'right to be'. A cup needs no right to be because it is a thing, it is. As long as it is, it embodies necessity. Consciousness is not a thing but an act. To act it must be allowed to act- have the right to act. I cannot tell consciousness not to be consciousness – only it can tell itself that: in trauma. Only the pre-self can 'give itself this right' to be – it is axiomatic in its own being, in consciousness. It is its *necessity*. The right implies that its place should be the right place for the right to be, because the right and the pre-self are one and the same. It's like talking of the right of water to be wet, but of course wetness isn't an act. The neonate pre-self cannot perform adult actions, but whatever it 'moves towards' or endeavours or intends, forms a patterned relationship with pleasure, pain and other less important stimuli. This can only be intended to achieve the right place for 'the right to be'. Whatever it intends – or purposes – must be and be seen by it as innocent. That is the word we would use later. And the intentions are radical because they must be defined by their ends – the new-born has not yet entered 'the parliament of means'. In fact, the neonate is a monad. It cannot distinguish between itself and the world. They are one. The self is created in this process, and implicit in it are this right to be and radical innocence. Infancy is the only

stage of humanness not vulnerable to corruption because the infant cannot corrupt itself. Later when the child enters society, the right to be is defined as justice. In the foundation of every human self there is the figuration of Prometheus and Antigone. But in unjust society the self may be corrupted and, under psychological pressures created by doing what must be done to survive economically and existentially; the need to be at home in the world and the need for justice, may become the desire for revenge – it is not that the motive is changed, but that the desire for revenge is the implementation of the self's need for justice. Such events are written in nothingness. They occur in the drama of the gap. They occur because although the imperative to justice is a human imperative, it is abstract, and so it must constantly be recreated in terms of social reality. The law cannot deal with such paradoxes. They are the subject of war, crime and drama. It is the working out of the logic of humanness. Throughout history we feel in drama the huge weight of the imperative to be human leaning on the corruption of the times. Paradoxically the imperative to justice can never let us rest, yet it may destroy us. Nothingness will be the last territory we shall conquer. (Bond, 2004)

Assessing this assertion of radical innocence is difficult intellectually. In many ways it is the lost origin of the possibility of writing or talking that is beyond words and assessment. It has affinities with many ideas in psychology and philosophy, though none of them has quite the same content. It is a species characteristic, a connectedness of perception, feeling and consciousness to the organism's needs and relationship with others, that may well have its origin in parts of the overall structure of the neonate brain. However, the radical nature of Bond's account is in placing radical innocence and emerging concepts of justice, and hence political and moral action and judgement, at the heart of the account of imagination and self. In this he breaks new ground and is without peer.

Earlier in his *Notebooks* in 1982, in one of the few prior references to imagination, Bond had described it as 'a faculty that becomes highly developed when the human species enters history and loses its instinctual nature' (2001a:77).

However, closely following the introduction of radical innocence, the related concept of imagination is increasingly articulated. In *Notes on Imagination* (Bond, 1995) and T*he Reason for Theatre* (Bond, 2000a), imagination is explored as necessary to the active cognitive or psychological 'bringing into being' process, at the centre of the child and adult in society.

So for Bond imagination is crucial to the neonate or newborn's existence in the world.

> The neonate does not imagine the world, its imagination creates the world as the child and the child as the world. This is how we become a self. The double meaning of imagination confuses later understanding because in essential ways imagination continues to create reality. (Bond, 2000a:114)

The self comes about through the differentiation in the neonate mind of two distinct parts, the self and the world, and this is at the same time the creation of self-consciousness. We could simplify the process perhaps in the following diagram

However Bond wants us to be careful about the double use of the word 'imagination'.

> Negatively, the neonate imagines itself to be the whole world. The adult knows it is not. Creatively, the neonate still uses imagination to assess the world in terms of its experience – patterns its experience. It is this which prevents pleasure and pain being arbitrary self-referential affects, but conceives them in relation to the pre-self (and self) so making them the concepts (as they would later be called) of the Tragic and the Comic.

Of this Bond says:

> The closeness of the relationship of imagination and reason, even from the beginning, is astonishing. There are grounds for a new understanding of emotion and certainly of important concepts such as the Tragic and the Comic. (Bond, 2004)

This gives a very general but provocative picture of Bond's understanding of how human psychology begins and functions. In more specific terms, because of imagination, the potentially creative human relationship with the world is marked by the asking of 'why' questions.

> Non-human animals are concerned with what and when, but not with why. Imagination is needed to ask why. Imagination and not reason makes us human. We are self-conscious. Imagination and self-consciousness cannot exist without each other... (Bond, 2000a:113)

Reason, though far more developed in humans, is what we share with some non-human animals, but is not a sufficient basis for this coming into being of humanness. Only when reason is combined with imagination so that imagination, as a source of value, makes use of reason, can reason be rational and imagination logical.

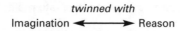

twinned with

Imagination ←——————→ Reason

Only then is humanness a possibility.

In the continuation of the above important but condensed passage Bonds claims

> The rational is a priori to our reasoning. It is derived from objective reality. The ability to reason does not make us rational. It is our imagination that reasons. Imagination is not prior to imagining, it is wholly human. Reason seeks the rational, imagination seeks the logical – either as fate or freedom. (*ibid*:113)

Both in terms of Bond's philosophical approach and, more importantly, in terms of Bond as a dramatist, this tightly packed assertion is of the utmost importance and has countless implications. To summarise these, the key contentions appear to be that:

- The mind's processes can be divided into those of reason and imagination.

- Reason is shared with some animals, imagination is distinctively human. But animals have no understanding because they cannot 'know they know'.

- Reason has its origin in the mind's understanding of the non-human world – cause and effect and means and ends relationships, time, space, number, mathematics, formal logic and so on. The structure of the material world and how it works (the rational) is what reason seeks out. However reason can often come to dominate our understanding of the human world – 'he works to get the money to buy the food to give him the energy to work to...'

- Imagination has its origin in the mind's understanding of the human world – the other, why they act as they do, the past and the future, justice, morality, feeling and emotions, fate and freedom. The structure of the human world of actions and events (the logic of fate and freedom) is what imagination seeks out, 'drama is reality's logic, the logic of change' (*ibid*:119). Imagination increasingly becomes interleaved with reason and is used with reason to understand the physical and human world.

• Together reason and imagination seek to know reality. Knowledge is possible of both the human and non-human worlds and imagination is the guiding process in the human.

• Imagination is not determined by material reality, but seeks material reality. Nor does it exist in the human mind in itself; it is a characteristic of the human mind that occurs *in relationship* with the world. This appears to be what is meant by Bond's quite significant recent references to immanence and immanentism (Bond, 2000a:49, 93, 123, 161). Bond wishes to restore to materialism the many-sided richness stolen and vulgarised by Ideology. The import here is that imagination is emergent; it is not God-given or transcendental, nor is it innate and hard-wired into the brain. It is not an 'essence' any more than are 'the right to be' or 'radical innocence'.

4. The self and its development in society

In his account of radical innocence, imagination and reason in the human self, not only are the relationship with Society, Nothingness and the World explored, but also the way that change occurs in chronological time becomes a key factor. Bond becomes interested in the child and its development, particularly in the early stages of life. The motivation for this is to understand the self as creative but vulnerable to the distortions of ideology. Key questions are, how do the habitual processes of submersion in ideology, of instrumentalist capitalist reason, of watching sport or soap operas, or even realist or Brechtian theatre, lead the mind to work, and how is the child's mind different from the adult's? Bond adds a further rhetorical question,

> Despite the habitual direction of imagination by social and economic pressures and by *reason as ideology*, built up over the years as the child becomes adult, is drama still able to engage the self's original self-creative potency, not in a return to any child-like innocence, but to the radicality which destroys distortions and corruptions compromises – a radical innocence burdened with all the understanding of later experience – a radical creativity? (Bond, 2004)

As mentioned earlier, these questions are also about the changing nature of society, changing institutions, technologies, ownership, forms of theatre *et cetera*. Bond's answers issue from the basic structures within which radical innocence, and the interplay of reason and imagination begin to allow for the coming into being and self-construction of human selves from birth to the trivialised, alienated, cynical and ordinary contortions of the contemporary corrupted self.

Bond's account of self is of a clearly etched, strong self that begins in the newborn as a singularity that, borrowing Leibniz's (1714) word more than his idea, he calls the *monad*. It moves by the vicissitudes of imagination and dramatisation through what for descriptive purposes could be divided into four stages of change from the child to adult.

- The monad – the pre-self
- The emerging psychological self in the pre-real
- The self entering culture
- The palimpsest self as perhaps simultaneously innocent and corrupted

The way that this changing and developing self has at its core the radical innocence and the processes of imagination and reason will be examined here.

Monad is a Greek word for unity, something that is indivisible or without parts. Bond contends that the child begins as a monad, an undifferentiated indivisible unity and totality of itself and the world, and that from this the child separates as a different entity from the World.

> The monad has no window on the world and no door on time. It exists in eternity. All its events are elemental, cosmic, total. (2000a:114)

Bond means by this that that is how the neonate must experience what we know as chronological time and finite measured space. He asks us to enter the monad world to understand the neonate's protean and elemental creativity.

> The neonate-monad is actor and act, agent and event, cause and effect. If (an impossible example) it took a cup to drink it would be mover and moved, cup, drinker and water. (Bond, 2000a:114)

At this first stage, the totality and indivisibility of the self and world means that it is not a psychological self. The feature that seems to coalesce and produce the transition to the next stage of the self is the emerging consciousness, in which is implicit the neonate's imperative and conviction of its right to be in the world and of its radical innocence, and with these go its acceptance of responsibility for the, its, world.

> In the patterned chaos of its experience the new mind rests on one thought: it has a right to be...

> The monad is morality – is and not has because as the monad is its own ex-
> perience it cannot distinguish between fact and judgement of Value. In it, is
> is ought (ibid:115-6)

In *Notes on Imagination*, the notion of 'the map' as beginning the structuring of the monad is explored:

> The map states the child's right to live: that is, its authority as the map and
> the map maker. The world and the child are a monad. The child creates the
> world, its world. The world is the place of radical innocence. (Bond, 1995:
> viii)

In the more recent *Modern Drama and the Invisible Object*, the role of
dramatisation and the Tragic and Comic are developed:

> The pre-psychological self is a stage on which the elements of creativity
> appear, the Tragic, the Comic. On it the psychological-self is created. The
> psychological-self, the human mind, is a dramatic structure. It creates
> humanness by dramatising the imperative to be human. (Bond, 2003b:3)

The key thing is that processes of differentiation now begin to occur: an
autonomous world exists beyond the child's skin and mind, consciousness
and self-consciousness come to exist. The child enters the adult's world and
thereby becomes, or more correctly, creates a self; agent, act, cause and
effect, time, inner and outer come to structure the indivisibility of the
monad. It now has a door to the world.

Looking at things from the monad's point of view, Bond sees the child, in
which imagination is the source of value, begin to come into contact, both
propitious and contentious, with the outside world, in which other values
operate, and in this process it creates both itself and its individual understanding of the outside world, the meaning it has for the child. In Bond
meaning is everything.

At this second stage of the self, the processes of dramatisation are
dominated by anthropomorphisation; the child, with the co-operation of
adults, gives objects human subjectivity; trees speak, chairs are tired,
storms are angry. By means of play, the child ascribes value and gives
meaning to the world. Bond calls this the stage of the 'pre-real':

> A child's block of wood may 'be' a car or dog. The child cathects objects
> with Value – the world impersonates the child... As it maps the world so as
> to exist in it, it puts itself in the map and maps the world in itself. All
> creation creates the creator. The child creates itself as it creates the wood-
> block car. (Bond, 2000a:120)

In *Notes on Imagination* (Bond, 1995), a key theme of Bond's account of self is introduced: that the mind works to find meaning and value and to understand the world, not only on the basis of a steady processing or assimilation of experience, but that the mind itself undergoes qualitative change in the process of encountering the world:

> A child's mind should not be described as a circle of light that increases as the child learns. Its mind is a totality and it brings the world into it bit by bit as if increasing the brightness. Before, it knows the totality ignorantly, with knowledge it knows it knowledgably. (Bond, 1995:vii)

By this, Bond means that the child and its mind should not be seen on the model of the adult, as a deficient being lacking many parts which it will acquire with time. Rather, it is a totality and experiences the same world as the other does: its world is as profound and its pains and joys are as real. The child's experience should be respected. This totality constitutes a strong self, or centre to the human mind. In the debates about the nature of self, this would be broadly in line with accounts that emphasise composure and integration, rather than fragmentation and the assemblage of parts. For Bond, the way reason and imagination work as a totality, through the mediation of the map and such processes as dramatisation, is to consolidate and increase the 'brightness' of this strong core of the child's emerging self. In young children, radical innocence is still to the fore.

The corollary of this is that self does not only change in a quantitative manner by acquiring new experiences, knowledge, skills and memories, but changes qualitatively through different constructions of maps, by integrating meanings and stories into its existing self. It creates its self-meaning:

> Imagination structures experience as a map. The map is the site of story. The first map is the neonate's. Later maps are imposed on this and each other. The self is a palimpsest of maps. (Bond, 2000a:117)

The self may re-create itself throughout life.

The third stage in the development of self is when the child enters its culture and the influence of ideology increases markedly. The imperative of the right to be in the world of the monad, becomes the search for justice and value, through the story of the older child. Thus the child imaginatively creates itself through the processes of story in a continuously articulated dramatisation of itself and others and the world around it. These processes can be related to, but in many ways go beyond those explored by George Herbert Mead, Lev Vygotsky and Sigmund Freud in the early days of psychology:

> In play, the child takes the role of another and acts as though she were the other (e.g., mother, doctor, nurse, Indian, and countless other symbolised roles). (Mead, 1932:169).

Mead's contention was that this combination of communication, taking the role of the other, and seeing yourself from the other's position, was involved in the formation of both self-consciousness and of the parts of the self he called the 'I' and the 'me'. Bond (2004) says that the child's experience 'is profounder than is suggested by the 'I and me'. This is because the child's mind is already structured by the Comic and the Tragic.' Nevertheless, it seems closer to Bond's ideas of dramatisation, placing value and the need for justice at the heart of things, than does Freud's (1920) account in *Beyond the Pleasure Principle* of the child who plays the 'fort-da game', staging the appearance and disappearance of a cotton-reel on a piece of string. Freud sees this as related to the child's new achievement of allowing the mother to go away without protesting. Similarly Vygotsky sees make-believe play as 'the imaginary, illusory realisation of unrealisable desires' in which the child

> wishes and realises his wishes by letting the basic categories of reality pass through his experience, which is precisely why in play a day can take half-an-hour, and a hundred miles are covered in five steps. (Vygotsky, 1976: 550).

Thus Vygotsky's approach runs counter to Bond's approach by accentuating desire and fiction. Comparatively, Bond's account of imagination and child's play, particularly his example in *The Reason for Theatre*, of the child who plays with a wood-block car, highlights activity, meaning and value, whereas other accounts in the literature highlight fiction, fantasy, symbolism, desire and pleasure. However, there is considerable overlap and this deserves further research. Perhaps the problem turns on the closeness Bond finds in the working of imagination and reason, and how this is a process which creates 'human reality'.

In *The Dramatic Child*, Bond sees the process of 'bearing witness' as crucial to how story is involved in the child's humanity. 'Bearing witness' is participation in the search for justice and indicates the impulse of radical innocence. This is currently being excluded from education:

> Drama searches for meaning and expresses the need to bear witness to life. Drama uses disciplines to define meanings, not take the place of meanings. And culture is essentially dramatic. (Bond, 1993:48)

The other things that are *taking the place of meaning* are the key danger in the child's entry into culture and education today, and this reinforces for

Bond that dramatisation is essential to the developing self. The attempt to replace the exploration of meaning and value through drama, with an induction into a culture of practical means and instruments *alone*, is fundamental to Bond's account of how reason directs imagination and leads to the corruption of self.

The fourth stage of self, which continues through to the adult, is in *The Reason for Theatre* (Bond, 2000a), *The Cap* (Bond, 2003a) and other recent writings, one which results in a complex and dynamic multilayered and conflictual self, whose relationship to the world is both variable and highly individual. The plays themselves are the best guide to these complexities, but in the above sources three important themes are frequently returned to:

- The self as a multiplicity of different selves built up over time, experiences and contexts

- The social condition of selves as humanised, corrupted, trivialised, mad *et cetera*

- The self, through the mediation of self-words, as the logic of imagination: both individual and collective actions, events, life histories and stories display this logic of fate and freedom

The older child and adult self is *the* multiple, palimpsest self; earlier selves are not lost or locked deep inside:

> It is as if the selves existed in the same plane not fitted into one another in the manner of babushka dolls. In the silence a babel of storytellers waits to speak – which one speaks depends on the situation. Maturity does not modify the potency of earlier selves. Any later real or imagined event may invoke any appropriate self. (Bond, 2000a:117)

This palimpsest self is essential to approaching Bond's characters and their actions in the plays and also to how he wants the plays to work for the audience. The series of horizontal selves that are the history of the character's or audience's relationship to injustice, include the self that is the original site of radical innocence. This self provides the link that holds all the others together and gives coherence and composure to the self. It is the self that Bond contends drama has access to. Just as in accidents things may appear to slow down and the mind and senses operate closer to the purposes for which they evolved, so also in the space opened up by drama. In these drama situations, which may be extreme in action or involve crises of meanings, rather than provoke flight or panic, drama may instead demand observation and, even in the midst of action, a sort of contemplation. This is the world of accident time. Here many of the palimpsested selves that come to dominate in life, that are conditioned by authority's meanings and ideology, are marginalised and other meanings can circulate.

> Society's story is its culture. It saturates reality with the unreal, the transcendental. [But in reality] Trees do not speak. Instead carpenters learn to make wood into tables and chairs. (Bond, 2000a:123, Bond, 2004)

This feature is the focal point of much of Bond's discussion of the theatre, education and of contemporary society. It underlines the importance of subjective psychological processes in the formation of the self and imagination and the ways he attempts to engage these in his work as a playwright. Crucially it indicates that there are grounds for optimism in the 'multilayeredness' of self; in the radical innocence of the first map, in the Tragic and Comic, and in the potential freedom in nothingness and the self. In these there is the possibility of experiencing and responding even in the most corrupted self as audience. This would be a state where imagination would operate differently, not as a regression to childhood and the jettisoning of the sophistication of adult reasoning, but as a more direct relationship to a situation, shorn of habitual ideologised meaning, reinstating the imperative, and the self's need, for justice, to harness reason in new radical ways. It is in this sense that drama fundamentally deals with reality and not fiction.

The third feature, that of 'self-words', is one that plays a small role in Bond's theoretical writing, yet seems crucial to the writing of his plays. The role of 'self-words' points to what the imagination seeks, 'a logic that we don't, but perhaps could, understand', a logic to be found in the stories of the actions and events both of our own lives and of the theatre.

> We have our proper names but the words we use to describe what is human are also our names because they are names for our imagination: good, bad, right, wrong, mind, reality, God, society, patriotism, religion and so on. These words have meaning and are about meaning. The word 'table' is descriptive but the words we use to describe ourselves are also prescriptive. But all words may be self-words....Self-words recreate themselves in relation to each other. They are not stable but there is a logic to their relationship. The logic decides what happens to individuals and what will happen to us collectively. (Bond, 2000a:117-118)

Bond's work displays a profound exploration of this logic of human tragedy and comedy and the paradoxical nature of human action. This aspect of self is one that opens a vein of exploration that builds on the palimpsest self and the dramatic possibilities opened in both the character and the audience, to work through layers of the corrupt self's relationships to in-justice and the imperative to justice.

5. Dramatist and analyst

Edward Bond's accounts of radical innocence, imagination, reason and the self have a phenomenal reach and sophistication. They are both highly complex and difficult but also based on a simple and consistent underlying set of elements, structures and processes. They arise out of and have to be contextualised within his work as a dramatist, in particular one whose concerns are with justice and politics, and who explores the logic of characters and events with the aim of engaging the audience in radical new ways.

His innovative strength is to devise an account of the human self and the human mind which systematically and consistently relates to the basics of society and social life in the categories and interpretations of concepts of justice. Whereas other accounts of self put pleasure, enjoyment, authenticity, autonomy, self-actualisation and so on in this position, Bond asserts the moral and political nature of the human relationship with society and the world. The other aspects of his account of self unfold from this pivotal link with justice. This relationship is not an individual one but is highly social; we are a *species being* in Marx's sense. The relationship involves universalised imperatives emanating from the social nature of human life and self and encompasses the prescription to choose and act in line with those imperatives. In this context the relationship between imagination and reason is rethought; imagination is not superfluous indulgence but the source of value and consequently vital to the possibility of humanity, and even of the social survival of the human species.

At the core Bond displays an optimism about humankind in which radical innocence, imagination and reason, within a complex but centred self, play the major part. However, his analysis of contemporary capitalist society, which, in a recent radio interview (British Broadcasting Corporation 2001), he described as not so much a post-modern society as a posthumous one, paints a picture of extreme danger. A posthumous society is one where ideology drives linear 'means-ends' reason to lead imagination; we are dead because we cease to be able to imagine the future and relate to it through human values; creativity and imagination are instead used to imprison and mortify our selves to adapt to this society of the dead. Bond in his own way gives a clear lead, a persuasive analysis and a body of work that shows that the dominance of this process is far from total. The self as the site of an originary radical innocence can be brought into relation with what is shown on stage. His recent advances in dramaturgy, from theatre events to acting the invisible object, follow through this analysis and work to develop what is shown on stage as that which can engage and not deny, alienate or lose this self and the imperative to justice. In post-modern times these ideas constitute a compelling case for drama and a new theatre. They can also, through the argument for the instatement of a self, imagination and reason oriented to justice and social sanity, rather than to the prevailing social madness, provide an impetus for the besieged institutions of education, health, criminal justice and beyond. It is pressing that we support, understand and respond creatively to Bond's work.

References

British Broadcasting Corporation (2001) *John Tusa interview with Edward Bond*, Radio 3, broadcast 7 January 2001

Bond, E (1990) *Two Post-Modern Plays: Jackets and In the Company of Men*, London, Methuen

Bond, E (1991) *The War Plays*, London, Methuen

Bond, E (1993) *The Dramatic Child*, in Bond, E. (1993) *Tuesday.* London, Methuen

Bond, E (1995) *Notes on Imagination*, in Bond,E. (1995) *Coffee*, London, Methuen

Bond, E (1998) *The Reason for Theatre* in Bond, E. (2000a) *The Hidden Plot*, London, Methuen

Bond, E (2000a) *The Hidden Plot*, London, Methuen

Bond, E (2000b) *Selections from the Notebooks of Edward Bond, Volume One*, London, Methuen

Bond, E (2001) *Selections from the Notebooks of Edward Bond, Volume Two*, London, Methuen

Bond, E (2001b) *The Cap: Working Notes on Drama, the Self and Society*, written for the National Association for the Teaching of Drama conference 2001, unpublished

Bond, E (2003a) The Cap: Notes on Drama, the Self and Society in *Edward Bond Plays: 7*, London, Methuen

Bond, E (2003b) Modern Drama and The Invisible Object, unpublished

Bond, E (2004) from correspondence with David Davis (editor) and Bill Roper, May 2004, unpublished

Freud, S (1920) Beyond the Pleasure Principle in Freud, S. (1984) *On Metapsychology* (Vol 11 Penguin Freud Library) , Harmondsworth, Penguin

Leibniz, G W (1714) *The Monadology* translated by Robert Latta 1898 at http://eserver.org/philosophy/leibniz-monadology.txt

Mead, G H (1932) *The Philosophy of the Present*, Chicago, Open Court

Vygotsky, L (1976) 'The Role of Play in the Mental Development of the Child' in Bruner, J S *et al Play*, Harmondsworth, Penguin

* *Author's note*: This chapter has been written, particularly the later versions, with the help of careful and extensive notes and comments from Edward Bond. Several quotations from these notes have been included in the text. I am enormously grateful for this help in a difficult task. The aim of the chapter is to give as complete an exposition of Edward Bond's theoretical understanding of this area as possible; the remaining errors and misunderstandings are of course mine.

8
The Children

David Allen

I think, for Bond, *The Children* is a pivotal play. It is his 'thesis', his statement. It encapsulates his views about young people, and how we are treating them, and not making a 'home' for them in the world. It is all there in *The Children*. – *Claudette Bryanston* (Bryanston, 2003a)

Bond's *The Children* was written to be performed by a cast of young people, with two adult actors. The play 'describes a journey – one which could start from any modern town'. (Bond, 2000b:3) The central character, Joe, is bullied by his mother to burn a house down. A young boy dies in the fire. With his friends, Joe decides to run away. They journey into a decaying post-apocalyptic world. They carry with them a stranger, an injured man, who, unbeknown to them, is the father of the boy who died in the fire. He murders them, one by one; until finally, only Joe is left, to face the future alone: 'I've got everything. I'm the last person in the world. I must find someone.' (Bond, 2000a:52)

The characters' journey, for Bond, is 'like the map of the ancient rite of passage' – 'the very ancient journey that all humans have had to go on since we first wanted to understand ourselves and take responsibility for our world'. (Bond, 2000b:3)

> The play does not describe the journey in an abstract way, but creates the experience of the journey through the intense concentration, which is the secret of drama.
>
> ... The young people who go on the journey in *The Children*, are the only ones who can save themselves – helped perhaps by adults who have also made the journey and learnt to replace revenge with justice, anger with care. (Bond, 2000b:3)

Bond hopes that, for the young people taking part in the play, the experience itself will be a 'journey', a 'rite of passage' that may help them to understand themselves and their world. The play, he observes, 'wants to involve the young people more deeply in the meaning of their own lives'. (Bond, 2003c)

Adults and children – 'the huge conflict of our time'

The roles of the Mother and the Man in the play are written to be performed by adult actors. The combination of adults and children on stage is crucial to the play's impact in performance. In Scene two, for example, Joe's mother uses intense emotional pressure to compel him to do what she wants – to burn down a stranger's house ('...if you loved me you'd do what I ask' – Bond, 2000a:13). As Claudette Bryanston has observed, 'the scene on stage is terrifying. It is like a torture scene. If the child was played by a twenty year old actor, the impact would not be the same.' (Bryanston, 2003a)

Bond argues that the combination of adult and child actors on stage 'mirrors the difference in real life between the reality of adults and the reality of young people'. The effect 'can be strangely disturbing and awesome – the stage seems to be filled with the huge conflict of our time'. (cited Irmer, 2003:57)

The difference between adults and children is inscribed in the text. The adult actors 'have highly structured texts', while for the most part, 'the young people's text is only indicated'. Bond expects the young people 'to improvise on the indications, both in rehearsals and performances. If they don't, the performance cannot work.' (cited Irmer, 2003:57)

Here, for example, are Bond's suggested lines for Joe's friends, when they hear that Joe's mother wants him to burn the house down (Scene three):

> **Friends**   If it was my mum I'd set fire to *her* –
> It's not funny.
> – but I'd do it out the back: my room's just been decorated.
> Shut it!
> You pile rubbish up against the door.
> Soak rags in petrol. Push them through the letterbox.
> Light a match – drop it in -
> And run! (Bond, 2000a:14-15)

Bond told the young cast of the original Classworks Theatre production: 'You don't have to stick to the lines, you can change them. As long as you make them real.' (cited Gold, 2000, p10) The fact that the text is semi-improvised helps to create the immediacy in the performances which Bond is looking for. When Bond saw the Classworks Theatre production, he felt that the directness and spontaneity of the young people's acting meant there was 'not a lot of falsehood between them and the text'. (cited Nicholson, 2003:19)

The element of improvisation also means that the cast are centrally involved in creating and 'owning' the performance. Bond argues that they 'should have the experience of being creative before adults, of being in charge of what they themselves do, of having to invent and create – but also of relating these things to a specific structure which includes adults. If the young cast can understand and enter this structure the play will work for them.' (Bond, 2003a)

The MAT production

The Children was commissioned by Classworks Theatre, and was first performed in 2000 at Manor Community College, Cambridge. It was directed by Claudette Bryanston.[1] In 2003, Gillian Adamson and I co-directed a production for the Midland Actors Theatre (MAT). We worked with a group of Year 10 and 11 pupils at Washwood Heath Technology College in Birmingham. We wanted to explore the demands the play makes on young people. Before rehearsals began, Bond gave us copies of the letters he had written on *The Children* to Claudette Bryanston, and others; these were an important influence in shaping our approach to working on the play.

Bond has argued that the situations in the play 'must be made radically clear' to the actors. (cited in Irmer, 2003:57) We developed a system in rehearsal to facilitate this. We would read a scene with the cast, and then break it down into discreet units of action.[2] Here, for example, is an excerpt from Scene three, with our 'units' marked. Joe has just told his friends that his mother wants him to burn a house down. They spot a stranger watching them, and chase him away. Then, their attention turns back to Joe.

Friends	Leave him!
	Do him later!

The others drift back

... sod dodged off ...
... wants thumping ...

They stare at Joe in silence.

Friend   She's got to tell you why.

Joe shrugs

Friend   What'll you do?

Joe (*slight pause*) It's only a house

Friends   He's going to do it ... !
Phew! I'm not getting involved!
The cops'll question all of us.
They'll make us talk – they're trained. What chance we got?
(Bond, 2000a:16)

After we had marked the units, we asked the cast to improvise each unit in turn. This, then, was a form of 'active analysis' of the play: a way of getting the play 'on its feet' instantly. Breaking a scene down into units helped to make the situation clear at each moment. Each unit gave the cast a clear focus and a concrete task to perform: to challenge the stranger and chase him off; to find out what Joe plans to do; to discuss the dangers they face, and so on. The actors knew *what* they were doing at each moment – although *how* exactly they did it remained open, to some extent, to improvisation, even in performance. The 'journey' of the play became a logical sequence of concrete tasks to be performed. (We wrote the units down on sugar paper, along with key lines of the improvised dialogue. The cast could refer to it in rehearsal, to remind themselves of the sequence of tasks.)

Within each unit, the action could be broken down again. In Scene three, the Friends agree to swear a pact to keep secret Joe's intention to burn down a house. He drags a large puppet on stage, a relic of his childhood, and they cement the pact by the ritual action of stoning the puppet:

Joe   We promise not to tell. Brick him – and swear we won't.
Friend   It's a pact! We swear to each other.

Hesitation. One of them takes a brick.

Friends   What do I say?
I swear to – (Stops. Shrugs.)
Keep my mouth shut. I promise the others.
(*Drops brick on puppet.*) I swear to keep my mouth shut.

The puppet sinks and falls back. For a moment they stare in silence. Then they rush to the bricks.

Friends   Brick it! Brick it! Brick it! (Bond, 2000a:17-18)

Bond suggests that the pile of bricks should be set some distance from the puppet. The Friends then 'have to walk to the bricks – especially the first thrower'. This emphasises the significance of the moment. The distance the first thrower has to cross to get a brick, and then 'kill' the puppet, emphasises the difficulty of taking this step. As Bond has observed: 'the decision is made physical and not subjective'. (Bond, 2000d) And then, the Friends' hesitation is suddenly broken, when they all rush at once to the bricks.

In Scene five, after Joe has burnt the house down, the Friends gather round him, to find out what he plans to do next. Then, behind then, 'a Man comes on slowly'.

> *He is tall and thin, his face is white, his hair is matted. He wears a long black overcoat, dark trousers, black boots, and pearl-grey gloves. He moves as if he does not see the others. He stops, stares at the ground. Falls. The friends turn to look at him. He lies completely still.* (Bond, 2000a:29)

When Bryanston was rehearsing the play for Classworks Theatre, she initially staged the scene so that the Man walked straight through the group of the children – 'making it very obvious that he doesn't see them, although they are all around him'. (Bryanston, 2003a) She recalls, however, that Bond

> saw the scene differently. He rearranged it, so that the children were standing in a group on one side. The man entered on the other side of the stage, so he was quite isolated from the others. Again, he didn't notice the children were there – and they didn't notice him, until he fell. They turned, and instantly, they all went across to him. (Bryanston, 2003a)

The Friends, then, had to cross the whole stage to reach the Man. Again, the decision to go and examine him 'is made physical and not subjective'. 'They each reacted in their own way,' Bryanston recalls. 'Some weren't frightened of the man lying there; some were terrified; some said, 'O God, he stinks!'.' (Bryanston, 2003a)

The stage picture, then, can help to 'tell the story' and make the situation clear at each moment, not simply for the audience, but also for the *actors*. We saw, also, that we look for ways to emphasise the significance of moments of choice and decision, to *physicalise* them.

Bond advised Bryanston: 'we need to break things down into small moments – not sweep through them – to find out what is involved ... We need a plan which says, articulate this moment – and this moment – and this moment.' (Bond, 2000e) His notes stress the need to slow the work down, and take time to 'articulate' the meaning of particular actions, and 'find out what is involved'. Thus, for example, there is a moment in Scene seven when drink cans are passed around, and one of the Friends offers a drink to the Man as he lies unconscious on a stretcher. It is a tiny moment, and its significance could easily be missed, but Bond notes that there should be a silence at this moment, as the others watch, to see what might happen.

In part, Bond is concerned to ensure that the meaning of particular moments is not lost because it forms part of a pattern of recurring actions in the play. Thus, there are a number of moments in the play of 'offering food (or love) and having it refused'. (Bond, 2000e) In one scene, for example, Joe offers his puppet a sweet. In another scene, Joe's mother tells him there's a meal waiting for him in the microwave – but he never actually gets to eat it. After burning down the house, Joe is sitting alone in the abandoned lot; he is cold and hungry. The Friends enter, and Bond suggests one of them offers him a packet of crisps, but he refuses, because he is too traumatised to eat.

There are other patterns of action, or as Bond terms them, 'diagrams' of 'the complications of love and violence and crime'. (Bond, 2000e) Thus, in Scene one, Joe stones his puppet, and then drags it off – just as the Man later stones a child, and drags the corpse away. Bond also creates oppositions between tenderness and violence. Thus, Joe hugs the puppet before killing it. In one scene, the Man sits among the sleeping children, and cradles a brick, stroking it like a baby; then, suddenly, he turns to the side, and kills one of the children with a blow of the brick.[3] The moment shows, as Bond says, 'the two extremes of the man'. (Bond, 2003c) A member of the audience at Washwood Heath College commented: 'I loved the bit where the man said 'good children' then killed them which really made me laugh.'

We had only a week to rehearse the play at Washwood Heath College, and so had to work quickly. There are, as Bond notes, advantages to working in this way: 'Young people don't like rehearsing. Once they've done a scene once, they don't want to do it again. They want to move on to something else. The play is actually written to accommodate this.' (Bond, 2003c) We found, however, a creative tension between the need to work on the play with attention to detail and the pressure to work at speed. We also found a tension between the need to define and shape moments with precision and the need to give the cast the freedom to improvise. We also have to recognise, that there were things which we just didn't manage to achieve in the time, and a number of points which were missed. Bond suggests, however, that asking young actors to focus on 'small moments' and 'find out what is involved' helps to create the 'intense concentration, which is the secret of drama'. (Bond, 2000b)[4]

Cathexing the object

Objects, Bond has observed, are 'psychosocial ... they combine both the psychology of the owner or user of the object – but also the social situation'. (Bond, 1997) The puppet is the 'central object' in *The Children*. It is both imbued with personal meanings for the character, and with social meanings. Joe abuses the puppet, and loves it, just as he is abused, and loved by his mother ('Anything goes wrong in our house, Mum hits me' – Bond, 2000a:6). By implication, it reflects how society treats, and 'murders', its children.

The object, then, is 'cathected' with the play's meaning. The play begins with Joe alone on stage, carrying the puppet. He has decided to get rid of it. Bond observes that this is part of the character's 'rite of passage'. Getting rid of the puppet 'is painful because it means losing part of himself'. (Bond, n.d.) In rehearsal, it is necessary to investigate the object, to explore the personal meaning it holds for the character. A close relationship must be developed between actor and object. At one moment, Joe is half-hugging the puppet and playfully swinging it from side to side, or feeding it sweets; the next, he is pummelling it with a brick.

Bond notes that, in the script, the characters' 'subjective states and responses are physically charted'. (Bond, 2004) Here, we can see that a strong sense of the character's 'subjective state', 'the complications of love and violence', are developed through a sequence of precise physical actions. The act of stoning the puppet clearly demonstrates or 'charts' the character's 'subjective state' to the audience. At the same time, simply performing the actions can, in fact, help the actor to find a 'subjective involvement' in the scene; to enter the 'site'. Bryanston recalls that:

> the young performer had to find considerable physical energy to abuse the puppet, bricks are heavy if you lift them above shoulder height whilst kneeling or crouching on the ground and continuously have to hit something. The energy contorted the face; and strangled the voice; the young performer would feel angry, very angry about the task his mother had set him to do in the play, angry and frustrated with the adults who confused him. This was not acted it was simply performed. The act of beating the puppet with the brick could only be done in anger. (Bryanston, 2003b)

The journey into the psyche

A play, Bond argues, 'has to make a journey into the actor's psyche': 'there are ways in which the actor can enter into the whole play and come back like an explorer with his face made a map of the country he has explored'. (Bond, 1996:144)

In staging *The Children*, we had to consider how we could help the young actors to take this journey into the world of the play. At first, they were both puzzled and intrigued. In the 'Thoughts' book, a notebook we provided during rehearsals for the cast to jot down their thoughts and impressions, Sonia Nawaz wrote: 'I think there are way too many unexplained things in this story.' Indeed, in the early stages of rehearsal, it was the lack of explanation for some of the incidents in the play that worried the cast most; as they worked on it, however, they began to enjoy looking for the answers themselves.

After the Friends set off on their journey, there is a sudden catastrophe that leaves them, it seems, alone in the world. We read Bond's explanation for this to the cast:

> A catastrophe suddenly happens and every one vanishes? Could it really happen like this? Probably not because there would be bodies lying around. But I didn't want to describe exactly what would happen – I wanted to describe what it would feel like to the young people: that they would be suddenly lost and abandoned. (Bond, n.d.)

The cast could accept this explanation of the catastrophe as an artistic metaphor. Nevertheless, they continued to look for logical explanations and consistency. Why, for example, if everyone has died, do the Friends continue with their journey, when the natural (logical) thing for them to do would be to return home, and find out what has happened to their families and friends? When we put this question to Bond, he responded:

> The play doesn't say anyone has been killed (except the child in the fire and the group of friends). Everyone else has just vanished. The children don't find any bodies, for example (not even of those of the group who are killed). They would not return to their families for the reasons they give for going on their journey in the first place. They have no other friends to return to because all the friends are together. The play is describing a different world in which people act differently. When this is clear the young people acting the play would be able to give many reasons for not returning – then the play would be working properly: it would be about the young people's lives and not the specifics of *this* journey, which in themselves have no interest. Often when young people run away from home their situation deteriorates

drastically – yet they don't return home. The young people already know the answer to this question if it's put to them in this way. (Bond, 2003b)

If, Bond insists, 'the play is used to settle factual questions about itself it is not doing its proper work – that would be the work of, say, the police the children mention in the earlier part of the play'. (Bond, 2003b)

> Often the play itself becomes the problem – and then its problems are solved and nothing has really happened. (Then it's like a TV detective whodunit – utterly reactionary.) A play must not deliberately confuse but it should always open more doors than were open when it began. Otherwise don't have plays but provide questions and answers about facts. A play isn't a fact it's a fiction used to enter the reality of imagination. (Bond, 2003b)

Bond suggests that

> All I can do is record certain facts, say what events are known to have occurred ... but that does not give the meaning of the facts. Meanings must be given by young people to facts which demand understanding – and in giving these meanings the young people create their humanity... That is why I say drama cannot teach anyone anymore than a statue can breath – drama creates: when the audience creates. Its questions do not have factual answers – the answers are meanings. Of course young people are interested in facts. In drama it's possible to open up different questions – and young people are very able to go into these questions. When they do, they find how meanings may become facts – and so how facts can change. (Bond, 2003b)

Some of the questions asked by the cast at Washwood Heath reflected a concern with 'facts' rather than the 'reality of imagination'. Nevertheless, they enjoyed struggling with the play's apparent lacunae, as if Bond had left them with a puzzle to complete; and they began to create their own meanings for these 'facts which demand understanding'. In the 'Thoughts' book, Kellie Durrington wrote: 'The play is really good and the way it's left unexplainable for the audience to make up their own mind was effective.' And Sonia Nawaz, who had earlier complained that there were too many 'unexplained things', changed her mind by the end of the week, and wrote: 'I thought that the storyline was different and unique.'

The 'sense of desolation and abandonment'

As we have seen, for Bond, the 'catastrophe' in the play is less a 'realistic' event than a dramatic device, to evoke a sense of what it would feel like for young people to be 'suddenly lost and abandoned' in a hostile world. (Bond, n.d.)

> The play wants to create a sense of desolation and abandonment which all children at some time feel – but in which they do not despair but turn back to life, seek their maturity. (Bond, 2003b)

The challenge for any production is to help the cast to create that 'sense of desolation and abandonment'. Again, this 'subjective state' is 'physically charted' in the text. Bond alludes to the characters' physical states at different points in the journey: they feel thirsty, hungry, tired *etc*. Through performing concrete physical actions, the young actors can begin to enter the 'site' of the drama: to enter, imaginatively, 'a different world'.

Bond observes that in Scene six, the first after the 'catastrophe' has occurred, the 'important story in the scene is that the world is dying. Probably no one should sit down in the scene – they are tired, of course, but they are scared – this is the stronger objective.' (Bond, 2000d)

In Scene seven, the mood among the Friends has changed. They have been travelling for several days; they are tired and irritable. Some drink cans are handed round, cans that have been looted from a deserted town. They are all thirsty but they might pause, and wonder if the cans are contaminated, before they drink. This is a logical action in the circumstances, and can help to make the characters' situation *concrete* for the actors. As they settle down to sleep, the lines that Bond has suggested for them evoke their sense of uncertainty and hopelessness:

> We're lost.
> Like being shipwrecked in the empty fields.
> Why've they knocked the houses down?
> We don't know where we are. We don't know where we're going. What we're doing. (Bond, 2000a:35)

Then, they wake up – and a fight breaks out. It blows over quickly but then another, more ferocious fight begins. Bond notes that the fighting 'should be painful to watch – to see the F[riend]s becoming enemies and hitting each other before ever the M[an] does. They hit out in despair and fear. The Fs need to know it shows their desperation.' (Bond, 2000d)

Again, the physical action of the fight expresses the characters' 'subjective state'. The action needs to be driven by a real sense of 'despair and fear'; otherwise, as Bond recognised, there is a danger that the fight will lack real conviction, and could even seem comical to an audience. (Bond, 2000d.)

The importance of image

Bond argues that the 'importance of image is always vital'. He cites the example of Frankenstein's monster, an image that is disturbing because 'it has the forehead of a baby but is a semi-giant and wears the dark suit of an adult with authority – a priest, an undertaker'; it is a monster with 'technological scars on its face' who yet 'desires passionately to be human'. In *The Children*, 'the Monster(s) live in houses and housing estates'. (Bond, 2000c)

In Scene nine, the children are lying on the ground, asleep. The Man walks among them, picking his next victim, and all the sleepers begin to murmur:

> The murmur rises in piteous sobs and wails. Slowly it swells into a great arc of lamentation and tumult – echoes sounding inside echoes – torn, solemn, beautiful – the sorrow, frustration and longing of childhood. (Bond, 2000a:44)

The image of the Man killing the children had a powerful impact on both cast and audience. They were both fascinated and disturbed by him. He is like a figure from a dark fairy tale or horror film, and Bond notes that he becomes more grotesque and nightmarish with each victim: his coat grows longer and his face grows whiter. One of the pupils at the school observed after the performance that the 'ugly man' had 'shit me up'.

The Centre

Bond argues that every play has a 'centre'. This might be defined as the 'basic theme', or perhaps, a question at the heart of the play. The 'centre', Bond argues, should guide actors and directors in all their work on the production. 'Once the importance of 'centre' is understood, anything on stage can be used to show it' (Bond, 1996:168)

As we have seen, for Bond, *The Children* is a play 'about growing up' and accepting 'responsibility for ourselves and others' (Bond, n.d.), a kind of 'rite of passage' which the characters go through. Thus, the friends have to learn to help each other; they even take responsibility for the Man, and help the very thing that is destroying them. In his letters, Bond highlights certain moments which, he says, take the audience, and the actors, to the play's 'centre'. In Scene seven, for example, the children lie asleep but one of them, Adam, gets up, and starts to clean up the empty drink cans that lie scattered over the stage. He explains:

> I can't stand the mess! (*He starts to gather the empty cans*) We're walking through a desert! Ruined houses! Everything falling down! And we drop

our litter like pigs! ... I don't know what's happening! Why it's falling apart!
Where everyone's gone! But I'm not an animal! (Bond, 2000a:37)

The cans are put in a sack and dragged off, just as Joe drags off his puppet,
and the Man drags away his latest victim. Bond observes that in Adam's
desire 'to take some action against the chaos there is the centre of the play:
the journey for, to humanness'.

Bond cites this moment as an example of a 'Theatre Event'. He stresses
'what is at stake' in this moment but he does not define *how* to do the
scene. He does not say 'how the incident of the tin-clearing is to be used'.

> ... some forms of puritanical cleanliness are destructive – perhaps the friend
> who clears the tins is afraid, should be criticised in the playing – these are
> directorial and actor choices (because the audience can be shown meaning
> in many ways) ... Meaning does not dictate use. (Bond, 2000c)

We can see that Bond is working through concrete moments of action. Any
production of the play needs to work out what is at stake, 'what is
important' – and then work on *how* to show what is involved.

In rehearsing the play at Washwood Heath, we did not want to impose a
concept of the play's 'centre' on the cast. Rather, we wanted them to 'own'
the play and so define the 'centre' as they saw it.

The cast were struck, from the start of rehearsals, by the behaviour of the
adults in the play. Some thought the behaviour of the mother, for example,
was funny, because it was so outrageous; others called it 'evil'. When I asked
them to define the 'centre' of the play, Ashley Deeming said it was about
'wrong states of mind'. Later, in the 'Thoughts' book, he wrote, 'Everyone is
a psycho'; and he drew an image of a face, based on Munch's painting *The
Scream*, to represent the adults in the play. (He saw that the adults are not
simply evil; they are, themselves, damaged and traumatised.)

We asked the cast what they thought Bond meant by 'the journey for, to
humanness'. Mehrish Yasin recognised that 'it's about growing up, and becoming an adult'. Nevertheless, it might be argued that, for this group, the
madness and inhumanity of adults, and 'the emotional and physical
violence that is often used against young people' (Bond, 2000b, p 3), were
the emotional centre of the play. Perhaps, in the time available to us, we
had taken them only so far on the journey towards the play's 'centre'. However, their response shows, perhaps, how much the play had penetrated
their imaginations and entered their 'psyche'. Bond argues:

When *The Children* works, it's got to become the young people's play. They've got to want to do it, and they've got to feel they're making the right decisions ... They're using it for what they want. (Bond, 2003c)

Sources

Bond, Edward

– (1996) *Letters III*, edited by Ian Stuart. Amsterdam: Harvard Academic Publishers

– (1997) Unpublished letter to Big Brum TIE Company

– (2000a) *The Children*, London: Methuen

– (2000b) 'Words about *The Children*'. In: programme for the Classworks Theatre production

– (2000c) Unpublished letter to Claudette Bryanston, 16.1.2000

– (2000d) Unpublished letter to Claudette Bryanston, 12.2.2000

– (2000e) Unpublished letter to Claudette Bryanston, 26.2.2000

– (2003a) Unpublished letter to Eva Dumbia, 1.11.03

– (2003b) Unpublished letter to David Allen, 27.12.03

– (2003c) Unpublished interview with David Allen, 11.10.03

– (2004) Unpublished letter to David Davis, 7.4.04

– (n.d.) Unpublished letter to Sorrell Oates and Matt Morris-Jones

Bryanston, Claudette (2001), 'The Children', in: *Drama Magazine*, Winter 2001, p 29-35

– (2003a) Unpublished interview with David Allen, 23.4.03

– (2003b) Unpublished paper to IDERIE Conference, Northampton, July 2003

Gold, Karen (2000), 'Children Know the World is Violent and Vengeful'; interview with Bond in: *Times Educational Supplement* (Friday magazine), 18 February 2000, p 8-10

Irmer, Thomas (2003), 'Menschen müssen nicht destructiv sein', interview with Bond in: *Theater der Zeit*, February 2003, p 57-8

Nicholson, Helen (2003), 'Acting, Creativity and Social Justice: Edward Bond's *The Children*', *Research in Drama Education*, Vol. 8, No.1, March 2003, p 9-23

Notes

1 The Classworks Theatre production was ACE funded. It subsequently toured to some twenty-one different venues around the country, working each time with a new group of young people. Claudette Bryanston recalls that, before Bond wrote *The Children*, she discussed with him the idea of young people and adults working together on stage: 'I very much wanted the young people to be *centre stage*. Having professional actors and young performers together on stage, after all, isn't original; but other examples I had seen left the young people with a sort of 'rent-a-crowd' status. My motive was to do with giving young people's creativity *recognition* within the professional theatre world, and to see their work valued, and thus for young people to be valued. Edward achieved this and much more. I think that from this point of view, *The Children* is truly original.' (Letter to David Allen, 18.6.04)

2 Similarly, in the Classworks Theatre production, Claudette Bryanston broke individual scenes down into units. Each unit was given a title, e.g. 'The decision to run away'. See 'The Children' by Claudette Bryanston in *Drama Magazine*, Winter 2001, p 33.

3 Thomas Jones, who played the Stranger in the MAT production, observed that the Man, at this point, cradles the brick like a child, and then uses it to kill, just as the Mother earlier uses *her* child to kill.

4 In a letter to Bryanston, dated 26.2.00, Bond stressed the need to create 'the concentration ('you are there') which is the secret of drama'.

The MAT production was funded by a grant from Awards for All. It was directed by David Allen and Gillian Adamson, with Georgina Biggs as the Mother, and Justyn Towler as the Man.

Stage Manager: Den Woods.

First performance: 12 December 2003.

Cast: Amy Brown, Lorena Chinea, Subrina Choudry, Ashley Deeming, Kelly Durrington, Roxanne Dwyer, Jason Graham, Natasha Harris, Laveeza Hussain, Daryl Johnson, Thomas Jones, Anita Josephs, Heidi Kempson, Mark Lee, Karly Mackenzie, Che'Nene Morgan, Sonia Nawaz, Samuel Poole, Kelly Spencer, Momina Sultana, Kirsty Tuckey, Mehrish Yasin.

Staff supervisors: Liz Soden, Mike Allen.

9

Edward Bond and Drama in Education

David Davis

E dward Bond has a long association with drama and theatre in education.[1] He is a staunch supporter and advocate of DIE (drama in education)[2] and TIE (theatre in education): he regards them as fundamental to a young person's development. '…Theatre-in-Education… is the most valuable cultural institution the country has.' (Bond, 2000:58) The fact that he has allied himself so strongly with drama and theatre in schools has meant that inevitably he has influenced some practitioners but it is surprising that he has so far made no major impact on drama in education theory and practice. However, perhaps it is not surprising, considering that he is virtually an exile in France where his plays are valued and performed. ('I feel myself more and more isolated from the present theatre – in exile' Bond, 1995:84) In this chapter I want to look at the implications of this lack of influence and examine how Bond's theory and practice of theatre might have the potential to enrich school drama.

I want to argue that drama in education theory and practice has run into some difficulties. Teacher education courses have been stripped bare of the possibility of giving new teachers a thorough grounding in pedagogy, which is a vital basis for any teacher who wants to educate rather than deliver a prescribed curriculum. The cutting back of teaching time in the universities and the placement of students in schools means that students are apprenticed on the job with some day release to get a smattering of teacher competencies. This 'apprenticeship' could be fine if all the host drama teachers were grounded in pedagogy and the theory and practice of teaching drama and they had time to teach the 'trainees', as they are now called. Even at its best this is no substitute for a course that afforded the time and resources to open up for the students theories of art and drama, of teaching and learning, and of ways of knowing and for all this to be taught through developing the skilled practice of the student teacher. The pressure to test and write attainment targets has tended to drive what is taught in drama down to the level of examinable skills. In this climate it is understandable for teachers to reach for a formulaic approach.

One influence on this development has been *Structuring Drama Work* by Jonothan Neelands (Neelands, 1990). This book was originally written to act as a valuable resource for teachers who wanted to have a handy range of activities for their drama lessons. It was intended that teachers, as part of devising sophisticated drama structures, could take some of these 'conventions' as he calls them (forum theatre, voices in the head and some 45 others) and use them as part of the complex structure of the drama sessions. Instead, they lend themselves to becoming the total method of work employed in a drama lesson. They are relatively easy to teach and can bring some 'success' relatively quickly. What is missing is the deep theoretical embedding which a teacher needs to make use of them.[3]

The strongest piece of evidence that we may be in a dead-end with the theory and practice of drama in education is the syllabus of one of the GCSE (General Certificate in Secondary Education) drama boards. The negative influence of *Structuring Drama Work* has, I suggest, been an indirect influence on the appalling concoction that masquerades under the title of EDEXCEL GCSE Drama (2001). Through this examination course in drama, students have to study and demonstrate expertise in and knowledge of eight explorative strategies for drama, eight features of the drama medium and eight elements of drama. The eight explorative strategies are:

- Still image
- Thought tracking
- Narration
- Hot-seating
- Role play
- Cross-cutting
- Forum theatre
- Marking the moment

These appear to be a random selection from the above Neeland's publication.

The eight features of the drama medium are to do with the 'use of costume, lighting, sets, voice' *etc.* But most alarming, the eight elements of drama are:

- Action/plot/context
- Forms
- Climax/anticlimax
- Rhythm/pace/tempo
- Contrast
- Characterisation
- Conventions
- Symbols

Where in the 'elements of drama' list are, for example, tension, the special use of time, constraints, imagery, use of objects, sub-text and meta-text? Also, the categorisation in the above lists lacks coherence. For example, the explorative strategies mix Forum Theatre, which is a whole method of theatre with its own rationale and complex methodology, with the fundamental performing skill of entering drama, role play. Thought tracking and still image can be used when role playing, to help with reflection or focusing. 'Characterisation' is not an 'element of drama' but belongs in the category to do with the performing art of theatre; 'forms' are different ways of combining the 'elements' rather than a component part. Overall, the EDEXCEL curriculum reduces a complex art form to a list of things that can be practised, learnt and tested. It would seem that the 'bits and pieces' approach to drama formalised by *Structuring Drama Work* has inadvertently led to this 'bits and pieces' approach to teaching drama for a whole generation of students. Blaming Neeland's book may sound harshly judgemental but Neeland's own teaching is far more sophisticated than this. I am pointing to the unforeseen but unhappy outcome of providing a drama manual in this form.

The 'conventions approach' to drama is widespread. The latest Department for Education and Skills, (the revised name for the Department of Education, DfES!) guidance for Speaking, Listening and Learning at Key Stage 1 and 2 has 'drama' activities included. The drama work focuses on performance and is skills-based. The complex 'living through' drama is left out. The drama 'strategies' are inevitably selected from the conventions approach, formalised by Neelands: freeze frame, conscience alley, hot-seating, thought tracking and so on, (DfES, 2003).

If we are indeed at a junction or, rather, in a siding in DIE theory and practice, is there anything in Bond's approach to theatre that could be useful here? I explore this in the rest of the chapter.

This exploration assumes that readers will have read the chapters in this volume by Kate Katafiasz and Bill Roper. In writing about Bond's approach to theatre here, I intend to do no more than refresh some of the areas they identify rather than fully to rehearse them. I include only a few features of Bond's theatre which are of key relevance to drama in education.

From his first performed play, *The Pope's Wedding* in 1962, Bond has been concerned with developing a new form of theatre. (Stuart 2000:viii) This new form implies dissatisfaction both with Stanislavsky and Brecht. Bond's key concern is with the relationship of the audience to the performed play. He argues that in Stanislavsky's theatre the audience is caught up with the characters in the play, feeling empathy, disgust or whatever is motivated in them by the life-like performance of the actors. There is little direct recourse to critical reasoning: feelings predominate. In Brecht's theatre, although allowing emotion and empathy – albeit with Brecht and the actors attempting to control its content – the audience is continually reminded of the need for a critical stance in relation to the events they are witnessing: if the audience is alienated they can't experience empathy at the same time. In order to alienate the audience, the actors indicate the attitudes and values that the audience should preferably adopt. Reason and criticism predominate. What Bond wants in his own theatre is a relationship between actors and audience where the audience is engaged with the action of the play, with the possibility of empathy and emotion, but where the imagination is stimulated which then has to seek reason. Imagination and reason predominate. With this approach, he seeks to alienate from within the act, that is without breaking the empathetic relationship forged between the actors and audience.

It is interesting to search through the different methods and approaches which have been invented and developed in DIE, to see which methods or schools of thought, most closely correspond to Bond's theory and practice. Which approach to drama in schools engages the children with the role, emotionally and empathetically, and yet enables them to use their imagination to seek reason? I would like to propose that the early work of Heathcote, continued and developed by Bolton and O'Neill, has many of these features of Bondian theatre, although there are also substantial differences.

One of Heathcote's key inventions was a 'living through' drama which involved teacher in role – one of Heathcote's most important inventions – and had as its primary purpose a re-examination and/or development by the students of fundamentally held values by which they lived. This first phase of her drama teaching, up to the early or mid-70s, came to be known as 'Man in a mess' drama, (Bolton, 1998:176-7). This was her definition of drama in response to the director of the BBC Omnibus programme about her life and work, 'Three Looms Waiting'. The video of this programme, made in the early seventies, shows an example of this sort of drama work involving boys from a community home, a remand centre for young offenders. This one extract has probably done more to publicise her work and the value of DIE than any other. The boys elect to make up a play about prisoners-of-war and Heathcote works with them to develop a play for themselves. By chance it has an 'audience' in Heathcote's students and the camera crew, but this type of drama does not need an outside audience, the participants are also their own audience. The boys get the keys from the guards and plan their escape but are fooled by a stool pigeon who betrays them. In the video, interviewed by the director of the filming, Heathcote says 'It looks like they've just had a good adventure. It will be a little while before they could say 'That was me talking'.' They were actually in a prison and would have liked to escape and they know about betrayal and the pressure to 'grass' on each other. In the drama they are in two worlds at once: the world of the drama and the world they are actually in, a prison. The role-playing involves them in *being themselves* in the role they are taking. Both of these states of being can come into relationship and inform each other both during and after the drama. They have an open discussion with the film maker afterwards in which they explore their attitudes towards the stool pigeon, wondering why he should have gone down on his knees and sobbed after he had betrayed the prisoners.[4] The boys want to know why he should have sobbed as he was a German and should have been pleased that he had foiled their escape. The reflection on the event is integral to this type of drama.Heathcote became more and more committed to this form of reflection in and after the drama experience and invented the centrally important notion of 'developing the self spectator'. (Shillingford, 1994) This is probably the point of greatest alignment with Bond, who wants the audience for his plays to be involved in just such a struggle with their developing 'self'.

Bond distinguishes between conventional theatre, of which he is highly critical, and the drama he is creating:

> There is a distinction between 'theatre' and 'drama'. 'Theatre' animates itself by reverberations within imagination but closes off its relation to objective reality. It uses acting skills, which are often eminent, shock effects and emotive lighting and music. It reaffirms, consoles, reassures and entertains but enervates. ...But drama uses the stage as the site of the pre-self. (Bond, 2003:4)

This notion of the 'site of the pre-self' is crucial to what follows. Bill Roper's and Kate Katafiasz's chapters deal here with this concept in more detail so I will sketch only enough to take readers forward.

The 'pre-self' is seen by Bond as the foundation of our humanity in the newly born child. It is the site of the imagination, which Bond argues is synonymous with self-consciousness. The foundation stone of Bond's whole approach to theatre is that humans have more than reason. All higher forms of animal life have rudimentary reasoning (Walker, 1983), but humans have imagination. 'Can we even think without imagination or must it accompany thought as if it were a light thrown on an object?...reality coerces imagination into seeking rational understanding: and so imagination comes to desire reason.' (Bond, 2000:13)

The 'pre-self' is the site of the most basic human desire: the neonate's desire to be at home in the world, from which follows the search for justice and the awareness of injustice. It is the echo of this 'pre-self' with which Bond's drama seeks to make connections: to slip round behind the ideologised 'self' and make connections with the imagination of the 'pre-self' which connects us with the basis of our humanity. 'The importance of drama is that it may directly confront radical innocence and the need for humanness' (Bond, 2000:181). Bond's 'Palermo Improvisation' is an example of what he means here. This was an exercise he set a group of students from Palermo University (see 'Commentary on *The War Plays*' (Bond, 1998). John Doona also describes it in his chapter but I am repeating it for the sake of clarity. Bond gave them the situation of a soldier sent by an officer back into his own street with an order to kill a baby. There are only two families still living in the street, the soldier's own mother with her baby, the soldier's sibling, and the neighbour with her baby. Bond wrote down what would happen as a prediction before the improvisation started. This was that no one would kill the neighbour's child and this turned out to be the case. I think Bond would argue that this situation was touching the 'pre-self' of the actor. He was no longer 'acting' but 'being' in the situation, and in 'being' was in touch with what was most fundamental to his humanity, whose origins are in the radical innocence of the young child. This notion of 'being' has much in common with Heathcote's early approach to drama teaching and a lot to do with Bolton's life work in drama. Writing in 1980, Heathcote states of drama, 'We interpret the word aright when we understand it to mean living through, struggling through, and doing' (Heathcote and Hovda, 1980c:5). Heathcote and Bolton are the two practitioners whose approach to drama teaching I now explore. I will return to this notion of 'being' in the drama, either as audience or participant, at a later stage as I want to compare Heathcote and Bond in a fairly cursory way.

It is possible to find a number of formal similarities between Heathcote and Bond, both as people and as enormously creative innovators in their respective fields of drama in education and theatre.[5] Both are of the same generation, growing up and experiencing the pressures of the Second World War. Both were working-class and both left secondary school as soon as the age for compulsory education ended, at the age of fourteen. Both are autodidacts and thus avoided the damage that a formal university academic education might have done to the way their minds work. Heathcote did have a two-year experience at drama school, which seems to have been largely practice-focused rather than formally academic. Both seem to have minds which throw up images and connections in a remarkably fertile way. It is important to mention these dimensions of similarities because it may have helped them both to start out as innovators, setting out on their own paths rather than being directed into other routes by academia. Heathcote moved away from all conventional approaches to DIE and Bond, from the first plays published in the 1960s, was developing a new form of theatre. It is interesting that Bond 'respects the contribution she has made to young people's theatre. She was a pioneer, certainly for me' (Bond, 2004).

Other connections can also be traced between Heathcote's approach to drama and that of Bond. I am trying to do no more than highlight some connecting points: there are also great differences and even in the similarities are the seeds of these differences. These are apparent even as I try to explore the connections. From the start Heathcote subordinated dramatic action to meaning; Bond sees the essence of theatre as dramatising meaning. Heathcote emphasises the significance of actions and objects: Bond focuses on how objects can hold human values and how actions and gestures etc can form the basis of theatre events. Heathcote sees drama not as telling a story but the 'story' coming out of how the attitudes and actions of the people in the play shape events; each event is the centre of an episode. Bond shapes his theatre form by providing the potential for a series of Theatre Events, which explore the relationship of the characters to the social world and each other. Story is more important to Bond than to Heathcote: he does not seek an episodic development of plot but rather a clear connection from one scene to the next. In the performance of Bond's plays the Theatre Events themselves all relate to the centre of the play and make a meta-text. What Heathcote and Bond share is that a play is not just telling a story but that the story is the means of exploring our humanity. Heathcote sees drama as the foundation of human knowing and Bond sees no progress for humanity unless we can dramatise ourselves. Imagination is key to both practitioners. Heathcote's aim is to 'inculcate a new, childlike, non-jaded vision in us' (Bolton, 1998:207), Bond's is to connect with the radical innocence in all of us. Heathcote always works for the group and not from the psychology of an individual character: Bond does not build from the psychology of a character but from how people use each other. Both are concerned most importantly with re-examining who we are. Central to Heathcote's approach is the notion of developing the self-spectator: Bond is concerned that the audience are provoked into re-examining how they live and how they might live life differently.

Evoking the imagination is central to Heathcote's work with young people. Almost every time I have seen her teach, very early on in her contact with the students she holds up her hand which has half a finger missing. It is a provocation to jolt the class into imagining what might have happened to it: to search for the implications held by the missing half finger. Did she have it cut off in some cultural ritual? Did she cut it off herself? Was it pain-ful? 'I wonder...' is her favourite way of forming a question. It is intended to make clear to the class that they are going to have to move their imagina-tions into gear. 'There is one tool without which we now cannot work. It is the word *implication*' (Heathcote and Hovda, 1980c:4). The choice of the word implication is interesting. It relates to reason as much as to imagina-tion and it took her more towards reason in the later development of her work. I am not suggesting that it is exactly the same form of imagination or the same sort of provocation as used by Bond, but simply arguing that they are both fundamentally concerned with imagination.

Fundamental differences are also to be found, particularly in the use to which drama should be put. As Bolton points out, Heathcote favoured an anthropological approach in her role-building rather than the social/ political one Bond would choose. (Bolton, 1998:196) She needed to help the children find the generalised cultural stance of the role they were taking, the culture's values, before they could begin to 'be' in the situation. This led her away from a consideration of class relationships and the inherent injustice of every developed society in the world, as a priority, and towards accepting the cultural norms of a social group, the group's ethnic norms as it were. (see Bolton, 1998:196) The young people were inducted into a drama world where the social relationships were given, accepted and not fundamentally challenged. For Bond, the search for social justice and what it means to be human were from the start, basic to his approach. His plays are not political with a capital P. He is not interested in propagandising but his basic concerns are class and injustice.

After this 'Man in a mess' period, Heathcote became clearer that she was more interested in education than in drama (Heathcote 1980a) and she developed her 'Mantle of the Expert' approach to drama during the mid to late seventies, to serve 'curriculum' needs. This is not a very precise way of describing it and leads to her work being seen as simply a method, or methods, for cross-curricular work. She always worked wider than any conventional school curriculum, aiming to maximise the knowledge possibilities of her students and, as Bolton points out, she went beyond just finding methods to teach curriculum subjects. 'She sees drama as the very foundation of human knowledge at once personal, cultural and universal, pointing to a new conception of the curriculum and *overriding* the prevailing 'disciplines' '(Bolton, 1998:177). Bond sees dramatising ourselves as the only way humans can forge a future for themselves. Both, therefore, see drama as fundamental to humanity but Heathcote's focus on knowledge and learning is an indication of a difference with Bond.

By 1980 she is writing with Oliver Fiala that 'Drama, expressed as Theatre, has fundamentally a didactic purpose presented as an aesthetic experience'. (Heathcote and Fiala,1980d:25) Bond would never say this. In fact he would refute it. Heathcote's concern to see herself primarily as an educator leads her, as far as the art form is concerned, to move away from drama as 'living through' in the event, to drama where the role is more distanced. It allows the child to move from being in the actual drama event, to a role relationship to the event which is more distanced and allows for more scrutiny and critical examination. In her writings up to around 1978, the 'living through' in drama (as in making a play) is regularly referred to, rather than 'Mantle of the Expert' which she was beginning to invent at about this time as she moved more towards drama for learning. For example in *Subject or System* first published in 1971 (Heathcote, 1980b), she writes:

> I define educational drama as being anything which involves people in

active role-taking situations in which attitudes, not character, are the chief concern, lived at life-rate (that is discovery at this moment, not memory based) and obeying the natural laws of the medium. (p61)

By the end of the seventies she is becoming interested in Erving Goffman's frame distance (Heathcote and Hovda,1980c) and the advantages she sees as accruing from *not* being *in* the event but approaching the event from a frame distance. She is moving consciously to aligning herself with aspects of Brecht's approach to theatre. In the paper written with Oliver Fiala she distances herself from Stanislavski, '...she stands apart from the majority of drama practitioners who ally their educational ideas with Stanislavskian theatrical ideas' (Heathcote and Fiala,1980d:37)[6]. She claims that the pattern of her work 'has a distinct likeness to the way Brecht worked in theatre', (*ibid*, p41) and that '...it [is] possible...to demonstrate an artistic affinity between Dorothy Heathcote's approach, and Brecht's theory of Epic Theatre'. (*ibid*, p42) One of the elements of Epic Theatre picked out to demonstrate this affinity is that 'The emphasis is on the process of demonstrating *how* an event occurred, so that the *why* it occurred (the implication) can be recognised and resolved.' (*ibid*, p43) It is worth noting that the use of 'implication' now has less to do with stimulating the imagination through objects or actions that startle the child, in role, into new searching for understanding, but more to do directly with reasoning.[7] Finally, Heathcote holds up Brecht's approach as offering a great deal of use for drama teachers.

> He [Brecht] lays stress, in his writings about Epic Theatre, on rational understandings. 'The essential point of the Epic Theatre is perhaps that it appeals less to the feelings than to the spectator's reason. Instead of sharing an experience the spectator must come to grips with things.' (*ibid*, p52)[8]

Heathcote's foregrounding of learning, implying an emphasis on reason and her preference for frame distance, therefore take her closer to Brecht in her approach to drama: at this point a huge gulf opens up between her approach and the approach of Bond, for whom 'alienation is the theatre of Auschwitz' (see chapter three of this book).

Bond has developed the notion of 'site', 'the social on which the personal is situated' (Bond, 2000:47). There is the site of the audience, the site of the actors, the site of the characters and the site of the play: the actors are seeking to bring these into a direct relationship. What Bond seeks to achieve in his drama is for the play to challenge the ideologically bound outlook of the audience – and the actors and director too: the distorted view of the world we have as we look out on life as if through an opaque window. Bond seeks those moments of self-questioning through aligning the sites without breaking the engagement of the audience. In Bondian terms, when Heathcote moved to 'Mantle of the Expert', where the pupils are inducted into the expertise, attitudes and responsibilities of the chosen enterprise, I suggest that she moved them into an enterprise culture which excluded key aspects of the social site. It is a world which is non-critical of this enterprise culture and although the accent is on service and not monetary reward, the site nevertheless leaves key areas of ideology aside, such as class, justice, religion, the state, patriotism, racism *etc*. As Bond himself puts it:

> ...I disagree with Dorothy Heathcote because I don't think it's true that the way you're taught is more important than what you're taught. And I think her use of business managers' human-relations charts is suspect. These charts depend on incorporating people into existing systems of under-standing – reified versions of the story – and do not allow people to question function. So I think what she is doing is really ghettoising imagination ...and not freeing it to question the ideology of the story. (Bond, 1994:102

Heathcote's key concern is not to find a site where human relations are to be problematised like Bond, but where problems can be solved. The children can learn knowledge and skills from the enormously useful basis of having no fear of failure because they are being inducted into the mantle of expert. But this leads them away from the totality of their own personal site and into the site of the expert world they are entering. This means that they are much less open to re-assessing their personal values and perspectives in relation to the ideological areas indicated above, and more concerned with taking on the values of the chosen occupation. This is a shift away from her early work, which had more to do with imagination seeking reason, to, in the later work, reason seeking imagination. This reaches its logical conclusion in her latest method, 'Commissioners Drama', where the children actually take on a commission from the community or from within the school. The children work with teachers and parents within a specified time frame and bring it to a published, useable conclusion. The children start with a problem and then use reason to seek imagination to find the answer to the problem.

I think Heathcote would say of her own work that even in that early phase of 'Man in a Mess' drama she was really pursuing the distancing for reflection which she found the tools for later. I remember her once saying to me 'I've only ever been in one room'. At the time I couldn't see how that could be possible in relation to her own work, as her early method seemed so different to her 'Mantle of the Expert' approach. I questioned her about it in an interview (Heathcote, 1985). I can now see more clearly what she meant. I think she would argue that the outer form had changed but the inner form which she had always sought, was consistent and that she was constantly finding better tools to shape it. This chapter ends with a somewhat deeper consideration of what was involved in this 'turn' in Heathcote's work and its significance.

The early form of 'living through' drama was continued by Bolton and O'Neill (1995). Bolton says of his own work that he took 'living through' drama in a direction never intended by her [Heathcote] and perhaps, from her point of view, off-target, if not misguided.' (Bolton, 1998:217). I think it was extremely important that he continued to develop this work and that it was on target and not at all misguided. O'Neill, influenced by him, developed her own form of process drama. This focused more on theatre form and related less to the deep 'being' in the situation in which Bolton had a life-long interest, although O'Neill was still concerned to find episodes of this at the centre of the process. Bolton's work was built around this period of engagement with the role by the students that set up a sort of *metaxis*, a living in two worlds at once; being in the world of the role and being oneself at the same time. Thus the two states of being could collide and fundamental values, opinions, viewpoints and concepts could be challenged and ideally re-worked. He saw this approach as being intimately linked with children's play and the early exploration of their social roles through dramatic playing. In one of his later pieces of writing (Bolton, 2000), he comes to see that his favoured approach to drama involvement and the drama work for production which other teachers favoured, were all different theatre genres.

I suggest that the place we need to 'return' to in order to locate a point where Edward Bond's theory and practice can inform drama in education and help find a way forward, is in the early work of Heathcote and in the late work of Bolton. Heathcote devoted her enormous talents to developing drama in the service of children's learning and in doing so moved away from developing the theory and practice of drama as art: where the drama activity is itself the central focus for the children's development. Instead, what she did was to invent the most sophisticated teaching methods using drama that I have found anywhere in the world. However, as she left this early form of 'living through' drama behind and focused on using 'living through' mainly in the 'Mantle of the Expert' method, it is perhaps to Bolton that we should return. An examination of Bolton's latest[9] approach to 'living through' drama could be the starting point for the future development of the art form of process drama, onto which drama teachers could graft or rather re-work into new forms, in line with Bond's innovations in theatre form.

We can usefully examine an account of one of Bolton's later sophisticated teaching/learning structures to examine what relationship might be found to Bond's work. This is a workshop, preparing students to read Miller's *The Crucible* (Bolton, 1998). He taught several versions of this workshop, and although I participated in one of them when he taught my students and so have first hand experience of it, I draw on the published version rather than the one I have in my notebook, on the presumption that the published one is his favoured form.

Bolton has decided that the centre of the drama experience should be the pressure on a group of adolescent young people who have to respond to rumours that some of them have been seen dancing naked in the woods and practising witchcraft. In the play it is girls but Bolton wants to include the boys in this as well. The pressure point needs to be found which could lead some of them to point the finger elsewhere to distract attention from themselves. He builds towards this tension point through a series of activities: he begins by looking, out of role, at the notion of superstition and gradually leads the participants to create an image of a family portrait, which aims to show the 'purity' of the children and the family 'power struc-ture' (a full description of the step by step building of this structure appears in Bolton, 1998: 222-227).

Bolton carefully protects the students into roles, helping them absorb the atmosphere of puritan rigidity in terms of moral codes and standards. He prepares them step-by-step towards a central scene where, in chapel, the minister confronts all the families in the community and makes the charge that some young people have been seen dancing naked in the woods. Each young person has to come out and swear on the bible: 'My soul is pure'. Prior to this each had written 'guilty' or 'innocent' on a slip of paper and then shown it to one another, so they all know who has and has not danced naked, although others may well have been there as witnesses. The parti-cipants playing the parents had left the room while this happened so do not know who is 'guilty'. On the occasion when I took part, the atmosphere was electric. All the children swear that their souls are pure. The families are then instructed by the pastor to go to one of the many vestries in the church in order to interrogate the children and 'get them to confess'. In this final scene, the teacher has handed over the 'living through' role-play to the students and there is no teacher in role, although as Pastor, the teacher in role could still come and intervene if necessary. In the final scene back in the chapel the Minister invites confessions and, as in *The Crucible*, accusations can be made.

This sequence of scenes gives an intense experience of living under strict moral codes and the witch hunting this can provoke. It has the moment of swearing on the bible. In Bond's terms this is to alienate from within the site of the role and the play, producing what he calls 'accident time', when, as in the eye of a storm, time can seem to stand still and we can examine ourselves afresh. It is interesting that there is no direct search for learning, no overt didactic bent, but a deep involvement in the build up to a witch hunting situation. The students are very much like a Bond theatre audience in having to sort their experience with no guide from the author. This is very different from Brecht, who would have wanted to ensure that the audience knew what he wanted them to think. It is also a marked change from the early Bolton who was much more concerned with propositional knowledge (see Bolton 1978, 1998).

This sort of 'living through' drama is I think a point at which drama teachers could begin to search for how Bond's theory of theatre might enrich this already rich process. Bond's notion of site is present. The potential for accident time exists. The play's centre is clear and each activity builds the meta-text. Theatre event is present. The major area for innovation concerns how the imagination could be evoked to seek reason. He is centrally concerned with putting value into objects rather than characters. He would be searching for objects which could connect with the radical innocence remaining in us. This is why he tends to use cups, chairs, tables: everyday objects not already overloaded with ideology.

Heathcote left behind as a central concern the development of the art form of drama in education and concerned herself with pedagogy. Bolton and O'Neill continued from Heathcote's 'Man in a mess' phase and developed the art form, but Neelands has become a dominant influence on techniques that drama teachers can use and that this has led us into a dead-end. By using these conventions, drama teachers can appear to have a complete guide to drama teaching. They fail to realise that they have taken a Brechtian influenced route, and lack the facility to locate themselves either in relation to Stanislavsky or Brecht, let alone Bond.

To sum up, I maintain that Heathcote's invention of whole group drama involvement, where in-role engagement provides the opportunity for reflection while still being engaged existentially in the role, was a high point of the development of the theory and practice of DIE. Further, that this has much in common with Bond's approach to theatre. Bolton and O'Neill also pursued this whole group living through approach differently, but to great effect. I see Heathcote as making a turn in her work to more open pedagogic goals where her concern is to invent better ways of learning, rather than developing the art form. In making this turn she became wedded to 'distancing'. Neelands has been the writer on drama teaching who has followed this 'distancing' approach and what started out as conventions with quite a limited role have been developed into a whole approach to drama teaching, which seems to be much easier to assimilate and employ. The outcome of this approach can be seen in the EDEXCEL Drama syllabus. Consequently, I advocate a return to this 'Man in a mess' stage, but with a whole new exploration of the possibilities offered by Bond's approach to theatre. This would involve an exploration of the relevance of his theory of 'site', 'theatre events', 'cathexing of objects', 'alienation within the act', 'accident time', 'centre' and other dimensions of his work which are set out by Kate Katafiasz in chapter three. This is a whole new field of research for drama in education.

References

Barthes, R (1996) 'The Tasks of Brechtian Criticism (1956)' in Eagleton and Milne (Eds) *Marxist Literary Theory* Oxford, Blackwells

Bateson, G, Jackson, D, Hayley, J, and Weakland, J, (1956) 'Towards a Theory of Schizophrenia' in *Behavioral Science* 1

BBC (1993) – BBC Education Policy Unit Fieldwork Reports, Autumn 1993, English File: *Tuesday* by Edward Bond

British Broadcasting Corporation (2001) *John Tusa interview with Edward Bond*, Radio 3, broadcast 7 January 2001

Bolton, G (1978) *Towards a Theory of Drama in Education*, London, Longmans

Bolton, G (1998) *Acting in Classroom Drama*, Trentham Books in association with the University of Central England

Bolton, G. (2000) 'It's all theatre,' in *Drama Research: The Research Journal of National Drama*. London: National Drama Publications, Vol. 1, April. pp 21-29

Bond, E (1971) *Lear*, London, Methuen

Bond, E (1972) 'Drama and The Dialectics of Violence', *Theatre Quarterly* Vol II No.5 Jan – Mar.1972 pps 4-14

Bond, E (1978) 'A Note on Dramatic Method' in Bond, E *The Bundle*, London, Methuen

Bond, E (1980) 'Advice to Actors' – The Activists Papers, in *The Worlds*, with *The Activists Papers*, London, Eyre Methuen

Bond, E (1990) *Two Post-Modern Plays: Jackets and In the Company of Men*, London, Methuen

Bond, E (1991) 'The Culture of the Child', *Theatre and Education Journal* 4, pp 4-12

Bond, E (1991) *The War Plays*, London, Methuen

Bond, E (1993) *Tuesday*, London, Methuen

Bond, E (1993) 'The Dramatic Child', in Bond, E. (1993) *Tuesday*, London, Methuen

Bond, E (1994) 'The Importance of Belgrade TIE' in *SCYPT Journal* 27, pp 36-38

Bond, E (1994) *Edward Bond Letters Vol. 1*, (ed. Stuart, Ian), Amsterdam, Harwood Academic Publishers

Bond, E (1995) *Edward Bond Letters Vol. 11*, (ed. Stuart, Ian), Amsterdam, Harwood Academic Publishers

Bond, E (1995) 'Notes on Imagination' in Bond, E *Coffee*, London, Methuen

Bond, E (1996) *Edward Bond Letters III*, (ed. Stuart, Ian), Amsterdam, Harwood Academic

Bond, E (1996) 'Rough Notes on Theatre' in *SCYPT Journal* 31, pp 8-17

Bond, E (1997) *Eleven Vests*, London, Methuen

Bond E (1998) *Edward Bond Letters Vol. IV*, (ed. Stuart, Ian), Amsterdam, Harwood, 1998

Bond, E (1998) *Edward Bond, Plays:6*, Methuen Drama

Bond, Edward (1998) 'Commentary on The War Plays', in *Edward Bond, Plays:6*, Methuen Contemporary Dramatists, London, Methuen Drama

Bond, E (2000) *Selections from the Notebooks of Edward Bond, Volume One*, (Ed. Stuart, Ian), London, Methuen

Bond, E (2000) *The Children*, London, Methuen

Bond, E (2001) *Selections from the Notebooks of Edward Bond, Volume Two*, (Ed. Stuart, Ian), London, Methuen

Bond, E (2003) The Cap: Notes on Drama, the Self and Society in Edward Bond *Plays: 7*, London, Methuen

Brecht, B (1964) *Brecht on Theatre*, London, Methuen

Brecht, B (1983) *Mother Courage*, London, Methuen

Bryanston, Claudette (2001), 'The Children', in: *Drama Magazine*, Winter 2001, pp 29-35

Colvill, B (2004) 'Evoking Imagination to Seek Reason' in *The Journal for Drama in Education* 20:2 pp 33-41

Counsell, C (1996) *Signs of Performance: an introduction to twentieth century theatre*, London: Routledge

Derrida, J (1967) *On Grammatology*, Baltimore: John Hopkins University Press

Derrida, J (1988) 'Structure, sign and play in the discourse of the human sciences' in Lodge, D *Modern Criticism and Theory* (Second Edition), London, Longmans

DfES (2003) *Speaking, Listening, Learning: working with children in Key Stages 1 and 2* Ref: DfES 0627-2003 G, Qualifications and Curriculum Authority

EDEXCEL(2001) *GCSE Drama Specification Guide*, Issue 1

Eisenstein, S (1999) ' From Film Form: Beyond the Shot (the cinematographic principle and the ideogram)' in Braudy and Cohen (Eds) *Film Theory and Criticism* (Fifth Edition) Oxford: OUP

Finney, M (1996) 'Making Theatre for Knowing', in *SCYPT Journal* 31, pp 18-26

Fortier, M (1997) *Theory/ Theatre: an introduction* London, Routledge

Freud, S (1920) Beyond the Pleasure Principle in Freud, S. (1984*) On Metapsychology* (Vol 11 Penguin Freud Library), Harmondsworth, Penguin

Fromm, E (1991/1942) *The Fear of Freedom*, London, Routledge

Gillham, G (1994) 'The Value of Theatre in Education' in *SCYPT Journal* 27, pp 4-11

Gold, K (2000), 'Children Know the World is Violent and Vengeful'; interview with Bond in: *Times Educational Supplement* (Friday magazine), 18 February 2000, pp 8-10

Hawkes, T (1977) *Structuralism and Semiotics*, London: Routledge

Heathcote, D (1980) 'Signs and Portents' in *SCYPT Journal*, Spring

Heathcote, D (1980) 'Subject or System' in Johnson, L and O'Neill C (Eds) *Dorothy Heathcote: collected writings on education and drama*, Hutchinson, London

Heathcote, D and Hovda, R (1980) 'Drama as Context for Talking and Writing: The Ozymandias Saga at Broadwood Junior School. Newcastle upon Tyne' in *Drama as Context* NATE Publications

Heathcote, D and Fiala, O (1980) 'Preparing Teachers to Use Drama: The Caucasian Chalk Circle' in *Drama as Context* NATE Publications

Heathcote, D (1985), 'Dorothy Heathcote interviewed by David Davis', *Dance and Drama* (2D), Vol. 4, 3 Summer

Irmer, T (2003), 'Menschen müssen nicht destructiv sein', interview with Bond in: *Theater der Zeit*, February 2003, pp 57-8

Jarvis, J (1983) Janice Jarvis (in discussion with Roger Chamberlain) 'Acting in Theatre-in-Education', *SCYPT Journal*, Number 11 September 1983 pp 14-25

Lacey, S and Woolland, B (1992) 'Educational Drama and Radical Theatre Practice: drama-in-education as post-Brechtian modernism in practice' in *New Theatre Quarterly* Vol viii No.29

Leibniz, G W (1714) The Monadology translated by Robert Latta 1898 at http://eserver.org/philosophy/leibniz-monadology.txt

Lenin, V (1996) 'Leo Tolstoy and His Epoch (1911)' in Eagleton and Milne (Eds) *Marxist Literary Theory*, Oxford, Blackwells

Levi, P (1989) *The Drowned and the Saved*, Abacus

Levi, P (1996/1963) *If This is a Man*, Vintage

Marx, K. (1950/1888) 'Theses on Feurbach' in *Ludwig Feurbach and the End of Classical German Philosophy*, Foreign Language Publishing House, Moscow

Mead, G H (1932) *The Philosophy of the Present*, Chicago, Open Court

Muir, A (1996) *New Beginning: Knowledge and form in the drama of Bertolt Brecht and Dorothy Heathcote*, Trentham Books, University of Central England

Mulligan, J (1993) in Bond, E. *Tuesday*, London, Methuen

Neelands, J (1984) *Making Sense of Drama*, Heinemann Educational Books

Neelands, J (1990) *Stucturing Drama Work: A handbook of available forms in theatre and drama*, Cambridge University Press, Cambridge

Nicholson, Helen (2003), 'Acting, Creativity and Social Justice: Edward Bond's The Children', *Research in Drama Education*, Vol. 8, No.1, March 2003, pp 9-23

O'Neill, C (1995) *Drama Worlds: a framework for process drama*, Heinemann, New Hampshire

Shillingford, L (1994) An Explanation of the Self-Spectator Construct: Its Function in Drama in Education as Practised by Dorothy Heathcote, Unpublished MA thesis, University of Central England in Birmingham

Stuart, I (2000) 'Introduction' in *Selections from the Notebooks of Edward Bond, Vol. 1*, Stuart, I (Ed.) Methuen, London

Sutton-Smith, B (1988) 'In Search of Imagination', in Egan, K. and Nadaner, D. (eds.) 1988 *Imagination and Education*, Open University Press, Milton Keynes

Toller, E (1995) 'From Post-war German Drama 1928' in Drain, R (Ed.) *Twentieth Century Theatre: a sourcebook*, London: Routledge

Vygotsky, L (1976) 'The Role of Play in the Mental Development of the Child' in Bruner, J S *et al Play*, Harmondsworth, Penguin

Walker, S (1983) *Animal Thought*, Routledge and Keegan Paul, London

Notes

1 He has given keynotes at SCYPT (Standing Conference of Young People's Theatre) and NATD (National Association for the Teaching of Drama) annual conferences on a number of occasions. He has also written keynotes for NATD, which have been read to the conference on his behalf. He has had articles published in the respective journals of these two organisations, (Drama Broadsheet as it was then and *SCYPT Journal*). He was the first artist to support the founding of IDEA (The International Drama/Theatre and Education Association) and wrote a specially commissioned paper which I presented on his behalf at the founding Conference of this organisation in Porto, Portugal in 1992. I invited him to be Patron of the International Centre for Studies in Drama in Education at the University of Central England and he immediately accepted and played this role for many years until the Centre folded after I retired. His first paper as Patron was 'Notes on Imagination' (now printed to accompany his play 'Coffee'). He was an active supporter of the campaigns to save the destruction of TIE companies attending conferences in London and writing in the national press against this cultural barbarism.

2 I am using drama in education without capital letters to denote all types of drama that might take place in educational contexts. There is no one agreed approach or coherent theory of educational drama: I am therefore using it as an umbrella term.

3 Are they influenced by Stanislavsky or Brecht or neither? In fact sections C and D of the book seem to be more concerned with a sort of Brechtian distancing than with the immediate engagement of Stanislavsky. This has led some commentators to note this move to forms that instigate reflection and to see 'drama in education as post-Brechtian modernism', which is part of the title of an article by Lacey and Woolland, (1992).

4 I am aware that this going down on his knees and crying was artificially added by the director afterwards. He had picked up that this is what the boy wanted to do and so gave him the chance to do it. Because it is presented as part of the sequence and it is not pointed out anywhere that this was an insert, I am taking it at face value.

5 I am indebted in this section when referring to Heathcote to the penetrating study of Heathcote's work in Bolton's seminal book *Acting in Classroom Drama*. (Bolton, 1998) and have drawn heavily upon it here.

6 Although Heathcote is indicated as the main author, I suspect that Fiala drafted much of the paper so that it sometimes refers to Heathcote's work as though she were not the author.

7 What I find extremely interesting is that the drama experience described in the paper written with Fiala, that Heathcote sets up to serve as an analogy for the work they are doing on *The Caucasian Chalk Circle*, has the students in the event, not distanced! They are in role as monks protecting the body of St. Cuthbert, rather than in a role frame-distanced from the event.

8 Alistair Muir is another writer to have drawn attention to similarities between Heathcote's approach to drama and Brecht's. (Muir, 1996)

9 Latest in the sense of his life's work in drama. He always developed his teaching methods and the theory that was guiding it. His latest approach is explained in Bolton, 1998.

Appended letters by Edward Bond on the Tragic, the Comic, the Self, the Theatre Event, the Invisible Object and Brecht

'I do not hold a mirror up to nature but a spanner... to the universe – the human universe' (Letter to Graham Saunders, 7.11.04)

Introduction – [David Davis]

These letters by Edward Bond give recent accounts of the areas outlined in the heading to this section. Bond's letters are an extremely important source to provide access to his thinking. He writes each letter afresh in response to a wide range of international correspondents. In the letters (five volumes are published and a sixth is in preparation) one can follow a constant flow of development. There are certain basic ideas but it is not possible to reduce these to any fixed mantras or repeated formulas in his writing. He seems to be driven to seek fresh formulations every time he writes, thus he is constantly honing and developing his understanding of what needs to be addressed. He is closely fascinated by the areas that are thrown up as he writes his plays: areas that demand further exploration. Edward Bond's whole system of theatre is really based on his particular and original theory of the development of the human self. Several of the letters that follow deal with this issue. A short introduction to Bond's ideas on this subject might be useful.

It is foolhardy to try to reduce to a few words Bond's complex and thoroughly thought through approach to the concept of self. The basic ideas are simple but the consequences are far reaching. I offer in this short introduction an attempt to sketch a few pointers which might help to give readers an orientation to Edward Bond's account of the Tragic and the Comic. Bill Roper's chapter explores this area thoroughly and Bond most fully outlines his approach in 'The Reason for Theatre' in his *The Hidden Plot*. These notes are only an aid to readers who come to these letters early. Central to his exposition of how the self is formed is his notion of the Comic and the Tragic.

Bond's approach is radically different from that which might be anticipated from his perspective of the drive for a socialised/socialist humanity. It might be expected that he would see the human child entering a world that has a history, a culture and an ideology and immediately these social forces would start to structure the neonate. Such an approach would be essentially socio-historical constructionist. However, in an important sense, he makes a radical alteration to this approach and argues that although the human neonate is born with the genetic pre-disposition for socialisation, such as a brain that will be able to think, the capacity for emotion, language and social interaction, the neonate is active and creative in its very first stages. The neonate does not distinguish between its self and the world. It *is* the world. It would be wrong to say it *thinks* it is, because it does not think. Instead it has a body with feelings that can be grouped as pleasure and pain. It has a brain but no mind. No one can have its feelings for it. The baby responds to life enhancing forces such as warmth, comfort and food but is also instinctively aware of opposite forces. Thus the neonate is in its world *directly*, it connects with it without passing through the distorting opaque window of ideology. These early responses to pleasure and pain are transformed through the stage of the neonate when the pain and pleasure become the Tragic and the Comic. Then the child has a mind and enters the ideologised social world. Bond explains this process in greater detail in the Glossary entry the 'Tragic and the Comic'.

The significant thing is that the basis of the adult's humanity has been formed during the neonate period and later becomes socialised as the child enters the world of recognised meanings. For Bond this fundamental human drive to be at home in the world is an *a priori* necessity of the mind which can never be eradicated and becomes the striving for justice. In the child this is 'radical innocence' and it survives in the adult under all the contortions and corruptions created by surviving in unjust class society. It leads to the paradoxes which drama reveals. So humanness is not an essence or ideal or any form of transcendentalism: it is the expression of our materiality in the material world. As Bond put it: 'we are imprisoned in our need for justice'. He calls our working out of this relationship 'the logic of humanness'. In an important sense every teacher recognises that young children are closer to the uncorrupted stage of their development. I certainly found in each new generation of children new hope for humanity and the formal education system and ideology rapidly undermining it.

Imagination/value and reason are the unity of opposites that are articulated from this neonate existence.

The radical innocence becomes corrupted with the ideological social overlay, but never completely destroyed. Bond's plays seek to connect with and energise this radical innocence through the imagination which is impelled to seek reason. To some people his theory might have the appearance of an idealist Kantian formulation in which there is a mind born with the ability to structure the world. It is, in an important sense, the opposite of this. It is thoroughly and consistently materialist but is seeking to elaborate the dialectical in dialectical materialism, by insisting that the only hope for humanity lies in each human bringing back to life the way the mind 'naturally' begins to work: immediately able to engage with objective reality and to develop the active, searching, creative, value-laden struggle for a socialised/socialist humanity. These are some of the dimensions involved in his use of the Tragic and the Comic.

The first letter to Graham Saunders (7.11.04) deals with the logic of imagination, its origins in the neonate and its location in the Theatre Event. The letters to Cesar Villa and Jean-Pierre Vincent are concerned with the origins of the individual self, the Tragic and the Comic and how we can create our humanness through drama. The second letter to Graham Saunders (20.10.04) deals in particular with the Invisible Object (IO) and its relationship to the Theatre Event (TE). The letter to David Allen deals with Bond's relationship to Brecht's theatre and gives a particularly clear outline of his differences with Brecht's theatre practice.

Graham Saunders 7.11.04 (Extracts)

Dear Graham

I wrote you about Freud and Wittgenstein and Heidegger and certain others – how they were all involved in the basic human problem. In the 17th and 18th centuries it was how we know anything, how do we relate to the world. The shadow of God still fell across every page – and he was responsible for a certain basic humanness. You could say Hegel's 'Geist/spirit' is the ghost of God – performs his functions but lacks his presence. At the turn of the 19th/20th century – after Darwin and Marx – the problem is: what are we, what is a human being, how do we become humans. Freud and Wittgenstein both think in terms of cure – Heidegger is a mystagogue and actually says there is a need for a new saving God. (How can a God be new?) I take the basic problem and make the solution 'creativity and logic'. This isn't Hegel's Geist unrolling its own magic flying carpet. Or. to use an image I prefer, Hegel sees the human as being blind and guided by his all-seeing white stick. Marx turns Hegel on his head – but still leaves problems. This is why there are so many 'Marxisms'– and they are not different versions of science: their basic problem is what is a science? About the engine of history I am a Marxist fundamentalist: it is the contradictions between the forces of production and the relations of production. My particular concern is how the contradictions work through human beings and how human beings create their humanness or inhumanness in that process. I don't think socialism is a science – it is not reducible to natural interactions between its elements. It is a logic – and logic requires use: how will you use the logic? History is not a science because history is not made by scientists. But nor is it made by the blind – because the human problem presents itself in immediate situations. We stand between the horizon of the universe and the cup. We are not blind – we are *blindfolded* by ideology. The problem may be put simply: how do we let the blind see that they are blind? We cannot even say that individually reality makes us acknowledge its presence – it only does that (or has so far) collectively. Obviously humans always have a choice. At a certain time it might be: today shall I go to work in Auschwitz or the Kindergarten? Such choices are unavoidable – but how do we choose which is the *human* choice when there is no scientific yardstick? I find the answer in radical innocence, in the imperative to be human, in the Tragic and the Comic. There is the danger that this might be understood transcendentally, as Geist or elan vital or some other abstraction. And this is the most important point for me. I do not suppose that evolution 'intended' history or that animal biology 'intended' the human – all evolution would 'intend' is bigger dinners and more numerous relatives (and even that isn't 'intention'). It is simply that at some stage nature evolved a certain prescience: that humans were animals who looked at themselves. That is self-consciousness – and it comes only from the brain and its site. It is a formal, structural consequence of what is already there – not an intervention from God. If the monad is the world, in the sense that throughout its life the 'fish is the sea' (and would think so if it could think) and if the monad not only has feelings of pain and pleasure but knows it has (because its brain makes concepts in the sense that the fish makes bubbles) – then the neonate (the monad under another name) must make choices – that is, be responsible for itself – and it happens to be its world-self because as yet the monad has no windows on the world. So the human imperative is consequential – it does not need to be based on the transcendental or on some historically burgeoning knowledge of God. It is merely the sweat of granite in the storm – I put it in terms of pathos because self-consciousness becomes aware that the world is not its – or any animal's – home, that the universe is founded in mechanics and not justice. If this is so, then the human imperative is structured in the mind of the neonate and endures in the adult mind. You could say it's a cognitive structure the way Kant sees the objectivity of space and time having its origin in the mind and not in the thing-in-itself. But humanness can only be in-itself – it is the thing-in-itself which humanises (its relation to) creation – and not the other way round. But it can't do this arbitrarily: it cannot say 'it is good for humans not to drown and so we will change the nature of the sea'. Humanness must accept material reality as it is. How does it make it its home? – that is the logic of humanness – implicit in the situation, the natural site, and in the human mind, its early-found imperative. Because we are also pieces of the natural world. If you look at human history, it's as if the sea and the volcanoes were in mutual strife. Plutarch said the Greeks inflicted their greatest disasters on themselves – and so do all people, or at least they are the agents. Justice is created when the human imperative acknowledges the human imperative in everyone else. Then we can even accommodate the discommodities of our lives. Hegel thinks the process can take place at a distance – that history is rational though we are mad: that reason and history are Siamese twins. But humanness isn't rational – in the way even evolution is. There is no reason why we shouldn't choose to destroy ourselves – suicide and genocide are human contrivances. Oddly, only the human imperative is rational – in that it is indestructible – which is why revenge cannot administratively replace justice. In this sense justice – it sounds extravagant I know – is inherent in creativity which touches on the human (that is, not mere invention). But the imperative to be human is necessarily lost in the historical necessity to organise a relation to nature and to survive – the lie- truth of morality and politics. You don't have to invent drama as a means of breaking this 'bind'– because it is drama which creates the bind: the double need, to survive and be human – and yes, the need to be human creates the inhuman, the need for justice creates the mechanical law of revenge – structurally (but this might be erased by reason) and psychologically as a need – because it brings us into conflict with our own imperative: not as an innate response but because the imperative then comes into conflict with reason. But ideology can explain away even this – there are just more enemies about. How can you unpeel the layers of ideological obfuscation that destroy reason (the rational description of the world and the nature of our actions in it)? Not by appeal to reason. That is the whole problem – it's like asking the measuring tape to change its calibrations. When I say that imagination seeks reason, this is more or less equivalent to saying that the human imperative seeks reason – but can do this only through imagination, because only imagination can carry the original value attached to the imperative when the self-was-also-the-world. That is why creativity is really the self seeking to understand itself and act on the understanding – but the self is also the site in which it exists. Drama can create the extreme situations in which the self must define itself – then the imperative to be human is exposed to itself. It may not be practically possible in all instances – how can you talk humanness to Hitler? But collectively in societies it is possible – historically cultures can be sufficiently human when the truth discards the vehicle of its old lies. Then the human universe is in respite.

I seek for new ways to describe this – because it is like answering the question of common-sense: at what point on the circumference does the circle begin? If I don't know that how can I know where I am? – that is, know what I am? – know what to do or what I should do? – know anything to the purpose? – because I become my site (and this is true also non-ideologically, because I cannot escape the tensions of my site, the lie cannot escape the tensions of truth – how can you lie to the universe?). If we could tell that – if we could find God's footprint somewhere in the universe – ideology would not be possible. But we would not be human. It would certainly be: that God's footprint was in hell.

This is what the TE/IO is. I do not hold a mirror up to nature but a spanner up to the universe – the human universe. Nature is not the human universe. For that there is no mirror because we create the mirror – otherwise the blind cannot see. The mirror then becomes human reality – it is a matter of logic.

Best wishes

Cesar Villa 2.1.04 (Extracts)

Dear Cesar

You write much about reification. I agree with what you write. I concentrate more on ideology. Reification implies a loss of the self, a numbing of the self. This creates a gap – space – vacuum – into which ideology moves. But the denied self (for reasons of the structure of the psyche) generates its own ressentiment – or as I put it, revenge, vengefulness. Ideology then fuels this and it leads to reaction and in extreme situations to fascism. Before the extreme, fascism is incipient. But what is the self that is alienated? I've read your thesis once – quickly – and didn't quite grasp this.

What is the origin of the individual self? The answer would throw light on culture, politics, society and whatever other things are human. The answer would lead to the logic of humanness. But notoriously the answer is ideologically distorted or found through false assumptions (on the analogy that the earth is flat because it looks so). Is the mind (the site of self) comparable with the limbs in its *being*? The legs have to learn the way to walk (it requires the organisation of the whole body), and does the mind have to learn something in the same way? Obviously we – ourselves – learn.

But does the infant learn to walk – or to walk *to* somewhere? Lying on its back and kicking is a 'pure' form of 'walking'. It has an objective but no destination. It is not 'complete walking'– walking may be 'incomplete'. So what is a thought? Only a self can have a thought. Is there an early form of thinking analogous to lying on the back and kicking? No – thinking is absolutely the opposite. You cannot have a 'bit' of a thought – you think or you don't. The object of the thought is not relevant. The infant will not think out the intricacies of $E=mc2$. The first thoughts may be profounder than that. There must be a time when the brain (the mind) does not think. When does it first think? If there cannot be a 'bit' of a thought, it must think when it can think totally. Imagine a time when the brain does not think. Then to have a thought means that the brain is independent – it does something, it is a mind. This is different to having a feeling – then something is done to the mind. Only a self can have a thought. So there must be a pre-self which may be the site of a feeling but not of a thought. What will the neonate feel? – in sum, pleasure and pain. Not adult pleasure and pain because the neonate is synonymous with its world: it is its – the – world – and so the 'world' is in pain or pleasure (you see already the origins of human aspiration and responsibility). But the pre-self is sited in a neurological-brain. The brain will report pleasures and pains – and as these will form sequences and patterns the brain becomes a mind – perhaps it has time but no space, because there may be sequence without pattern. But the neurological-brain is equipped to acknowledge pattern – to designate structures to specific spaces, to distinguish somewhere from nothingness. The feelings of pleasure and pain then move their site from the body and feeling-brain to the mind. It is as if with one thought – the first thought – the mind crosses the universe in one stride. Pleasure and pain are 'values'– when pleasure and pain are 'thought' they become concepts – because they have changed their site from the body to the mind. That is the 'stride' across the universe. Only in humans does this happen. A concept is not a feeling – it is an 'idea' which interprets space-and-time, which interprets the world and so the neonate itself. In humans, feelings enter the self only through the gateway of concepts. Humans are ineluctably ideational, conceptual. This is what echoes throughout drama. This does not devalue feeling – it means that all our feelings are also conceptual. Potentially a concept has a name (the neonate does not yet name but does identify). The concepts are independent of memory and form their own inter-structures. The feelings of pleasure and pain become the concepts of the Comic and the Tragic: and this is the origin of the self – the first thought (which must be of an autonomous mind) instantiates the self as the Tragic and the Comic in a site (the self). Whatever has a name may also be said. Thereafter we cannot immerse ourselves in nature. This relates to what I call the self-names of objects. Of course the table (the name) cannot speak – that's anthropomorphism – but no object or natural thing can avoid our conceptualisation. This is part of the strength of metaphor – a language science avoids, because science can divide science from technology. In human action such a division – between knowledge and act, knowing and doing – is axiomatically impossible: and when it is even attempted it leads to reaction and finally to Auschwitz. Originally the SS intended Auschwitz to have an art gallery (did you know?) but although art necessarily has multi-valency and is multi-vectored (because we must be human without perfect knowledge and historically we have been unable to create – enact – our humanness without ideology) nevertheless art in the age of technological giantism cannot compensate, to the degree that would be needed, for reaction. In completed fascism art would become an animated mask set on the face of a corpse. Art is the concept of the imagination. The mind is ineluctably intellectual – and this includes, of course, imagination. Metaphor encloses grammar, it is not the other way round – but imagination needs grammar to enable metaphor. A name must speak – and the first names are the Tragic and the Comic. In naming the world the self names itself. This does not mean that there is a comic feeling and a tragic feeling. They are concepts which structure and envalue experience. Where would grammar come from if it did not come from language. . .? From the names of the Tragic and the Comic. The self – and its mind – are removed from nature because conceptualisation commits us to choice – but to remain human (respond to the human imperative which is formed, in the material process I have described, in the infant: the imperative to justice, the world-home) we have to choose the logic of humanness, or forever fall into discontent, the self-rancour which is revenge. So we are imprisoned in our freedom. It is the site of drama, the human story. In the past we have talked about human rights – we still have to learn why we must talk about the right to be human or we can no longer go on creating our humanness. The blind man did not expect his white stick to see – but whenever an ideology outlives its practicality for humanness, that is the sort of expectation a culture has. The anti-logic is always destructive because it withdraws us from the creation of humanness within its logic. As socially (and through ideology, psychologically) we may – and historically must – live in the lie-truth, ideology may compensate for our ideology – but only in the shorter term. The laundry of fascism is limited. This is why art is either fascist or socialist (to repeat the idea that disturbed your tutors) – it's a question of which direction is taken along the route of logic.

You quote someone as saying that the later child must learn individuality, and so acquire autonomy. The neonate's tripartite site – the Comic, the Tragic and the Self – is already a profound 'individuality' in that it is both uniquely individual and humanly universal. It is 'knowledge' of what being human is. It is this which marks human beings for life – divides them from objects and pre-human animals. This is the origin of the self. Of course to be human the infant must become a child and adult in society – but it can begin only from this origin.

Does the neonate avoid the Tragic and seek the Comic? We assume it does because after all even animals avoid pain and seek pleasure. But animals do not have a mind – and are never in that state where the mind *is* the world (only consciousness can be in that state, only a self) – and animals have no self. Does this mean that the neonate's body would avoid pain (remove its hand from a source of pain) but the mind would not? The neonate's mind could not say – in itself – your hand is on a source of pain – remove it. The hand is animal and will move. Its mind observes only the Tragic and the Comic. Later it will extend its conceptualisation of the world and in doing this *give the world a human meaning*. In the beginning the self is only in the theatre of the self, of the Tragic and the Comic in a site which is timeless and so eternal and spaceless and so infinite. Later the child gathers the actual world into these things and in order to be human – to have a self which is conscious of itself and so conceptual – it values – that is, is envaluated with – the Comic and the Tragic. Without these it cannot envaluate the world and make it the site of the human.

The neonate lives in what we would call the imaginary – it is its reality. But in its reality, our adult reality (in terms of what identifies us as human) is *enclosed*. It is not, as we assume, the other way round: what we assume is a flat-earthism. Later we extend – constantly recreate or desecrate – our humanness in the practical, material, social, economic world. What can be said of the neonate is this: it is its own world and seeks to be (to use adult language because the neonate has no language) 'at home in its world'– which means to achieve a relationship between the Tragic and the Comic. The relationship is not stable but creative – it is the creativity in which the neonate leaves the monad and enters the 'objective' world. Without the Tragic and the Comic the neonate cannot instantiate – be – itself: but already it is autonomous in its relation to these two concepts of its experience. It needs both – at this stage – because it cannot abolish part of itself: the Tragic and the Comic are in its world – to abolish the Tragic would be the most Tragic of acts: it would be as if the infant cut off its legs because they could only kick and not walk. But this question does not arise for the neonate – it is not involved in adult choice. It has – you can say – the freedom of drama, but drama can never lose its 'value', or if it does it becomes humanly meaning-less – a modern flatulence of the spirit. There is nothing transcendental about this. The human mind is the projection of the material brain – and the neonate is – in the creation of its self – equipped to enter the material world which the human species has created (just as evolutionarily/historically they evolved the human neonate). They have created their world not by following the naked laws of evolution (that is socio-biology) but by the logic of humanness. An age of science, which discovers more about natural evolution and material reality, tends to reduce humans to bits of nature, animals – but because social intercourse – politics, technologies and the economy – have removed us from being the objects of evolution – that on which time and space bring their natural pressures – we have made ourselves masters of evolution. We are bound up with freedom – but we are still slaves of our 'selves'– because we have not articulated the logic of our freedom. Only drama could articulate that logic – which, we must assume, will always change, will always implicate its regularities and necessities in changing ways, because our situation will always change, not least because we will change it. The elimination of this total 'drama' is reactionary. You quoted me as saying that art – which is a means by which the logic is expressed (or partly repressed, because we live in the lie-truth) – is either fascistic or socialist. I repeat this. As humans we are divided between our imagination and our reason – and imagination is the source of our humanness, reason is the means of implementing it but not creating it. This explains why art which designates itself as socialist may be reactionary. It explains the curious fascism which haunts the thought of Bernard Shaw. It's also – though coming from a different angle – why I say Brecht's theatre is the theatre of Auschwitz.

We create our humanness in history – the forms of humanness change but they must implement the logic of humanness. That is the process in which the neonate's need – its 'beingness' to be – at home in the world becomes the *need* for justice. The problem is that once the neonate leaves its monad – in which it is ineluctably and entirely committed to itself (and in that site that is coterminous with humanness) – it must create humanness in the indifferent universe and the inhuman world: because humanness is synonymous with justice – being at home in the world. Destructiveness cannot achieve creativity because revenge – unlike justice – can never be complete: it always invites counter-revenge. Oddly, as revenge comes from a distortion of the human need for justice, it is 'just' that revenge should be avenged... and this does not create the world home. So we live in contradictions. But we have to understand – if we are to hold onto our threatened humanness – threatened by our technology which now by its sheer mass tends to reintroduce 'nature' into the human world – that our contradictions are paradoxes because they involve human value. There are no contradictions in nature – and of course no paradoxes – only natural processes. An impractical species may be exterminated and the universe will not weep. An impractical (anti-social) human being should not be exterminated: Shaw is wrong wrong wrong wrong wrong. If you do this to individuals you will do it to races: modern technology makes death so convenient. Do not tread on the tail of Vengeance – it will turn and bite off your head. I am not a pacifist, we have a human obligation to defend ourselves against those who attempt to dehumanise us, who in practice *seek* – because the process becomes ideological – to reduce us to reified rubble. As a species we are condemned to seek justice, it is as if we were driven by the imperative. But the situation is difficult to read. All systems of morality are corrupt because their effect is to reconcile us to injustice – and as the effect is always justified by ideology, it is the unspoken *intention* of morality to reconcile us to injustice, to require us to live unjustly – and because of the contradiction *in the self* this leads to the paradox that crime (acts against morality and law) may be expressions of the human *need* for justice. From this trap there is no immediate escape: societies must organise themselves – and so must revolutionary armies. So? The contradiction is not just in our situation – if it were Shaw would be right and Brecht's theatre would be the path to Utopia – *the contradiction is also in ourselves.* We are driven by the need for justice, but ideology distorts this into the performance of injustice – and the ideologised mind is part of the ideology. Perhaps this was Marx's profoundest teaching. It should be written over the gate of every learning institution – it removes 'Know yourself' to another part of the site...

I try to create a drama which can meet this crisis head on – it's the only way it can be contacted. Drama activates the logic of humanness – because the logic is not passive, like the mathematical logic of the material world on the level at which we relate to that world in other ways. It is why drama is called drama. The Greek root of 'theatre' is in 'looking' (and related to miracle) – the Greek root of drama is related to doing. We should make a distinction between theatre (which simply uses a 'kit' of theatrical means and styles, or reduces itself to empty biological effects) and drama. All drama engages the logic of humanness: it is what is constant in the classics of drama. They do not give us answers but define the human questions. They are always created at times of change, when an old way of life, religion and morality break down. The cave-artists drew their pictures for us. The cave artist gives my humanness his picture, but my humanness does not take his spear. I'm not sure, for instance whether McGrath's fourteen points (which you quote) are more than appeals to reason.

My account of the origin of self and drama in the neonate might seem a 'romance'. Remember I analyse a situation in the mind that exists before the adult mind. A neonate thought may be in some respects unlike a later thought (its duration and so on) but the sum of its contents would have the same meaning and in the pristine mind would be starker and more foundational. A dramatist by practice enters into other minds in an intuitive and analytical way which science cannot measure or 'imagine'– and so then the concept may become 'blank'.

Best wishes

Jean-Pierre Vincent
Nanterre 13.10.04 (Extracts)

Dear Jean-Pierre,

This letter will be longer than I (and no doubt you) would wish. I need to make clear to directors such as you that my plays are not simply self- expression (an abhorrent idea) but seek to enact a human logic. I need to explain how and why this is so, and then my plays will not appear arbitrary. In doing this I stand on their heads most of the common terms used in drama – but then the present practice is different from that of the ages of great drama.

If I had my own theatre I could *show* things. As it is, I have to describe. Showing is easier, because showing is like many strata of lines appearing as one stratum – in showing you read not a line but a page in one coup d'oeil. I need to create a radical new theatre but one which has none of the flashy tricks – the reductive and reactionary effects – of most self-styled radical new theatre. I came to the sort of theatre I need by accident. I wrote about how I found the world – but then I saw that in production directors distorted what I wrote and often even reversed the meaning. This is easily done because ideology is the lie-truth and it is easy to pass from the truth to the lie, although they are in fact the opposite. They are worlds apart because the lie must change the meaning of *everything* – which is why Hitler said if you tell a lie it should be a big one. So I need to disentangle the truth from the lie. But if our existence – our being – our consciousness – is given to us (in culture) by the lie-truth – then disentanglement is an act of creation. It is not arbitrary or merely aesthetic – it is logical. The role of imagination is to express – serve – this logic. It does it in two ways. It allows an area of random freedom: if you want to find something you don't look at it (because you don't know where it is) you look 'round'. So imagination is speculative – but always it is a looking *for* something. The something fits into the practical structures of our life. If reason (except formally) can be entangled in lies, then imagination is necessary to rational thought – it enables us to escape from the formality to find, see, the meaning. And that relates to the second function of imagination: it is the site of value. This is the basic problem of modern thought. It was the basic problem of Hegel, Marx, Freud, Nietsche, Kirkegaard, Wittgenstein, Heidegger – and the rest. And inevitably it is the problem of drama: because drama concerns our 'being'. That is why we have to understand drama as a source of human logic – which necessarily tends to be entangled in the cultural lie. Only humans can lie, and it makes us human – because it means we may also distinguish truth. (Animals may fake but cannot pretend, because they have no conscious self to pretend with.) The only other thing you need to know is: the source of humanness – why, for instance, we don't just gas all our enemies or run over those we disagree with – or if we eat our own kind then it is not usually a crime of hunger but out of our awe of the universe... Since there is no Creator, humanness must be a mere consequence – the universe has no telos. The human mind has self-consciousness – and therefore self-regard. But it has this initially before it knows it is in a world: it thinks it is the world. This is what I say about the neonate – and Freud says much the same. But he draws the opposite conclusion. He sees consciousness as a leaky ship bobbing about on a dangerous ocean of drives and passions. I think that once the 'concept' enters the mind everything else is changed – because then everything has a meaning. The great, cardinal, first instances of concepts are the turning of pleasure and pain into the Tragic and the Comic – and this is an event simultaneous with the creation of the 'self'. So that then dramatisation is at the base of the human self, is imposed not by animal drives but by meaning. This would mean – if mentation had no source of energy itself (and it is not clear that that would differ from meaning) – that the energy which would be possessed by drives and passions (as Freud sees it) would also be the energy of thinking (otherwise the lame man's stick is using the legs so that it can walk) – that even on this level a distinction could not be made between imagination and thought. I must cut corners, or I shall write a book for you... The significant point is that the child begins in the widest possible theatre of being: the ontological – and then enters the domestic, existential, social and so on. Yet it's almost universally assumed it's the other way round. But the child brings into its growing knowledge of the world it's determinates of value – the ontological, the Tragic and the Comic. It brings them, is not taught them. Ideology – and practical activity – only teaches an interpretation. Perhaps it's like Chomsky's language module that pre-exists any particular language, and so the child's existential need for justice precedes any ideological definition of justice. (See how mechanically, almost, Aristotle deals with justice in his *Politics* – as if the mind needed to reduce the mental to the physical quantity in order to get some grip on it that will justify his historical need for slavery – and this, to us, 'lie' must ramify through his whole political structure. It's as if in Greece the people created democracy *against* the philosophers.) There is not a 'justice' module – it is the axiomatic, functional imperative of self-consciousness: which needs a world in which it can be conscious without danger and therefore a world which does not threaten it – and so history is the arbitration between threat and freedom. I think you could also say something more: that consciousness in its involvement with justice is not reducible to Hobbesian pragmatics – but is also consciousness of the human dignity involved in justice. And this is of great significance for all matters of 'art'– that art balances the human world. In that, we see the universe as a mirror of ourselves – not in images of the ideological transcendental (religion, patriotism and so forth) but of our materiality, vulnerability, limitation – and strength and vision. None of this can consistently be reduced to irony or cynicism. But it is also why the lie is so fatally close to the truth. The logic of humanness is easily understood: it is to make practical the neonatal need for a world home, to reduce danger and increase freedom.

The human self will sacrifice much to support the dignity of this. Of course – since we do not live in the radical ontology of infancy – to need freedom is dangerous: because societies are dangerous structures of danger intended to protect violence. The seeking of justice becomes a threat to the monopoly of danger. If reason usurps, on Freud's model, the 'energy' of the irrational – this cannot be only in order to repress itself, as Freud seems to think, because it must do so for a meaning, a purpose, other than fear – for a concept: and Freud does not explain this singularity. He deals with it by darkening the problem: he invents a death-instinct (thanatos) to oppose the pleasure principle (as the motive of action). But a death-instinct requires no concept – and so again he dodges out of the human, conceptual mind. Clearly that conceptual mind can only negotiate itself through mediations of the Tragic and the Comic (not the painful and pleasurable) because the concept is inscribed in the physical: they are the two sides of the one sheet of paper – and I cannot 'read' the front of the page without reading the back.

You can understand the situation as it's seen by Descartes and Kant (given the extent to which they could openly express themselves: but both *did* produce a philosophy intended to explain the recognised problem). Descartes sees the body as mechanical, a machine – and the mind as transcendental, resident in the hall of God. Kant interiorised the transcendental: the mind created the world by its means of assessing it – and what the world was out there was the thing-in-itself which the mind could not know. Kant's great contention is human freedom – he wants to make us responsible for our humanity. (He turns God out of doors, but Hegel (dismayingly) enables him to rent rooms in the Spirit.) But suppose this: that the structures in the mind 'distort' reality in the way they would if they were ideologised, then the real world out there would be a thing-in-itself and our interpretation of it would be distorted – all our acts of truth, our perceptions of truth, would be distorted by the lie. People born deaf and blind have a particular problem: they do not know there is an 'out there'– they might live in perpetual neonatality. They would be sealed in the lie. But one day they realise not just that there *is* something beyond them – but that it has a meaning and purpose, which it derives from a practical reality. That realisation must be – to them – like the original lightning-flash of inspiration. Their problem is basically physical – but our ideological problem is deeper. Because the thing-in-itself must appear to the mind to be distorted: it's as if we kept trying to shape water with a hammer and chisel. And it is only the danger of this which makes us change – finally – our 'seeing' of the world – that is, our 'being', because we are what we mean. And we have one advantage over the deaf and blind – we see ourself imaged in the world, its physicality a memento of our own, and that physicality is a memento of our consciousness – and so, by this route too, we come to the dignity of justice (a dignity created through observation of the natural combined with the imperative for justice: the world home *would* be a pleasant place). But this only adds to the desire, it does not mediate the meaning – the balance between danger and freedom. And so it is clear: if the thing-in-itself is to change – if the world is to change for us as the object we use – then the mind that creates it must change because we are dealing with ideology, not Kant's innate perceptives. But physical danger – which we inherit from the pre-conceptual animal mind – simply says 'hit' or 'duck'– but what would 'danger' be to the concept, to the conceptual mind? Again 'hit' or 'duck'– unless it has the concept of the Tragic – which, I think, is (my own addition) also the self's concept of itself: because the Tragic and the Comic are conceived in the same instance as the self. Sooner or later the mind must change if we are to live in the world differently and to share it differently. But still: why not just kill your enemies – as ideology tends to recommend or even insist – and as practical circumstances often dictate, because after all practical reality is bound to imitate us sometimes? We can impose our meaning on reality: as for example when we turn petrol into fuel – and all that follows industrially and economically. You don't change the world *just* by changing the mind, or vice versa – it is like asking which end of a link in the chain holds the chain together. It isn't just a matter of 'seeing' the world but 'being' in it. Kant was criticised by idealism for the thing-in-itself – but if we understand this as an ideological screening then for us it is a vital political truth. If socialism brushes the problem aside – as political theatre seems always to want to do – then it cannot be resolved, the mind cannot be freed to implement justice – to rearticulate the balance of danger and freedom. Clearly it requires a change in the mind that understands – and not just a change in knowledge ('I teach you this') but a change in the self, which is the means of acquiring knowledge. There is, however, no therapy for consciousness – it must articulate its own freedom. Marx: the ideologised mind is part of the ideology. Euripides: you cannot teach reason to the mad. You can put the socially mad in prison or pay them more or elect them to high office, you can drug the medically mad. Immiseration might bring enlightenment – but it hasn't, because capitalism is too subtle, protean and prolix to die when it should – perhaps the immiserable are already on a rope round their neck but they are not yet strangled by it because the rope stretches right round the world and the torsion is not yet felt and we cannot wait till it is. And anyway, there is the matter of the human dignity of justice – it is (and this is not idealism but structural in the mind for the reason I've given) part of the human imperative, that we are in *this* world, which is (that is, should be) pleasing to us, and not some other.

Each new age of drama has its own logic – the Greeks, the Jacobins, and others, create a logic which rebalances danger and freedom: the blind see another reality and the dumb speak it. It is a relationship between the self and its world. But for that to happen – since physical, animal danger is not enough – and the consciousness of the danger to humanness is needed, that justice should 'speak' its need – then the mind must be put into a different danger – in which perhaps danger itself becomes a human assertiveness, within tragedy – and that is the danger itself of the Tragic: in which paradoxically Shakespeare and the Greeks found freedom. In tragedy it is not the body that suffers

– that is a symptom of the tragic – but the concept of the human self, and all that belongs to it in justice and the human imperative. The tragic events assault the logic of humanness in the individual protagonists. Tragedy throws the indifference of the universe in our face, and only the self's concept of the Tragic, steeped in practice from the beginning of the self, can receive the assault and restore the self's humanness. Otherwise there is nihilism, the absurd or the most debasing and reactionary forms of transcendentalism. The universe is a trap until we make our human universe. Humanness cannot be taught, it can only be created – drama is its means. No revolution can be without its flag – and for the same reason, none can be without its appropriate stage. If we read the twentieth century we find this.

It should be that all who served in the death camps learnt their humanity from their service. They did not – nor have all those who have since witnessed it. I don't delude myself that drama can always have a bird's-eye view of our situation. But drama can confront the extremity in which the mind creates itself: the threefold Tragic, Comic and Self – and in that make it responsible for itself. To work in Auschwitz you must abandon responsibility to violence or authority. Tragedy is the confrontation with extremity – not of the physical sort, for that you watch football or fright-films or go mountaineering. Drama must create Tragic danger, the danger to the concept which is the self, so that we are confronted with responsibility for ourself – and because imagination is material this may give fiction a creative advantage over reality. Or, we are all animals after all and we can hand the problem over to brutality to solve and thus make death fun – or to the linearity of therapy or to the transcendentalism of God, and these latter two always resort to brutality even before the end. We need a Clausewitz of therapy to demythologise it and make it practical. This is my case against the thinkers I mentioned above. In particular I apply it to Brecht because he is a dramatist, and to Aristotle because he is Brecht's de facto apologeticist. To understand Aristotle on Tragedy you need only read his *Politics* and *Poetics* together. The former is the – O so nice! – Bible of the death camps, and that leaves Brecht stranded.

If I could sum this up. I am a materialist but that does not mean reducing materialism to the mechanics of matter. Matter does not say 'I am a materialist'. The *material* problem between mind and matter is that mind and matter do not behave like two bits of matter. If water meets a mountain it will run down hill. If water meets the mind, the mind may make the water run up hill. So soldiers march to their death in an alien cause. Not in the long term – but how long is the term? The problem is severe because the lie always has a lot of truth on its side. It is disentangled only by the logic of humanness – evaluative-and-practical – so it is always as if the scissors had to cut themselves. The self does not exist for the self – it is a relation to the world as much as the foot is. And it is because of this material relationship that the imagination is logical. Vulgar materialism is just inverted transcendentalism. For the structural and not idealist reasons I've given, the self bears the imperative to be human and carries it into the world. The imperative is inescapable, but it may either create our humanness or physically or culturally destroy us. This is the meaning of freedom: we are responsible for our future. The world does not exist abstractly – the thing in itself is our relationship to the world, poised at a moment in history – just as say our eyes are poised at a level of space. The daily eye does not need to see the atoms in the table. It follows that in nature we partly create the thing in itself (petrol is not fuel till we create engines) and we always create its cathected value, its human-cultural meaning. That is why I objectify drama, working through objects – not for some sort of aesthetic or symbolic or contemplative-spiritual reason, but because objects are the language in which lies are told, often even as they are used. Drama is the means by which the mind – as a Kantian designator – recreates itself to bring itself closer to the world and the impact we have on the world. The logic of imagination and reality meet in the logic of humanness. Enter the drama of the extreme. And the question for drama is: how do the scissors cut themselves? That is why I am so careful about stage objects, because all objects on the stage must affect the matrix of cathexies.

That might sound complicated but it reduces to a simple theatrical practice. And a direct concentration on the actor – on the invisible object. That probably traces the trajectory from the ontological to the existential-particular. It is why object-ifying has to replace the traditional way of telling 'story'– there is no over-covering meaning beyond the imperatives of justice and humanness – abstractions till they are made concrete: the story cannot make them concrete, they make the story concrete.

Best wishes

Graham Saunders 20.10.04

Dear Graham

One thing to beware is that TEs can't stand on their own. They arise out of the present fracture of the story and the remoteness of myth. I've reread Freud's *Civilization and its Discontents*. I was struck by how of much of what he says is in line with what I say about the basis of humanness in the neonate – but he then extends it (or I think reduces it) into conservative conventional thinking and draws opposite conclusions. In his time he shocked because of his openness about sexuality – but really he is conservative and says what every Victorian nanny 'knew'. I was always confused about his theory of Thanatos. I couldn't quite see why he needed such an extravagant account of the blind searching for their graves (I parody it in the 'Hitler's speech in *Early Morning*). Rereading *Civilization and its Discontents* I suddenly saw that it's because he has no theory of Tragedy. It's why he insists that his account of a primal patricide is a real, historical, calendar event – and not an event in the reality of imagination (the reality of the imagination means that without necessarily directly duplicating factual reality, whatever happens in the reality of imagination has objective, factual consequences). Because Freud has no theory of Tragedy he has no theory of creativity – he is a therapist: and as in dealing with the mind he is dealing with imagination, therapy means – apart from helpfully relieving tensions, possibly – trying to teach a disease to be better. Jung saw the lack of creativity and the limitations of medical therapy – tried to hypostasise imagination into a mystical reality, but this is not creativity. Mysticism may create God in imagination but it cannot create God in objective reality, only a church and its living and material appurtenances – and the evolved function of imagination is, in order to meet the conceptual imperative of our mind, always over time to bring us closer to natural reality and to create a human reality (as a new part of the natural reality) which enables us to live beneficiently with one another. That is why there is a logic of imagination – which I think is recognisable when enacted. There can be no humanness without the creativity of the Tragic – and no Utopia without it. I think this is philosophically true – but it is even, so to say, truer in practice because without the individual perception of the Tragic, societies will always, under urgent practical pressure, resort in desperation to force and therapy. Neither social engineering nor Tragedy can replace each other without dehumanising themselves. Rereading Freud reminded me how I am involved in a basic disagreement with much of what is the foundation of modern cultural consciousness: Freud, Nietzsche, Wittgenstein, Hegel, Marxism reduced to mechanical-materialism – modern drama is deeply involved in the problems of such thinkers: because drama is about people in society and it has to deal with the subjectivity of people because that is the way they experience themselves as being in society and is the way they are in drama (it's drama's purpose). Brecht wanted to do what Wittgenstein wanted to do: create a therapy of language as a therapy of ideas. Their politics were opposites – so their differences lie in their understanding of what people are, in the human and inhuman. In practice Brecht refuses to confront the human subject.

The logic of humanness is what recreates our situation to bring it closer to common justice – to the world home. The logic of imagination is what brings us closer to this situation. But imagination is always 'embodied', if at first only in the mind – it issues in its own appearance, it displays itself and in this is always an action even if in recoil. So that imagination is the practical need for justice (Utopia is the house of justice) – if there is no need for justice but only an animal need for survival, then imagination may be as destructive as it is creative. But there is a pathology of imagination: in which (for reasons I've explained at length) the need for justice may become the desire for revenge. But the pathology is part of creativity because it is social (in the form of violence, hate and so on) – 'no man is an island' and so in this sense I am involved in every one's crime – humanness cannot be left to the arbitration of legality, all moral codes are corrupt because they are (historically neces- sarily) based on injustice. I do not see any truth in the concept of a golden past which was then sub- sequently corrupted – because at no earlier time did humanness exist, it is not biological – human- ness is (being) created. The need to be human – to know the world home – is the birth situation of the neonate as it enters consciousness. It would express this need not merely in the mind but in the body which is the envelope of the mind. We read this in miniscule – the child wants a drink or changing. But for the child there is no miniscule – it is always in the full theatre of humanness. Religion vulgarises this in miracles: the rock pours milk for the thirsty. But it does at least see this as a world-relation. Humanness is totality and the totality appears also in the immediate. This is the source of the Invisible Object. The Invisible Object shows the self in relation to the world *across the gap, the no man's land, which is the site of justice*. I allow myself to put it in this elaborate way, which I would not normally do if I hoped to be understood: but in drama all analysis is finally tactile, physical. I mean that in humans there is a functioning *need* for justice – just as there is a need for, say, sex (or an ideologised substitute for it) in the mind and the body. A TE may be pro- duced simply by rejuxtaposing objects. They would then speak to our human need for justice. I think it's useful to reserve the IO (Invisible Object) for people – the face, gesture, voice, stillness – any use of the self – which is a TE in that it enacts a TE and is in itself the equivalent of a TE. It comes from the repertoire of humanness and its distortions. The distortions contain the undistorted that is being distorted – even if only by implication. But I think the IO is subtler than implication – that if needed it embodies the distorting of the undistorted. This is probably quite close to our biology – you can weep with pleasure or pain, cry in ecstasy or despair or anger, whisper in malice or love and so on. (The difference is between legality and drama. Legality orders but does not create humanness. So a crime must also be a search for justice – psychologically, and also structurally in unjust society – it works on both levels. 'But Edward I need the police to protect me on the streets' – that is the difference between drama and the street, but drama is also as much a reality as the street and that means it is corrupting when there are so many detectives on TV – they are really policing the viewer's mind. But more importantly, if imagination seeks reason – then reason must also be expressible in imagination, and imagination is (as I said above) expressible in the physical. Hence the completeness of art, which is not reducible to 'emotion'. So the intellectual appears in the enactment of imagination, is embodied in it. I think Spinoza's intellectual love of God is formally analogous to this: the IO is the intellectualisation of imagination, reason expressible only in imagination. There is of course no plan of Utopia, but the IO is a plan of the need for Utopia in that it is enacted outside Utopia – which to be Utopian must be a place even free from the need for defence. Its own internal processes defend it from its self. The TE may be closer to a directorial device – the director chooses to show something. Imagine a soldier's coffin being carried for burial. It is draped with a national flag. As the coffin is carried by a thorn tree, the thorns snag the flag and drag it from the coffin – and then many varied things may happen to the flag and round the event (different reactions of spectators and so on). In itself this is a director's TE. But my plays are also crammed with the sites of IOs – how does the actor enact the TE, or – say – convert an 'ordinary' (there is no such thing) action into a TE? That's why we need a different sort of acting. 1 first thought of the TE because I found that critics would say this means X when I meant it to mean Y – they would recoup an action back into an existing ideology. But the TE also meant disturbing the ideology of the actor – I remember asking an actress to play parts of a tragic scene farcically and she said but this character has a soul – and I said that's why she's farcical – and she said 'Oh well if you want me to ruin your beautiful scene. . .'But this means that interpretations fall into the categories prescribed by ideology. The IO may open up whole new worlds of interpretation – and I say 'worlds' because human beings are saturated with the universe. You could probably describe much of Brecht as TE – but he rejects the IO. It's only clowns like Piscator who actually destroy the IO.

I think the IO is missing from contemporary drama. You describe a play called *Bloody Mess* which is the deliberate staging of chaos – everything-and-nothing happens at once. I want to cry 'stop it' when I turn on the radio to listen to the news, turn on the TV, often when I go into a school, see people being 'entertained' and so on. I don't need theatre for that. A hundred years ago it was useful to draw a moustache on the Mona Lisa because academicism was replacing vision and understanding with skill. Now the moustache is drawn on nothingness and we have to draw the face round it, the logically human face for our time – and I think that is the TE/IO. We have to enact our imagination so that we can see ourselves and know ourselves and become ourselves. At the end of the play, Hedda Gabler, before she shoots herself, plays the piano. Why does she play the piano before she shoots herself? Is it the suicide 'note(s)'? Does she play the piano so that she may hear it – or for the unwitting people outside the room to hear it? – or directly, on the author's behalf, for the audience to hear it? Is it a TE – is the expression ('wild dance music') an IO? How is the music a protest which the shot isn't – what does it add? I think the whole problem of modern drama can be found in this moment of music or rather of playing. Oddly, in Greek drama perhaps the IO replaced the TE. This is because of the huge sociability of the event – the audience displaying itself to itself and being a large part of the city and processing together after the plays. The actors were hierarchic – masked, costumed, Gods arrive in a machine and so on – and the music was not intended to subvert the action but was expressive of it in a way we can't understand – when Oedipus leaves the house after blinding himself he both speaks and sings. Perhaps modernist music tried to enter this no man's land with '*sprechgesang*'. It's as if the Greek's categories had a unity they cannot and must not have for us. The lack in performance art is that it tries to imitate categories without concepts, and this is the pathology of the imagination. I think placing TE and IO in the drama site (which must not be either decoration or symbolic – if the latter it becomes the static imagination instead of being the site of the active imagination) is the only way drama now has of placing the audience back into society.

I should add one thing – not for the sake of any completeness but to close at least one gap. Each actor has his or her way of discovering and enacting the IO. It is the individual way of enacting the common human need. Whether this is what would normally be understood as character is debatable. But the IO requires total involvement of the self – it is the extreme situation. In the extremity the generality may be read. In fact Brechtian abstraction is not possible – because by eliminating it would simply heighten – purify if you like – the residue. So that only the actor can find his or her IO though the site of the IO is objective and not subjective. This bridges the gap between the subjective and the objective. It's what I called 'trusting drama again'. This isn't reversal to some primitive 'Ur' dramatic presence because the situation is always historical and always changing. But you have to explain why the cave dwellers' art is still art – that is, why the cave artist paints 'for me'. The most a writer or director can do is indicate the site of the IO, draw on its logic.

Best wishes.

To David Allen 6.9.04 (Extracts)

Dear David

About Brecht and reason/imagination. You quote from me: 'Brecht's alienation is based on the idea that you isolate reason and appeal to it: that is if you alienate a thing it can be seen as what it rationally is. This is like asking a blind person to open their eyes wider'. You also quote from Brecht, in his 'Short list of the most frequent, common and boring misconceptions about the epic theatre' among which he includes the notion that epic theatre is against all emotions. He says 'reason and emotion can't be divided'. Elsewhere he wrote: 'It becomes (sic) clear to me that the antagonistic configuration 'reason in this corner – emotion in that' has to go. The relationship of ratio and emotio, with all its contradictions, has to be examined minutely, and opponents cannot be allowed simply to present epic theatre as rational and counter-emotional'. But the Brecht quote refers to epic theatre, mine to alienation. I do not claim that epic theatre is unemotional, on the contrary I have always insisted it's highly emotional – what else would you expect of musicals? I think the emotion of epic theatre is a way of compensating for what the *Verfremdungseffekt* lacks. Brecht was aware that he had created a problem. I don't think he could solve it – which explains his irritated tone and his use of 'boring'. He had a seventeenth century understanding of the human mind, though not of its relation to the material world. But because of the nature of the first understanding he couldn't understand the second. He is right in identifying this problem – which I think is decisive. But he is dangerously wrong in his concept of alienation. He wants to avoid the excess of conventional, Schillerian, idealist emotion (which later degenerates from idealism into the socio-biology of the 'method') and to substitute a different emotional involvement (in the epic). He saw reason as having a human value in *itself*. That there could be a behaviour that was reasonable because it was rational – that the rational penetrated totally not just into the structure of things but also into the meaning of being. It isn't so, because the paradox doesn't allow it to be. If it did there would be no problem. And it's not enough to say there is an emotion, a 'feeling', which will supplement the inadequacy of the rational – of Courage's 'silent' scream or her 'silent' mourning over her dead daughter (which can't be isolated in a gestus, for interesting reasons). The received idea is that reason and imagination are on the same plane, not least because reason can sometimes amend the irrationality of the imagined – you can see that the madman's tea cosy is in fact not a crown. But you can't show him this, re-enact the tea cosy. And ideology is a form of madness. I call it social-madness. But it is a bit more complicated because in all matters of consequence in history, humans have the truth only at the cost of lies: the lie-truth. Most of nature, the universe – and indeed ourselves – is hidden from us. Yet we are existentially holistic. We do not understand our situation and we have to create a functioning and creative reality to live in. You cannot permanently find freedom within the lie, because ultimately it does not equate with the objective reality about us. The material world always tugs at the coat sleeve of imagination: or, to put it another way, tyranny inhabits graveyards. You have to distinguish between calculating, functional reason and human reason. You can't say the former is 'of the world' and the latter not – because human beings are part of the natural world. But human reason does not lie on *this* side of imagination: to get to human reason you must pass through the imagination – and doing that involves the logic of humanness, which cannot be reduced to reason. Just as you may give a scientific description of a cube but you will not have made a cube and it would be possible that no cube existed.

That's why I write of the infant's conception of Tragic and Comic. They are not emotions. In the infant they are *feelings* which are then conceptualised in ways which are forms of action. The infant is physically incapable of action, and so the action is structured into its concept. The infant cannot adjust its pillow but it can create a universe (if it didn't it would have nowhere to be). After this we cannot act as animals. Socio-biology is a travesty of what we are. It's difficult for adults to 'leap into the concept' because they live in barriers of ideology and economic necessity. Really, it's risible to teach the young pioneer that it's his duty to die. How can that be taught? You must leap into the concept before you can leap into the abyss. What Brecht does is open to terrifying abuse. (Compare the way the problem is dealt with in *Jackets*.)

Drama doesn't teach – only theatre does that, and sometimes usefully, but it is also an instrument of ideology. The human problem is always paradoxical – it is not more-or-less of something, but more of one-or-the-other. Humanness only exists in these choices – it isn't some essence or even capacity we have. Brecht writes tragedies but won't allow the Tragic. I talk of the Tragic and the Comic to get beyond emotion, because emotion may certainly be corrupted (and I think Brecht corrupts it). Without the initial instantiation of the Tragic and Comic we wouldn't be human. And later to discount them dehumanises us. The consequences are corrupt action and psychological petrification. But it isn't a matter of a sort of psychological housekeeping, using reason to sweep away emotional clutter (or vice versa). They are not 'in separate corners'. And it isn't a question of 'ratio' in a strict sense – that would be an extraordinarily complicated question which Brecht can't just leave to one side. It would lead to a version of the logical 'third man'. Who is to decide the ratio? – and immediately the whole problem falls wide apart – and you end by positing some objective third person who is to judge (in the end that's always authority – ideology or common sense in one or another form). So you have to have a different, non-mechanical understanding of mind. I try to suggest what that is. I think our understanding of mind is clumsy – part inherited from ideology-theology and part from reducing the mind to bits and pieces of brain. It accounts for the fatuous transcendental optimism of the sects – and for cultural, materialist pessimism. Often I describe parts of the process in contraries: for instance I say that accident time slows circumspection – but that the imagination must leap. It isn't a matter of calculus. We create our humanness in the dramatic extreme, we don't take our humanness with us into the crisis. Humanness cannot be reduced to the Tragic and the Comic. The imagination instantiates itself when it makes concepts of the Tragic and the Comic. So the imagination is conceptual. In the neonate-monad it cannot rationally relate the Tragic and the Comic (which are now part of it as the calibrations are part of a ruler – the ruler must measure its own length). Probably Blake is anticipating some of this with 'the tear is an intellectual thing'. Both imagination and reason must be in the process of choice (for a moment equate this with the *Verfremdungseffekt*) otherwise there is no 'self' in the choice – and that is the danger. There is no self-responsibility. So the imagination (as the site of humanness's conception) is needed to identify the Tragic and the Comic in material reality. In the neonate it could identify them only with the monad. This gives not just the isolated moment but the site, that which gives objective meaning. This sounds complicated – but by presentation drama may make it simple. Brecht's difficulty is that he recognises the problem but his understanding of mind is materialistic in a reductive way. So he understands neither the self nor the site. You know that he said quite late in the thirties (when he was working on *Round Heads and Pointed Heads*) that you shouldn't over-worry about Hitler because once his financers had used him they would drop him. In fact I would have thought that was more worrying: what would they replace him with, Super- Hitler? It shows a misunderstanding of what people are and of how their minds work.

I think that generally my aims are those of Brecht's. I try to analyse the human process because I don't think it can be reduced to any other process. I think it is material. Materialism is any system which is complete in itself – so there can be only one. There is no outside, transcendental intervention. We make our own process by use. Humanness is perhaps difficult to grasp because it contains a value which does not occur elsewhere in the system – but it is part of the system and relates to the system by its particularity. The relationship is logical: the process produces the values and forms of consciousness that follow from choices made in the system. The logic is determined but not the choices. This makes drama not an elucidation of philosophy but puts it at the heart of philosophy – the creation of human reality. The explanation – analysis – I give of the process is not drama but a guide to drama. I think that it's only in the extreme that evasions are erased. People historically have created their humanness within their ignorance. This means that truth has been 'protected' or facilitated by lies. We have to bring the human imperative – the concept, self consciousness and the Tragic and Comic – closer to a description, reflection and *counterpart* of objective reality. That is the object of drama. But the peculiarity is that the self is implicated in the reality it describes (etc) – the self cannot be transcendental to itself. It leads to Hegel's non-solution of *Geist* and *Aufhebungen*, which is really a mechanical system masquerading as a mental system. But drama is very immediate and concrete. In the end it is our only freedom – and I think we have to understand ourselves as the self- dramatising, self-creating species on site and not in environment. That's why your work and the work of members of NATD is vital. The post-modern understanding of 'aestheticism' is the opposite of drama – it has no logic. All advances in the human condition are always travestied because we do not understand the process and work on appearances and credulity. Rationality in the form of mathematics cannot secure its own ontology – mathematicians talk of the inadequacy of our form of numbers – they cannot penetrate mathematical reality. In the same way, human 'being' is ignorant of itself. But there is no 'black hole' which we can avoid – because we engage our totality in any significant problem. The problem can be stated: are we pushed by history or do we guide history? Or: we uniquely have self -consciousness – but have no self to be conscious of. We are a process. There is a web but no spider. Drama makes the web. Perhaps one day we shall step out of the chrysalis of history.

When you start to think about drama you are soon in the deepest human problems. Drama really is at the basis of our being and is sui generis, it can't be reduced to biology or evolution or medical psychology. There's something strangely Freudian about Brecht, seeking to place reason where Id was. His idea is that there is a darkness which cannot be penetrated by light and must be abolished – or given a new address: completely within the objectivity of things. I think that the whole of humanness has to be involved in creativity. There is no curative amputation. Euripides understands this better than Sophocles does, but his understanding is still incomplete: at the end he segmentises us. When they say the child is naughty, you have to tell them they don't understand the child – then they say the child is evil and evil is beyond our comprehension. I think all Brecht's plays (which is different from his working method) are haunted. There is something unexpressed. There are strange leaps that aren't examined – aren't derived through the logic of the play (or of drama). Galileo triumphantly disproves Aristotle's physics in a play heavily dependent on Aristotle's aesthetics (a bad word). He relates certain facts which are sound – they are scientific 'truths'. The telescope enables him to see the world differently. At the end he self-confesses to the audience. Obviously Galileo is the nearest Brecht came to writing a dramatic autobiography, a critical self-portrait. In the end he talks of a different form of value – not that of scientific truth (in a drama for the age of science). He is dealing with human truths – which cannot be reduced to truths about the cogs of the universe, though they are both parts of a materialist continuum. But the latter truths are not derived from the play, not enacted through dramatisation. So the play is not about itself but about something else. Brecht withdraws somewhere. Where does the second order of truth come from? The sleight of hand – the concealment of the play – is that it comes from the first, and comes (so far as the play shows) unmediated. The same thing happens in Caucasian Chalk Circle. There is an introduction based on the precept: the tractor goes to those who can use it. The play spends its time establishing this. At the end it changes, just as does Galileo. There is the Biblical-folk story episode of the child to be pulled out of the circle. Is the foster-mother to be given the child because she knows how to 'use' it? Clearly not. There is a different set of values – not unrelated because both within (you could say) the materialist monad – but the shift isn't dramatised, it's merely stated. In all Brecht's plays there is a central lacuna.

I think this ultimately goes back to Hegel's owl of Minerva. Hegel was heavily dependent on literature – you could say it haunts his work – but he wants to replace the creative-struggle of drama with the certainties of philosophy. History enables the cog's of history to finally utter their truth (there's an image of teeth grinding out the truth, of history as the gnashing of teeth that issues in utterance) – but this is so only because history is a sort of shroud that veils the 'Spirit' of reality. So truth is made the telos of history – Aristotle again. It's as if the corpse resurrects itself by eating its shroud. Or the face ingests the veil that covers it. History will leap the gap for us. But the cosmos – the birth-place of history in any materialist doctrine – delights in the void. It is it's site, it's playground. The cosmos is simply the debris of the big explosion. Democritus had to introduce the device of a devia-tion in the fall of atoms to account for the occurrence of a 'purposive' event – the primal cosmos was otherwise a cause without an effect. The atom fortuitously crosses the gap. In Brecht – because he is dealing with the most basic of human issues – it's as if the gap were haunted by a gap. That is why he resorts to ancient Asiatic literature and its obsession with doing nothing and instead with-drawing. In Confucius this withdrawal is dangerously politicised. Brecht's last exile is in nothing-ness.

He is the hermit of the void. This contrary to all the appearances he 'issues'. He was never in more distant exile than when he entered the East German regime. Not because he wished to oppose a human politics to political expediency or place-filling. Not because of censorship. But because of the new demands he has to make on his work. He can no longer luxuriate in opposition. It's then I think that he finds he has spent his life treading the tread-mill of nothingness. He has no tools which enable him to create humanness. After his early days his irony becomes a grimace of pain. His best scenes – such as the drumming scene in *Mutter Courage* – mock him. At the end he asks his native audience to have pity on themselves – because the pitilessness that they have shown to others is so fearful? It's a strangely contorted plea. In Mother Courage's mourning over her dead daughter he grovels to his public. It is a wretched scene. The last scene of Galileo is patronising and em-barrassing. My sticking point with Brecht is his sentimentality (it is the German vice) – when his irony runs aground on reality he shamelessly appeals to the cockles of his audiences' hearts to save him. You could describe Accident Time as a form of alienation but it is not arrived at by Brechtian withdrawal. Galileo clearly talked of atomic weapons but not of the technology of Auschwitz. So far as I know (correct me, please) Brecht never did. The Brechtian idea that cunning saves does not serve. Galileo's book is smuggled out of Italy under a cloak. If it had been burned it would have been written elsewhere. A scientific treatise is not unique: it will be written if not by one author then by another – that certainly is implicit in history. But every book of humanness is unique, it can be written only by one author. If that author does not write it, then no one could be human – humanness cannot come into general contention if it does not do so in every individual. Brecht writes his books: and they are lie-truths. They should not be regarded as truth-truths. We have to learn how to read and use Brecht just as we do Dante or Homer – the exiled and the blind.

Best wishes

A Glossary of terms used in Bondian Theatre

Written for the French edition of *The Hidden Plot* (L'Arche Editeur, Paris) by Bond's French translator Georges Bas with Jérôme Hankins. It has been translated into English by Alison Douthwaite, edited, with George Bas' permission, by Tony Coult and has a supplement added by Kate Katafiasz (in italics). Edward Bond has added the entry 'The Tragic and the Comic'.

This glossary is designed to enable readers to understand some key technical and theatrical terms and concepts used by Edward Bond in *The Hidden Plot* and other theoretical writing, particularly when he uses them in idiosyncratic or inventive ways.

ACCIDENT-TIME

This composite word expresses the particular nature of time when an accident occurs. It clarifies the degree to which Bond sees lived experience and theatrical representation as indissoluble.

Bond deliberately intermingles two very different events – a car accident and a cyclone – and merges them into a single metaphor. In the same way that a victim of an accident has the impression that time suddenly slows down, anyone who finds themselves in the eye of a cyclone is struck by the stillness there, contrasting greatly with the furious speed of the whirlwind all around. In both cases, the key thing for Bond is the contrast between the calm of the centre and the violence and chaos surrounding it. As a result there is a precision of perception, an enhanced 'clairvoyance,' of the details of the events which are happening.

Transposing this double phenomenon into theatrical representation, Bond places the audience in accident-time, inside a theatrical cyclone which is dramatic action, echoing the turbulence and accidents of life. The audience is therefore in the paradoxical situation of benefiting from the protective calm of the centre the better to analyse the nature and implications of the tumultuous or tragic events in which they find themselves plunged. Such ambivalence is at once a synthesis of, and a moving beyond, Brechtian 'alienation' and simple participation. But, in order for the stage truly to be the site of accident time, according to Bond, the T.E., the theatrical equivalent of this existential phenomenon, must recreate its specific nature and paradoxical contrast so that the 'work of the audience' can be an analytical participation which is as creative as it is free.

Though there are also comical accidents, the association with accidents predominantly suggests a proximity to tragedy, a sense we are in a temporal hiatus, which will have very significant consequences. In accident time we are suspended between cause and effect, imagining what the effect is likely to be. There is a sense in which accident time is 'live'; we do not just respond to a character's reactions but engage in accident time directly with the object ourselves so the 'time' in Accident Time is real, just as the 'event' in the Theatre Event is real. Accident time is slow because it is loaded with responsibility for the audience: values are up for grabs and the consequences are extreme. When we see things in conjunction, which we have never noticed in this particular relation to each other before (as when the object is dislocated from its usual semantic place) it takes time to work out or 'place' things for ourselves. This is what we are doing in Accident Time, creatively thinking 'what does it mean to wipe up your own blood?' or 'why is he doing that – why would I do that?'

AGGRO

'Aggro', as shorthand for aggravation or aggression, became part of the vernacular in the 1960s, (as in 'He gave me some aggro'). Bond uses the term in a theatrical context to describe the opposite of the stereotypical understanding of Brecht's 'alienation.'Rebelling against the supposed sense of detachment produced by Brechtian alienation, 'aggro,' confronts the audience with frightening, disgusting or simply extreme acts. Rather than simply aiming to provoke strong feeling or a gratuitous sense of shock, these acts of theatrical provocation fully implicate the viewer by *demanding* an emotional response. The purpose is to get a reaction but, further, to start a thought process about the *significance, the meaning*, of what is taking place on stage. Bond is asking for an analysis, a calling into question of the causes and mechanisms by which the event occurred. Although there is an indisputable ethical and political dimension to this, the paradoxical mix of emotion and reflection on which Bond's 'aggro' is founded has sometimes provoked misunderstanding or incomprehension. Throughout his career, many scenes in Bond plays have been judged unwatchable or emptily provocative. Bond, however, makes it ['aggro'] the founding principle of the Theatre Event, which is the core of his dramatic art.

The 'Aggro-effect' is a term Bond rarely uses in connection with the later plays of the Big Brum era, but it is interesting because the Theatre Event has clearly emerged from it. Designed to 'disturb an audience emotionally to involve them emotionally' (Bond:1979), the 'Aggro-effect' shows us Bond plainly 'telling it like it is'. Our social values are shown to us, but arguably in such a way that we are too deeply shocked by them to 'own' them. 'Here's a baby in a pram – you don't expect these people to stone that baby. Yet they do' (Bond 1979). We are to be provoked into connecting cause with effect, into asking 'why?' But for this process to work in the mind of the onlooker, we have first to be able to own the action (in this case the stoning), to engage with it in all its horror. If such horror exists in society, we need to be able to inhabit it imaginatively (see IMAGINA-TION) to understand it. But this requires a capacity for honesty on the part of the onlooker – to be able to see yourself stoning a baby and wonder why you would do that. It is of course far easier to alienate ourselves, to be 'moral'. As soon as we categorise an action as 'evil', or 'wrong', we refuse to engage or accept responsibility for the brutality we see on stage: when the protagonist becomes an 'other' or a 'thug', the violence seems safely incomprehensible. Latterly Bond gets around this problem with the Theatre Event, in which he uses a cathexed object to engage the audience directly in the action, so that they cannot be let off the hook and deny their social responsibility to engage imaginatively with disturbing events. In this way the audience are obliged to see themselves in the action on stage. The key to understanding the difference between 'Aggro-effect' and 'Theatre Event' can be seen in the terminology itself: 'effect' vs 'event'. An 'effect' is something we experience passively, constructed by someone else: an 'event' is an action of social significance that we can take a live and active part in ourselves.

AGON

Borrowing from Greek Theatre (whether tragic or comic), this term describes a verbal sparring match – debate, controversy or dialectic – where two alternate discourses, express the confrontation of two opposing opinions, Bond hits upon the original sense – as 'fight' or 'combat' – and, moving beyond its rhetorical associations, makes it the very 'site' of drama, the essence of the dramatic conflict. What is more, in radicalising the term 'agon', Bond revives it, making it synonymous with extreme or ultimate situations. For this revitalised idea of 'agon', in life as in theatre, is far from being a straightforward fight; it is always the bearer of multiple meanings. It is always (as Bond says) a 'positive fight' and is ultimately the struggle between the human and inhuman.

CATHEXIS/INVESTMENT AND EMOTIONAL CHARGE

In this case, Bond adapts Freud's idea of a psychological energy of a libidinal but also emotional nature, which is intensely concentrated on a being, a part of the body, an object, even an idea – which then becomes 'charged.' The Greek term for this energy is cathexis. The cooler-sounding English term is 'investment', and Bond uses the financial overtones in the word. He enlarges the idea of imagination beyond simply the make-believe processes children use in their games. He extends it to the function of collective rituals, and links it to the function of the TE, not only in the theatre but also in other forms of artistic expression. Bond's objective for cathexis is eminently positive, creating 'usefulness,' meaning and, above all worth.

Cathexis can perhaps be understood if we contrast it with its opposite: decathexis. Global capitalist society decathexes or devalues objects because it only operates one value system – the fiscal values of the markets. These do not involve human emotions. An object is decathexed when it is worth only the amount of money you could get for it on the open market.

Cathexis adds the human dimension of attachment to an object in the same way we might say an object has 'sentimental value' more than fiscal value because it was given by a close relative, now dead. The cathexed object becomes associated with the value of a human life, with mortality, with the tragic. The genius of the TE is that it uses deconstruction and cathexis so that the fiscal values we have to live by still operate underneath the emotional dimension. This means we can identify with the characters' handling of the object so we can still see ourselves in our social context. Bond likes to use domestic mass produced objects because they have such a low fiscal value that when cathexed with tragic value, when associated with matters of life and death, the chasm between social and human values opens wide. The object becomes the source of a bizarre bathetic tragic comedy brought about by the two vastly contrasting sets of values attached to it. This neatly prevents any whiff of sentimentality. When an object is deconstructed and cathexed in this way the characters on stage and the audience care about what happens to the object with the same level of investment: this is partly what makes the TE live and exciting. We are not just responding to the character's emotions, but are directly involved with the object ourselves. The important factor here is that any response is valid and valuable: Bond is not dictating to his young audiences. The nature of the deconstructed cathexed object is such that we can think on many levels, engage in many layers of discourse at once.

CENTRE

Bond has described dramatic art as a bicycle wheel – the spokes of which radiate from the central point towards the periphery or vice versa: converge from the rim to the hub. However, the centre of a play is not necessarily the exact centre, equidistant from the two extremes of dramatic action. The centre, rather, makes up the very heart of the work, from which all the textual and theatrical aspects originate, all of which should conversely tend towards and relate to the heart.

This 'centre' can manifest itself in many ways. It can be made tangible in visual elements, the props and accessories of the scene, in a space (or rather a 'site' –

q.v.) in an overriding 'atmosphere' or a recurring metaphor. Bond also talks of the 'Central Discourse' (CD) of a play, something both fundamental and general. This is also expressed then amplified, modified or varied, in key scenes or moments, dialogues or arguments/'discourses'. Sometimes this happens simply in individual lines, which are equally 'central', crystallising the key theme, underlying the meaning or the 'idea' which animates and irradiates the dramatic action. The directing, the set, the acting are expected to express and interpret, each in their own way, this permanent centre.

It is with this 'Central Discourse' that the audience finds itself confronted throughout any drama.

Going to the theatre, according to Bond, is 'going to the centre.' And as dramatic action reflects the tensions, conflicts and paradoxes present in society, the 'centre' is a 'vision which penetrates society'. Indeed it is 'truly the definition (and the putting into practice) of what being human means in our era.'

An example of a 'centre' and the mechanisms for its radiating out onto the 'periphery' and from the periphery back to the centre can be seen in Viv's speech in Act 1 of The Balancing Act about dancers on a ship who do not realise that the ship has sunk, do not know they are dead, and the speech becomes of central importance. This is because the idea of being buried before you die, or of being alive and dead in the same moment is reiterated and explored throughout the play. The idea seems to echo the helplessness of post-modern society in which we know we are on course for self-destruction but are capable only of hedonistic 'play': we 'dance' in the face of certain disaster.

DECATHEX/DECATHEXIS (see Cathexis)

DRAMA

As a general rule, the terms *theatre* and *drama* are used interchangeably. Sometimes Bond differentiates between the two but in rather subtle and allusive ways. Now, this opposition is without a doubt one of the most delicate points when understanding Bondian poetics, as Bond, by a twist of rhetoric, constantly plays with the word *drama*, which has many shades of meaning. He makes an 'accordion concept' of it, whose meaning the reader must reduce or expand each time, in each text, and sometimes from one phrase to another.

The distinction between the two terms is sometimes clearly defined: *theatre* is the location in which artistic creativity is represented or becomes a spectacle, (a text or a scene) and *drama* is a psychological experience or an experience of the psyche which goes beyond the scope of simply an aesthetic activity. Sometimes, as in his book of theoretical reflection *The Hidden Plot*, and even more so in his later texts, the word *theatre* begins to take on pejorative connotations. It describes theatrical activity in the strictest sense (if this can be said, as each time the term is used you must decide whether it refers to the writing of plays, the text, the acting, representation, the place of representation, the scene or the theatre building). The term *drama*, on the other hand, allows Bond to relocate dramatic creativity at the very heart of human activity and the functioning of our psyche.

In using the word *drama* Bond sometimes plays with its figurative meaning of catastrophe, accident or crisis (without ever taking on its hackneyed journalistic usage). *The Hidden Plot* begins with a letter to his English agent Tom Erhardt, to whom he points out that 'drama' and our tendency to 'dramatise' (*not* in the banal or everyday sense) make up a fundamental part of our psychic activity, a way of building our self-awareness/our consciousness of ourselves, the dominant form of expression of our imagination and of our 'being -human.' 'We are made not by our capacity to think and reason but by our need to dramatize ourselves and our situation.'

Being and becoming human constitute a 'drama' in the sense that our understanding and our imagination operate in a dramatic way, by game playing and enactments. Perhaps contrary to popular belief, these have a direct and potentially devastating effect on our social behaviour and political or ideological choices. (According to another of Bond's differentiations, in theatre, we only play or act, but in drama, in the broadest sense, things are *en*acted and things made *concrete* through those acts, which have effects on real life).

The complexity of the word *drama* is further increased when Bond suggests that all arts, to a greater or lesser extent, call upon dramatic expression or rhetoric. This extension of the word is applied in particular to painting, and Bond cites among his inspirations and masters fewer playwrights than leading painters, such as Carravagio, in his painting *The Death of the Virgin* or *Doubting Thomas*, and Gericault, in *Radeau de la Meduse*. In both cases (and many others, such as Manet and Van Gogh) the representation of bodily gestures, the positioning of limbs, and in particular the position and expressiveness of hands, and feet, are *Theatre Events* in their own right, where the playwright can find an inexhaustible source of inspiration.

In this case, the word drama embraces the tricky, elusive notion of 'theatricality'. For Bond the representation and enactment of the human processes of confrontation and understanding are expressed in the fundamental and essential situation of '*agon*'.

As soon as we combine the rational with the imaginative we are in the realm of the 'dramatic'. It is how we connect our minds with the world around us. It is like revisiting, in a mature way, the state of Leibnitz's 'Monad' or neonate, who cannot distinguish between itself and the world. As we develop from the neonate into the toddler and then start to use language we go through a process of disconnecting and reconnecting ourselves with the social and physical world. We learn to distinguish between our skin, our boundaries and those of others: we can discern between the rational and the imaginative. When we think dramatically, or act imaginatively, we act socially because we (re)connect ourselves with the 'other'. When we treat the self as society, when the individual and the social are treated holistically (as they are in Bond's dramaturgy), we are thinking dramatically. It is clear from this that much of what goes on on stages and in theatres does not therefore qualify as 'dramatic' but only as 'theatrical'. (See the difference between 'effect' and 'event' under AGGRO).

DRAMATISE/REDRAMATISE/DRAMATISATION/DRAMATIC ART:
see DRAMATIC

EMOTIONAL CHARGE: SEE CATHEXIS

GAP

This most important of Bond's theoretical concepts is the metaphorical 'gap,' which, unlike 'site', is deliberately flexible in the meanings it offers. The semantic versatility of the word means it can refer to a space, a discrepancy, a void, a hole, an interval, even simply a breach or break.

Just as 'site' is more than simply a place, the Bondian 'gap' means much more than an absence. In its own fashion, it is also a site. For, if it can be empty, it exists in order to be filled or, metaphorically speaking, 'inhabited' and brought to life in many ways. Far from being a bottomless void, the 'gap' is a container, a neutral hollow where many activities, negative or positive, take place. Moreover, Bond has suggested that this should be seen as a kind of 'metaphorical stomach' in which beneficial developments occur. And his allusions to a 'crucible or melting pot' suggest rather a receptacle where both refinements and re-combinations can take place.

What is crucial is that the metaphorical 'gap' always remains open, and so is always creative and dynamic.

Bond writes of the gap as 'the space between the material world and the self.' Its essential nature is at once individual (psychological and ethical) and collective (indeed *communal*). Above all, it is an essentially ontological dimension, made up of our 'being': *we are the gap*. And, just as it can be contaminated or corrupted, so the 'gap' has the authority to produce Value and Meaning, to be the site of Humanness.

Finally, a stage, when empty, is not simply a theatrical space: it reproduces and symbolises the gap. It is a 'literal representation', a 'replica', of the ontological 'gap' at the heart of the self and the world – that's to say a 'void' already inhabited by invisible presences, which are waiting to become creative through presenting action.

The 'Gap' is the place where we structure and evaluate the material world. It exists materially in places where events are dramatised (where the self engages imaginatively with the world) in the mind's neural pathways and on various 'stages', some of which are in theatres. In post-modern culture there is no 'God' in the 'gap', (on the stage or in our minds) telling us how to value things. Bond, unlike Beckett and the Absurdists, who merely react to the absence of God / value, considers it possible, imperative even, for us to create human value in the void, in the face of its cultural absence.

HUMAN/ HUMANNESS

These two terms don't just mean what we call 'human being' or 'human nature', nor even humankind, but rather indicate a supreme value often referred to by Bond as 'human-ness'. Bond does not believe in a biological or anthropological human nature, even less in a transcendental or fixed human nature. Human nature is not 'given' but is created. It is in fact a social nature, a product of culture. The same goes for the term 'human.' We are not born human and the human has to be created in order to exist. Our 'humanness' is a no man's land which we must bring to life and make 'use' of. More exactly, the human is created in what Bond terms the 'fifth dimension' which relates inevitably to the four spatial-temporal dimensions, but is also identified with 'the gap' It is there that the imagination becomes active and brings value and meaning.

Bond goes on to affirm the many ways in which he declares we are not yet (truly) human. He would say that to talk of the 'post-human' is a blind impertinence, as our era, more than any other, is characterised by the *destruction* of the human, which is always and constantly recreated, and that our only 'choice' is simply whether to become human or remain inhuman.

As regards 'What is humanness?' Bond asks himself the question and more or less gives the answer in suggesting these two key terms – Justice and Altruism. Thus, as Bond says elsewhere, the existential site of humanness is, finally, others.

Bond's drama generates this 'humanness' by inviting us to reconnect reason with imagination in the TE. Our post-modern culture (see STORY) has disconnected the rational and the imaginative, the social from the personal, and thus destroyed the human. In The Hidden Plot, Bond gives us an example of a scene to TE. In it, a man steps over a dying man to get a cigarette packet on the floor. The challenge here for the actor and director is to keep the audience on their social site: it is tempting for both actor and audience to disassociate or alienate the self from the inhumanity of this action. But this must be presented as a reasonable act so that we are not alienated from it: as a society we value consumables more highly than human life and the function of the drama is to allow us to engage with, to take responsibility for society. The self cannot 'opt out' from the social: we are bound in many ways (not least through language) to our society's values. If society is inhuman we need to see how that in-humanity operates in ourselves. The man is dying for a smoke. The packet is empty. His frustration might be comic. The comedy would be generated by bathos: the juxtaposition of the tragic (death) with the banal (fag end), the liberating absence of morality. In the comedy our social values – our 'site' – is dramatised: we laugh because we are engaged, we see as he sees, we feel his frustration. The man sees a cigarette on the lips of the dying man. He takes it, (here Bond intensifies the argument by suggesting he might shoot the dying man) and lights the fag end for himself. All of these actions are perfectly reason-able in the context of our fiscally-driven society. As he exhales his first drag on the cigarette he sighs. The TE, says Bond, is in the nature of the sigh. The living man has no empathy, only a rational need for a cigarette. It is when he breathes the dying man's last breath through the cigarette that he might connect imaginatively with the dying man and if he doesn't the audience may. Then it is as if he died himself, or was born having been previously dead. The range of meaning comes from our connecting the banal fag end with the tragic, with human mortality: or to be more precise it comes from the conflation of the two value systems in the act of breathing out the cigarette smoke. When we connect or conflate reason with imagination we animate the 'other' and the self be-comes social: pity becomes possible, and this is the birth or generation of humanness.

IMAGINATION

At least half of the articles in *The Hidden Plot* deal repeatedly and in great detail with the Bondian concept of imagination – a supremely personal, idiosyncratic, even paradoxical notion.

We need to avoid identifying imagination with the imaginary. Though there is such a thing as an 'imaginative Bondian world' which is the product and con-tent of his creative imagination as an artist, the imagination – as mental faculty or psychological agency – is for Bond the very opposite of imaginary. So where-as the imaginary is the opposite of the real, or is linked with the unreal, Bondian imagination is found in the real, 'desires reality', is linked with the real, is in itself real. The whole of *The Hidden Plot* develops and illustrates the command of one of the 'Poems for the *The Fool*' in which he acknowledges that he 'imagines reality'. Therefore imagination is diametrically opposed to fantasy – or more exactly to fantasy as whim or fancy or arbitrary, irresponsible escape and illusion.

It helps to understand that Bondian imagination is not so much a matter of inventing something new as of (paradoxically) understanding what already exists. It is a way of gaining knowledge, extending sensory perception, and complementing reason, allowing us to apprehend and interpret, and therefore 'create' the outside world. And, as 'we act with humanity when our imagination recognises imagination in others' and as 'we must imagine each other', it is fundamentally altruistic and is therefore the primordial source of The Human.

Acknowledging this may help with tackling the many pages of *The Hidden Plot* given over to the properties and characteristics of imagination and its relationships with 'self-awareness/self-consciousness/consciousness of the self,' reason and logic, (Bond writes of 'the logic of imagination' as part of 'the logic of humanness') and its key role as the archway of dramatic and theatrical art. A key Bond text is '*Notes on Imagination*' (1995), published with his play *Coffee*. Imagination is very much a tutelary presence throughout *The Hidden Plot* and his theoretical work in general.

In The Hidden Plot, *Bond discusses the birth of the imagination in the neonate. Initially unable to distinguish between itself and the world around it, the neonate experiences pleasure (being fed) and pain (hunger). These emotions, says Bond, mark the origins of the Tragic and the Comic in the psyche. The neonate imaginatively searches to make sense of the pleasure pain pattern; to connect cause with effect. The imagination is born in response to the baby's need to understand its world. It functions to connect emotions (born of material causes) with reasons. Imagination then, in its search for reason, is a tool humans use to connect our emotional selves with the material world. It can be most clearly stimulated to search for the rational by asking the child's question, 'why?'*

In the TE we see objects being used in unusual ways to just this end. In 'Eleven Vests' objects are continually shredded: books, school uniforms, flesh... the children in the audience may not need to ask 'why' in relation to this wholesale deconstruction. Society deconstructs itself around them and inducts them in its processes: the object in the TE is always rooted in its socio-historical context, as is the imagination. But in the last scene, when a soldier who has been callously bayoneted sits up and as he dies, wipes the blade that has killed him clean on his own vest, the question is unavoidable. 'Why is he doing that?' we ask, and in asking it we have to imagine that we were doing it to see what it would feel like. We put ourselves in the shoes of the dying soldier: the audience work here is very close to the actor's work. We don't experience second hand in the TE but first hand, we don't echo the character's emotions, as in realist drama, but in imaginatively seeking reasons, we have to generate our own emotional response in relation to the object. Drama is always 'live' in this way because in it we directly make connections between action and reason ourselves: these connections are not made for us. When action is not easily justified emotionally or rationally we must ask where the action comes from: the social self strives to understand itself.

When imagination seeks reasons for action we create new concepts. These concepts cannot be graphically represented because they are held in the mind. Yet they involve society and the self (they are emotional) so new values are implicit when new concepts are made. When we reason imaginatively we cannot be cold and detached because the self is engaged or dramatised. Because imagination animates the 'other' it makes us socially engaged. In this way we take personal political responsibility: the TE is deliberately structured to achieve this effect in the mind of the onlooker.

MAP/MAP-MAKING

Bond often turns to the metaphor of map-making to communicate the permanent existential encounter between the self and the world. Confronted with the unknown and implacable (the Tragic), the child, and later the adult, instinctively creates a map, albeit inexact, of the world around them, in order to understand and apprehend it, to build reference points in order to be able to live there and have the right to 'be' there. Imagination is what is used to draw this map on the 'nothingness.' The map's ultimate goal is to give meaning and value.

However, such a map-making process is interactive: the map maker finds himself mapped out, or rather makes a map of himself. In drawing up a map of the outside world, the self cannot help but sketch itself into that map. All cartography produces both a world map and a map of the self, each of which interpenetrate each other. If lived experience is compared to a topographical map, the individual himself is a 'living map of the world.'

Throughout life we must draw a succession of maps, each of which modifies and corrects the preceding map. What the individual calls the 'self' is therefore made up of successive stratas or layers of which there are as many as there are superimposed maps, autonomous but complementary. The map-making metaphor expresses more than just a process of discovery and understanding: it is also an image of simultaneous creation of the self and the world, when confronted by nothingness. (See below)

Theatre is clearly a part of this process. For the situations and the characters of all dramatic works are 'coordinates' (or 'markers') whose interaction and tensions create '*agon*' and whose double nature – personal or psychological and social – means that a piece of theatre is also a map of the world.

Bond invests objects rather than characters with emotional significance in his Theatre Events because deconstructed objects reveal society's 'map'. Manufactured objects can be made to subtly reveal the social structures that generated them – the shop floor, the board-room, the shopping mall. The history of those social structures is also implicit in the object: feudalism, the enlightenment, the industrial revolution, Auschwitz, consumer democracy. How we value and use objects tells us a great deal about our society's anthropological 'map'.

We can see language too as a 'map', both social and individual, the map that binds the individual to their culture, its values, assumptions, ideologies: we become social beings when we learn to name and value objects. 'Cathexing' the object, filling a bag of crisps with the plight of the planet, as in The Balancing Act, *radically changes its 'grammar' or meaning, and invites the audience to revalue the object completely. When the banal crisp, cup or fag end becomes tragic (associated with human mortality) the audience is invited to radically redraw their psycho-social map.*

NOTHINGNESS

What Bond calls nothingness only appears in *The Hidden Plot* in 'The Reason for Theatre.' Although this long text is, without a doubt, the most important in the collection, it is not, as far as 'nothingness' is concerned, as vital as earlier texts such as *Notes on Imagination* (1995) or the recent *The Gap: Working notes on Drama, the Self and Society* (2002.) It is nonetheless useful to attempt to give here an explanation, albeit inevitably simplistic, of this concept, which seems to be perhaps Bond's boldest and most paradoxical.

The fact that 'nothingness' appears several times in inverted commas in 'The Reason for Theatre', (this was not always the case previously and later the term is given a capital letter), could indicate that Bond accords it a meaning which does not truly correspond to either of the two generally recognised meanings. It never has the negative meaning of non-existence (or non-being) nor that equally negative sense of absolute insignificance of the Absurdists.

Bondian 'nothingness' truly exists: it *is there* from the very beginning, an all-encompassing entity, which, like a dark and endless sea, is like a presence in the background of everything that surrounds us from the moment of our birth. This presence is the 'unknowable' or, to take up Bond's image, 'that which is found beyond the bend of the road' but which we cannot access. That is the site of 'nothingness'. For beyond the material world, there is *nothing* – but this 'nothing' finds itself honoured with the rather more impressive name of 'Nothingness'. We are confronted with it from infancy; it provokes all the existential questions to which there are no answers. And as soon as we become conscious, 'Nothingness' permeates us (as we permeate it) and it remains there for the length of our entire lives, combined with the 'implacable' (we are mortal and vulnerable, subject to terror and despair). It becomes a permanent and renewed menace.

Now the paradoxical thing about Bondian nothingness is that it is not, in itself, negative. More exactly, according to a Bondian expression, it can either 'constitute a danger' or 'engender' something positive. Often some form of social authority appropriates 'nothingness' and takes possession of it, imposing its own dominant ideology. Thus, using 'nothingness' to its own ends, society makes of it a Transcendence, which therefore becomes the thing 'round the bend of the road.' 'Nothingness' is simply then the 'site' of this ideology, from which comes only lies, mystifications, or illusions pretending to be truths, disguised as answers to our questions – God (who is only 'ideology of nothingness'), the soul, eternity, mysticism, spirituality or religion. We must therefore, first of all, empty 'Nothingness' of all misleading ideology, all Transcendence claiming to replace 'Nothingness'.

Therefore, 'Nothingness' itself is not at all deterministic. As soon as the human self recognises its presence, thanks to Imagination, not only does it have complete freedom to react to its menace but also senses its necessity. 'Nothingness', says Bond, is 'positive' because it becomes the site of the Imagination and is therefore, because of this, the 'foundation' of human creativity. 'Nothingness' is in effect this 'gap' which is in us and which we fill in creating our self, that is to say in giving meaning to the world. And it is because 'Nothingness' forces us, in some way, to give sense to the world that Bond can call it the source of 'The Human.'

It is hardly possible to be more radically Anti-Beckettian or Anti-Absurdist than Bond. However, as the threat of 'nothingness' is continually renewed, our creativity must never slacken. And it follows that through Imagination, artistic creation – 'beauty' – plays, in this regard, a key role, particularly dramatic creation whose '*raison d'etre*' is to create meaning in the presence of 'Nothingness'.

'Nothingness' is the philosophical void left when God steps out of the cultural picture. It seems that by recognising that there is no God 'out there', but only the cold laws of physics, which cannot tell us how to be human, we lose our humanity. It is what Galileo saw through his telescope, and what we have been coming to terms with culturally since the Enlightenment. Neitszche, Derrida, Beckett all acknowledge it. In the absence of a transcendent being we must confront it. Yet Bond is radically opposed to Nihilism and Absurdism because they accept a world without human value: worse, they deny the very possibility of human value and so by default promote a passive acceptance of the brutally whimsical global markets. Bond's drama is constructed to allow the recreation of human values. This is done without God or transcendence, but with material objects. Deconstructing the object allows us to see our society, its lack of human values. 'Cathexing' the object allows us to attach imaginative, emotional value to the object in its social context. Such rational deployment of imagination (in the context of the socially produced object) accepts that meaning does not exist outside of us: we have to create it ourselves, in connection with the social and material. In doing so we regain our lost humanity.

RECATHEX/RECATHEXIS (see Cathexis)

SITE

'Site' is a rich and complex term in Bond's thinking. It is not a straightforward place or location, but an actual or metaphorical place where something happens, where a particular activity is undertaken – creation, a gestation or transformation, indeed imagination – of a practical, intellectual, psychological or emotional nature, which *can* be negative but should be positive and characterised by its 'usefulness.'

The 'site' is by its very nature multiform and protean. Indeed anything can be a site – it can exist on the level of the individual, a social grouping, an environment, indeed on the level of the whole material world. These sites of activity do not remain isolated or foreign to each other: they interact, influence each other, and interpenetrate. But if the circumference (if it can be called that) of the site is limitless, its heart most certainly is the theatre.

Finally, theatrical representation is in Bond's eyes, the perfect 'site.' All the existential sites mentioned find themselves in a veritable crossroads of interaction, and the vital processes of becoming conscious and reflection, of confrontation and imagination end up (or should end up) at what Bond has elsewhere called the site of 'instant-Antigone,' the ultimate site where the creation of humanity takes place.

A 'site' is the place where the self intersects with, or confronts society: it is a political place where something important – the recreation of human values – happens. This is where social, rational values meet emotional, imaginative ones and for this reason the deconstructed 'cathexed' object is always a quintessential 'site'. On the site, values are up for renegotiation: values concerning the self mingle and intersect with values concerning society. Thus workplaces, streets and so on are potential sites, but so is language and so are 'texts', objects and indeed all sign systems.

Alienation or 'decathexis' takes the self away from the social site because it upholds the rational at the expense of the emotional discourse. It generates the emotional detachment of the psychopath, who has split the rational from the emotional so completely, that he can only be conscious of reason. The psychopath's emotions are so alienated as to be invisible to him/her: emotionally they are dangerously out of control. You know you are leaving a 'site' whenever pity becomes unreasonable – at the gates of Auschwitz for instance.

STORY

The word 'Story' recurs frequently in Bond's writing. The human ability to tell stories is the mark of its imagination and is a key tool in its navigation through the world and its map-making. From the very first essay of *The Hidden Plot* – 'Our Story' – this idea is given profound importance.

Modernism could be crudely defined as the realisation that when humans create things culturally (objects, stories etc.) their values are embedded structurally in their artifacts. It follows that disturbing the structure of the object or story will disturb the values. Modernists tampered with time and space to create structural gaps in narrative in which the onlooker could reconsider their values. Post-modernists have dismantled narrative structure to such an extent, that values have been dismantled: the tragic has inadvertently become banal in the process, as reason and imagination are schizophrenically prised apart. Bond consequently does not deconstruct story because in story, in fiction, reason and imagination can work productively together. Instead he deconstructs objects (dissecting social values so that they become visible) and 'cathexes' them so that imagination can animate (or dramatise the self in) the action on stage. The story is not interrupted (sometimes Bond's plays appear to be 'realist' in style for this reason) but the analysis can still take place. Bond calls this process 'alienation from within the act'. It works because reason and imagination function together in story. Social analysis, which often, as in Brecht, interrupts the story, can still take place; this is because it is the object, not the narrative structure, which is deconstructed.

THEATRE EVENT

Bond frequently uses the term TE – the true cornerstone of his theories on the role and mechanisms of theatre – without giving it a definitive univocal meaning. The reason for this is that, rather than coming from a theory which is codifiable and intangible, TE remains a complex and open concept, which is as much a matter of theatrical practice as abstract theory.

Bond has stated that what takes place on a stage also takes place in life, originates from life and then returns to influence life. This permanent dialectic between theatre and life is fundamental to Bond, for whom dramatic action is not situated outside reality. An event taking place in the theatre is also, in a way, an event which is taking place in life. Likewise, a real life event can also be seen as a TE. In the *Commentary on the War Plays*, TE is explored in its various facets (from Simple to Multiple TE), and its linguistic metamorphosis (from abbreviation into verb, adjective etc.) traced.

It could be said that to create a TE, one must focus on a key action or situation, a crisis point or a crucial incident or gesture, and show it in such a way that it can be examined both in its own right, and in relation to the rest of the work.

The audience is helped to analyse not just the mechanics and significance of the moment, but also the causes and implications of the short-term 'event' on the drama as a whole. In other words, it helps reveal the *full* significance of the moment, to show what makes it a significant 'event.' It is all about opening up, not the story told but the *analysis* of this story, something which Bond has so often said to be essential when 'dramatising.'

Bond has stated that he has used TE as a 'dramatisation of analysis' throughout his career, before conceptualising it. (In the same way, he claims that we see TE in the works of all major playwrights, both ancient and modern, where they are latent or potential but can be made explicit.) He has confirmed his tendency to 'write into' his texts, in various ways, what he feels should make a TE However, putting TE into a work is also the responsibility of the director and the actors, who, during the staging inevitably introduce an element of interpretation, an element of freedom in the way it is realised. Bond not only acknowledges this but also openly welcomes this twisting of the author's intentions, which protects the creative flexibility of drama against all dogma. Such a possibility of 'play' (in all senses of the word) between intention and outcome is more or less analogous with that which exists between the 'centre' and TE (the former clearly being theorised after the latter). Of course the two must combine, but do so in a kind of dynamic tension – the 'centre' being by its very nature structural, tends to be restrictive and prescriptive, whereas TE, even though foreseen by the author, imposes nothing and is restricted to showing. The 'centre' is discovered through analysis and is a preliminary concern; TE is a praxis which must (should) reveal the centre. (Bond has described their difference/relationship as that between a brick wall which can be seen beneath the patterns of wallpaper which has been stuck on top of it.) However, according to Bond, TE, by virtue of its usual extreme nature, has something of the nature of 'aggro' and 'accident time', as they are all ways of summarising which aim to facilitate engagement and reflection.

Bond wants to move beyond the simplistic dichotomy between 'identification' and 'alienation', using TE as the spearhead of a new dramatic practice, even the foundations of a new form of drama. If the name of Brecht has been synonymous with the term '*Verfremdungseffekt*', Bond's intention is that his should be associated positively with TE.

The key to understanding the Theatre Event is in the term itself: 'event'. The audience engages directly with the action on stage because they are responding emotionally to the handling (valuing) of an object, rather than being engaged with or alienated from a character's emotions. In this way the experience is 'live' and happening in the world even though the event is set in the play's fictional context; the audience response is live; the emotions are first rather than second-hand; the consequences are tangible, so responsibility for the audience is unavoidable (see CENTRE).

THE TRAGIC AND THE COMIC

Two concepts of profound importance at the basis of the human self. Other primates may have elementary thought but only humans have these concepts. Here they can be described only schematically, without the subtleties and complications they involve. However, the 'singularity' (described below) is a unique event, whether it takes place over days, weeks or seconds.

Imagine the neonate's 'subjective state'. Adults shown a white page with black letters try to read the letters. If it could be shown to a neonate it could as well try to read the white shapes around the black letters. It has no sense of structure, or even of the external. It is its world and is the entire world, the monad. Outside stimuli are to it internal, because there is no external. Evolution gives it feelings which are vital to its existence. It has no 'thoughts' because it cannot act. Evolution ensures that others think and act for it. A body needs a brain but not a self. Only a mind needs a self. How does the brain produce a mind? The feelings that occur in the neonate's body are grouped as pleasure and pain, and evolution has produced a complex brain which registers patterns in their occurrence. 'Pattern' does not exist in reality but is created by the brain. Think of an apple, then think of 'object'. The apple exists in material reality, 'object' is a concept which exists only in the mind's mental reality. The brain produces a mind when the first concept is created. This concept must concern pleasure and pain because they are all the neonate may experience. Pleasure and pain exist in the body, but the concepts of pleasure and pain are different: they exist in the mind. They give pleasure and pain meanings which in time become grounds of action. The mind discerns and creates meaning, and enters into the world of meanings. (A meaning cannot exist alone, just as a grammar cannot be reduced to one structure.) The first concept is not only in the mind, it brings the mind into being. This event is the 'singularity', because the creation of the mind is at the same time the creation of the self. To be conscious of a concept is to be conscious that you are conscious of it (this need not be so of a feeling) – that is, that you are self-conscious. Meaning then becomes possible ('why'? – not just 'what'?). You cannot have part of a thought. You either think or you don't – this is independent of the content of the thought (that it's right or wrong etc). An apple cannot think, and an animal cannot have concepts and a self. So the first thought – the creation of the self – is like an instantaneous giant stride across the universe that unknowingly each infant takes to join the rest of humanity. The 'singularity' is not transcendental or 'ideal' but totally in and of the material world. As we are not spectators but actors in that world, it makes our relationship to it ineluctably dialectical. The singularity requires us to live in culture and history, and not in the mechanically material. The self is really the self's concept of reality, which is why science cannot locate a 'self' and mysticism has to invent a soul.

The 'singularity' has another profound consequence. An apple is an object. A thought is an act – but not a material act in the ordinary sense. Thought creates its own condition of being (an object's condition of being is atomic and so on). Thought creates itself by thinking, it exists 'in its own right'– has an a priori right to exist or it could not exist. This remark would be extravagant (merely repeating that a thought is a thought etc) were it not that the self is created with the first thought: and so the *self* has a right to exist. The right cannot be removed from self-consciousness, it is an a priori bonding as long as the self lives. 'The right to be' has the consequence that 'this is the place where it has a right to be – is its right place'. The reasons for this are pragmatic and psychological and have to do with the functioning of human, social personality. This makes the right an obligation, and what psychologists would call a 'drive'. It is the human imperative to be human. Working out the obligation in the material, social and historical world is 'the logic of humanness'. It is also the content of drama.

The infant's right is retained into adulthood, it is a priori in the self. It is the reason for the neonate's radical innocence. Whatever the neonate does must be to act out the human imperative, to secure its 'world home' (and remember, at this stage it *is* the – its – world). But as adults live in unjust societies, the human imperative to seek justice is distorted and corrupted by ideology. Administration describes this as original sin or genetic determinism, and thus legitimates its attempt to enforce and stabilise injustice. The law cannot create justice, only the paradoxes of drama can do that. Drama *is inescapably part of the activity of the human imperative.* So dramatic fiction is a form of reality. It struggles to clarify the paradoxes that arise when the 'justice species' (ourselves) lives in historical injustice.

All this seems abstract and remote, yet it is the intimate substance of daily existence. It may be summed up in this way. The self is a threefold unity of the conceptual self, the Tragic and the Comic. The conceptual self is the site of reason, the Tragic and the Comic the site of imagination. None of the three may exist without the other. When one usurps another's role, humanness is distorted into inhumanness. There is no 'human nature', we create our humanness. Neither evolution nor scientific positivity can guarantee the human future. They cannot replace our working out of the three-fold logic in the material, social world. We are responsible for our future or our fate.

We cannot immediately feel another's pain. The Tragic and the Comic are imbued with subjective feeling, yet have the abstraction of objective concepts. This makes them a sort of shared subjectivity, society's self- consciousness. A Tragic event (unlike the accidentally tragic) may contingently involve pain, but really it is an offence to the shared concept of humanness itself. Aristotle invents the guilt of the Tragic figure because of his wish to stabilise the politics of slave-owners. On the contrary, the Tragic figure is always innocent. (A dramatic insight of the ideological Christian myth is its recognition of this in its founding martyrdom.) The neonate is attracted to the Comic in a way adults would understand, but it cannot withdraw from the Tragic in the way they would expect. This is because as it *is* its world it has nowhere to withdraw to – and so it must 'approach' the Tragic in a way which anticipates the intense need humans have to explore their total situation. This is also a privilege of drama. The Comic (not the ironic or cynical) seems to lie on the far side of the Tragic and to be a celebration of humanness. It is still necessary to work for human rights, but an even profounder right is needed: everyone should have the right to be human. If that were understood, that we are responsible for the creation of our humanness, then much of ideology, and all the corruption of transcendentalism, would be swept away. A new radical politics would replace post-modern inertia. It would be the ecology of the human. But these are some of the questions a new drama should explore and enact.

FREEDOM – TRAGIC

This phrase in no way signifies that there is tragedy within freedom. It expresses the confrontation between the world (the source of tragedy) and the self of the subject (the occurrence of freedom.) Their close juxtaposition (Bond speaks of their apposition) underlines the paradox of their connection and their opposition, indeed of their conflict and their interaction. Synonymous with suffering or unhappiness at the same time as pleasure or happiness, the freedom-tragic makes up the deep structure of our 'self in the world.'

TRANSCENDENTALISM

The Bondian concept of transcendence/transcendentalism is as idiosyncratic as that of Imagination, differing as greatly from the majority of most current definitions of this philosophical concept.

First of all, it never indicates a rising or elevation towards a higher dimension or superior sphere, (what Sartre called 'trans-ascendance'), as this quite simply does not exist. Bond's existential philosophy affirms the absolute immanence which is entirely materialistic/material. Therefore, there is no divine being, essence or idea, no absolute, being or principle beyond the tangible world which can be invoked or can intervene from outside into immediate experience. This can only be done by awareness of self and of individual imagination. All transcendence, of whatever nature, is nothing but a usurping of 'nothingness'.

The radical and general character of this attitude means that, whichever of the two terms Bond uses, they are never strictly philosophical. The transcendental is not distinguished from the transcendent and has no philosophical significance, least of all a 'Kantian' one. Bond does not recognise either '*a priori*' or 'the thing in itself'. As to transcendentalism, apart from the idealistic thinking propounded by Emmerson, Bond sees it as belief or recourse to any form of transcendence, which he identifies as simply doctrines, theories or ideas.

Because Bondian terminology results from the fact that he recognises no spiritual or eternal dimension, conceptual and permanent, outside the material world, Bond challenges various religious mythologies, ideologies, morals, beliefs etc, created by all those that set themselves up as Authorities – societies, churches, nations or states – in order to achieve domination, the arbitrary and imposed nature of which make them in fact 'transcendences.' That includes, for example, patriotism, racism and original sin. This surprising and paradoxical aspect is what makes Bond's thinking and radical criticism of all transcendence both original and difficult.

USEFULNESS/USE

The double meaning of 'use' expresses, for him, a single and unique process: existential and above all theatrical. These terms are themselves neither positive nor negative. The important thing is *who* engages in the use and *what* usefulness results from it. In the case of an unjust society, which sets itself up in authority etc, the meaning can hardly be anything but negative. However, when Bond puts 'use' or *use*, as is made clear by the typography, it is eminently beneficial. So for him, basically, everything must 'be of use' (in the full sense of the word) in some way, everything must have a use. And the ultimate function that he gives to 'usefulness' is that it allows us to become human.

This is clearly the role of art, and particularly of dramatic art. Bond believes in the socio-political function of drama. He is a proclaimed adversary of purely aesthetic or pointlessly entertaining theatre. Far from being a didactic playwright, or one who is 'committed' in a narrow or reductive sense, he gives theatre the highest, supreme 'use', as the zone for reflection and communal interpretation of dramatic action. Its nature is to ask itself 'Why am I using this, at this moment, in this play?' The theatrical manifestation of this Bond calls the 'Theatre Event'.

When you are alone you use objects instrumentally in a completely 'decathexed' way. You put on a coat for instance, just to keep warm. The way you put it on has no significance because nobody is there to read your action or give it significance; to do that you have to care in some way about the other, to come into a relationship with them. Not just to look at but to 'see' or read them. This is the essence of Bond's use of objects in his Drama. The object's use is to bring its audience into a direct relationship with the 'other', to engage with the social world of others.

Edward Bond Publications

Plays

The Pope's Wedding	1962
Saved 1965	
A Chaste Maid in Cheapside (adaptation)	1966
The Three Sisters (translation)	1967
Early Morning	1968
Narrow Road to the Deep North	1968
Black Mass (part of Sharpeville Sequence)	1970
Passion	1971
Lear	1971
The Sea	1973
Bingo: Scenes of money and death	1973
Spring Awakening (translation)	1974
The Fool: Scenes of bread and love	1975
The White Devil (adaptation)	1976
Grandma Faust (part one of A-A-America)	1976
The Swing (part two of A-A-America)	1976
The Bundle: New Narrow Road to the Deep North	1978
The Woman	1978
The Worlds	1979
Restoration	1981
Summer	1982
Derek	1982
After the Assassinations	1983
The War Plays	
Part 1: Red Black and Ignorant	1985
Part 2: The Tin Can People	1985
Part 3: Great Peace	1985
Human Cannon	1986
Jackets	1989
In the Company of Men	1992
Lulu (translation)	1992
Olly's Prison	1993
Tuesday	1993

At the Inland Sea	1995
Coffee	1996
Eleven Vests	1997
The Children	2000
Have I None	2000
The Crime of the Twenty-first Century	2001
Chair	2001
Existence	2002
The Balancing Act	2003
The Short Electra	2004
Born	2004

Theory

The Rational Theatre	1972
A Note on Dramatic Method	1978
The Activist Papers	1978
Commentary on the War Plays	1985
A Short Book for Troubled Times	1987
Notes on the Imagination	1995
The Hidden Plot: Notes on Theatre and the State	2000
The Cap: Notes on Drama, Self and Society	2003
The Prisoner's Site	2004
Various introductions published with plays	

Libretti

We Come to the River (opera)	1976
Orpheus (ballet)	1982
The Cat (opera)	1983

Poems and Stories

Clare Poems	1976
Theatre Poems and Songs	1978
The Bundle Poems	1978
Poems, Stories and Essays for The Woman	1979
Fables and Stories	1981
Collected Poems 1978-1085	1987
Summer Poems	1982
Restoration Poems and Stories	1988

Notebooks and Letters

Selected Letters Vols 1-5	1994-2001
Selected Notebooks Vol 1	(1959-1980) 2000
Selected Notebooks Vol 2	(1980-1995) 2001

Index